THEOLOGY IN DIALOGUE

John W. de Gruchy

THEOLOGY IN DIALOGUE

The Impact of the Arts, Humanities,
and Science on Contemporary Religious Thought

• •

ESSAYS IN HONOR OF

John W. de Gruchy

Edited by

Lyn Holness and Ralf K. Wüstenberg

WILLIAM B. EERDMANS PUBLISHING COMPANY
GRAND RAPIDS, MICHIGAN / CAMBRIDGE, U.K.

DAVID PHILIP PUBLISHERS
CLAREMONT, REPUBLIC OF SOUTH AFRICA

Published jointly 2002 by
Wm. B. Eerdmans Publishing Co.
255 Jefferson Ave. S.E., Grand Rapids, Michigan 49503 /
P.O. Box 163, Cambridge CB3 9PU U.K.
www.eerdmans.com
and in South Africa by
David Philip Publishers
an imprint of New Africa Books (Pty) Ltd
PO Box 23408, Claremont 7735, Republic of South Africa

Printed in the United States of America

07 06 05 04 03 02   7 6 5 4 3 2 1

Library of Congress Cataloging-in-Publication Data

Theology in dialogue: the impact of the arts, humanities, and science
on contemporary religious thought: essays in honor of John W. de Gruchy /
edited by Lyn Holness and Ralf K. Wüstenberg.
p.   cm.
Includes bibliographical references.
Eerdmans ISBN 0-8028-3916-9 (pbk.)
1. Theology. 2. Christianity and culture.
I. De Gruchy, John W. II. Holness, Lyn.
III. Wüstenberg, Ralf K., 1965-

BR50.T445 2002
261.5 — dc21

2002073885

David Philip ISBN 0-86486-605-4 (pbk.)

Contents

CONTENTS

Theology in Dialogue with Science

Theological Engagement with the Public Sphere

Theological Perspectives on Socio-Cultural and Political Reality

Contents

Letter from Renate Bethge

Dear John

It is hard to believe that you are now on the point of retirement. When we came to know you, you had not long finished your dissertation on Dietrich Bonhoeffer and were in negotiations with Cape Town University. You had invited us to South Africa, and it was during our stay that your appointment to the university was confirmed. At this stage you were still in Johannesburg, and it was here that we started our marvelous tour through South Africa, which you had arranged for us. At the time I had not thought very much about the trouble you must had taken — nor had Eberhard, I think — to make that journey possible for the two of us. We were overwhelmed by all that we came to see - so much so that I didn't write down anything in my diary, different from my usual way!

I vividly remember your house and garden (and what for us were its strange plants and flowers), with Isobel and the three lively children. You were then Director of Communications and Studies in the SACC and you took us there to meet some of your colleagues and other interesting people. You arranged for your friend John Rees to drive us through Soweto, a striking and lingering experience for us: the many unpaved streets, the small houses, the crowds in the streets. Later we also saw other black townships. I remember one school being a worn-out street-car. Black children didn't need to go to school, yet many did, though they had to pay for their schoolbooks, while white children got them free.

You told us that black men could usually get jobs with the whites and then could move to Soweto or other black townships near white towns, but that they had to leave their families back in the so-called homelands, often several hundred miles away. There were many incidents that you told us about. But there were also positive examples, for instance the role of Helen Suzman, "our parliamentary opposition," because she was the only one who spoke out against the wrongs of the government. We met Beyers Naudé, the outstanding Afrikaner, and also other fearless and brave people

You and Isobel were very active in fighting apartheid in your church and otherwise. One of your activities against apartheid was to bring Eberhard over to speak about Dietrich Bonhoeffer, who had fought the NS regime in Germany. There were obvious similarities between the NS and your apartheid regime, especially the deprivation of rights to people of "another race" — the Jews with the Nazis, the black people in South Africa. Thus you hoped that people in South Africa, especially in the churches, would follow Bonhoeffer's example. To strengthen the effect of Eberhard's talks you published them under the title *Bonhoeffer: Exile and Martyr* in 1975.

With our experience of the NS-time in Germany we were afraid of how your governmemt would develop and what that could mean for you. But you would not in the least think of leaving South Africa, though there would not have been any difficulty for you to get work in the USA or England or anywhere else. Yet you often traveled in different countries, including Germany, so we were very fortunate to see you time and again.

Looking back now we realize with gratitude how much has changed in South Africa in the meantime, not least by your tireless and courageous efforts and those of your friends.

January 2002

Renate Bethge

Introduction

Lyn Holness and Ralf K. Wüstenberg

In the Beginning . . .

This book was born of enthusiasm and cappuccino — followed by hundreds of e-mails. Early in 2000 we discovered, in conversation after church one day, that we shared the similar vision of putting together a festschrift for John. The mutual delight occasioned by this discovery forged an instant bond, and we parted committed to thinking about the prospect in the months ahead. The next time we met was in Berlin — in August that year at the International Bonhoeffer Congress. Conversation here was difficult, mainly because John de Gruchy somehow materialized everywhere! We eventually agreed to attend the premier of the Bonhoeffer film, *Agent of Grace,* together and to discuss our project afterwards. With this in mind, we duly gate-crashed a post-viewing party, found ourselves a quiet corner of the restaurant, and fueled by several cups of cappuccino, brought our ideas together. Thus was born a most interesting, challenging, and ultimately rewarding long-distance partnership. This book is its outcome.

There Was John de Gruchy . . .

John W. de Gruchy had his sixtieth birthday in 1999, the year that also marked the twentieth anniversary of his first major publication, *The*

Church Struggle in South Africa.[1] The year 2000 began for John with the
news that the Evangelical Church of the Union (EKU) in Germany had
elected him to be the recipient of the prestigious Karl Barth Prize for
2000.[2] This year, 2002, began in a similar way for John, with the news
that in recognition of his work he is to receive an honorary doctorate
from his alma mater, Chicago Theological Seminary. During 2003 John
will retire from formal academic life. In view of all of this it seems an
appropriate moment to recognize his contribution to theology with
this collection of essays in his honor.

The Karl Barth Prize was created in 1986 to mark the centenary of
Karl Barth, in order to "honour outstanding works on the Theological
Declaration of Barmen and the tradition created by it."[3] The jury made
its decision in favor of John in recognition of his forward-thinking in
the transmission of this tradition, "as well as of the theological impetus of Dietrich Bonhoeffer and Karl Barth in the ecclesiastical and social contexts of South Africa." The citation continues: "Through his
Reformed theology John W. de Gruchy has contributed with prophetic
impulses to the overcoming of apartheid mentality as well as to the de-
mocratisation of South African society and the renewal of his church,
thus playing an outstanding role for a culture of international and in-
tercontinental theological exchanges." In being awarded this prize
John joins the ranks of a number of illustrious previous winners, each a
scholar of note. In view of the thirty-four-year friendship between
them, it is significant that the announcement of John as prize winner
for 2000 took place in the same EKU Council Session in which tribute
was paid to his mentor, Eberhard Bethge, who, poignantly, had died on
John's birthday that year.

We are privileged to introduce this volume with a letter to John
from Renate Bethge and to include the Laudatio delivered by Wolfgang
Huber at the prize-giving ceremony in Berlin.

John de Gruchy is a person of many facets, both in his personal
and public life. We are here dealing with an exceptionally gifted person,

1. Grand Rapids: Eerdmans, 1979.
2. See the Laudatio by Wolfgang Huber (Berlin) in this volume. In his contribution, Huber both introduces de Gruchy's major works and connects them with his
vita.
3. Quote from the letter received by John informing him of the award.

but also a whole person — one in whom intellectual pursuits and more practical forms of creativity blend together to make him the extraordinarily productive and creative person that he is: in work and relaxation, in public responsibility and personal commitment, in church and society. John is also someone who has demonstrated a remarkable openness to change, with the ability to assimilate new insights into his understanding and exposition of the faith, and to its practical outworking in a very challenging context. Along with this goes a stubborn persistence in understanding connections between things that he instinctively knows to be there, and his dogged determination to reach goals he has set for himself. Those who know John well experience, in addition, a person aware of his own shortcomings and eager to avoid mistakes previously made. They know too that here we have a free spirit, one who is open to exploring boundaries and taking risks, all the while remaining firmly grounded in what constitutes for him the core of faith and life.

Over the past two years John has written, spoken, and found himself in dialogue on a wide range of subjects that have positioned him at the interface of theology and a number of other disciplines and areas of life. His topics range from the dilemma of violent resistance to the reality of religious pluralism, and to theological perspectives on the relationship between transformation, art, and culture. John is currently exploring the theme of reconciliation — in tandem with discourse on the social and theological significance of food! It was not difficult therefore to link John de Gruchy with the theme that had begun to take shape in our minds.

And All of Life . . .

The growing awareness of what has been described as humankind's "new sensibility"[4] draws attention to the fact that on every level we as human beings are living in a time of transition. We have indeed reached a watershed. This new sensibility, although difficult to define, has a number of distinctive features. Among these are a greater appreciation for nature; a recognition of the importance of language to human exis-

---

4. Sallie McFague, *Models of God* (Philadelphia: Fortress Press, 1987), ch. 1.

tence; a "chastened admiration" for technology, as we acknowledge our capacity to extinguish all life on earth; an acceptance of religious and cultural plurality (which includes the decentralization of Western Christianity); the displacement of white, Western males and the corresponding rise of those previously marginalized because of gender, class, race, sexual orientation, etc.; and a growing sensitivity to the interdependence of all life.[5]

Contemporary situations of social, economic, and political transition are overarched by this spirit, felt most keenly in the realities of pluralism and ambiguity.[6] All this impacts considerably on theology, both in terms of its methodology and its content. Increasingly theology is being done in conversation with other disciplines, and in the process Christians are being challenged with respect to their hitherto narrow concept of God's working in the world. What does this mean for the centrality of Christ? Does it weaken the faith of the Christian, or does commitment to Christ give us the freedom to engage others in what can be mutually beneficial dialogue?

It is our belief that such exchange is a theological imperative in our contemporary world, and there are many theologians already interacting with other disciplines. We have seen that John de Gruchy is among them. With his Christological *cantus firmus* intact, John has reached out into a number of areas, allowing new insights both to inform and transform his theology. In this festschrift our aim is both to honor John's theological contribution and, in continuity with the model he himself has adopted, to stimulate further thought and praxis along these lines. We have tried to put together in one volume a number of different perspectives on the theme of theology for the twenty-first century as it responds to the challenge of the new consciousness. A single volume cannot cover every relevant area of theology's contemporary dialogue, and we have not been able to include all those qualified to contribute. In both there are significant and regrettable omissions. We are aware, therefore, of the shortcomings of this volume, but offer it nonetheless as a contribution to the ongoing conversation.

5. Sallie McFague, *Metaphorical Theology* (Philadelphia: Fortress Press, 1982), pp. x-xi.

6. See David Tracy, *Plurality and Ambiguity: Hermeneutics, Religion, Hope* (San Francisco: Harper and Row, 1987).

Among the consequences of interdisciplinarity is that sharp distinctions are less and less possible. For we are not only concerned with theology in dialogue with other disciplines, but also with the reality of interaction between the other disciplines themselves. Hence, for example, in more than one of the articles we see a meshing of science, culture, politics, and ethics, as well as theology. Theology's specific contribution to this conversation is the introduction of an explicit religious, and in most cases Christological, *cantus firmus*. In this way theology grounds the link between the disciplines along Barthian lines in the relationship between creation and covenant.[7] This situation, while certainly desirable, has complicated our task. No matter how we have tried to distinguish categories and group articles we have been confronted by the fact that several essays slot with equal ease into two or more areas. This has to do with the fact that while dialogue establishes networks with interweaving threads, we are compelled to assemble our material here in linear form.

Our categorizing and grouping therefore involve compromise, and others presented with the same material might well arrange it differently. We eventually — and tentatively — settled on three sections to the book, each reflecting a dimension of theology-in-conversation — with the arts, the humanities, and the sciences. The content we give to each of these areas might in itself be open to question. Of some concern to us has been the clear overload of what we have named the humanities, and initially we considered this a flaw. Perhaps it is. But on reflection we realized that this situation symbolizes a particular reality. The natural starting place for theology's dialogical stepping out would be the humanities, in which we include themes relating to culture, politics, ethics, sociology, history, and so on. These disciplines are, after all, "closest to home." And so there is a longer and more widespread history here than of theology's conscious interaction with the visual and performing arts, for example, and particularly with the sciences — old enemies who only relatively recently have stretched out tentative arms towards each other.

For our current purposes we have deviated somewhat from the classical definition of the arts to a more contemporary application to

---

7. Barth understood the covenant to be the internal ground of creation, while creation was the external ground of the covenant. See *Church Dogmatics* II/2.

those disciplines associated in one way or another with the senses — to aesthetics, that is. The question may justifiably be asked why it is that in our volume only music features in the section on theology in dialogue with the arts. In John's most recent book, *Christianity, Art and Transformation,*[8] he acknowledges the theological significance of the arts generally, but then opts to concentrate on the visual arts as a way into the area of theological aesthetics. In our volume music has come to play this role — an appropriate if not intended development, not least because of the important role played by music in Bonhoeffer's life and theology. And after all, is not Barth reported to have acknowledged that while Calvin was his "special revelation," it was Mozart who provided the "general revelation"?[9]

The word "dialogue" features not only in the title but frequently in this introduction as well. It is a term that falls easily from our lips, but which is nevertheless a highly charged one that can no longer be used lightly. We both have concerns about the term. These could be described as existential on the one hand and epistemological on the other. The postcolonial context of Africa brings both an awareness that dialogue is not a monolithic entity understood in the same way by all, and the concern that it be understood as one of equal partnership with no hidden agenda on the part of theology. That is, we ought not to be trying to harness the other disciplines in the service of theology, but seeking to interact with them for the well-being of all life on earth, and along with this to broaden the understanding and appreciation of our faith. From a different perspective, although in continuity with what has been said, comes the concern to acknowledge that dialogue also has to do with encountering and confronting different insights. It has to do with change and different ontological settings. When we discover a theological insight through, for example, music, there is an ontological shift, so that in effect we have the outworking of a hermeneutical circulation, changing from that point on how we see things. As Christians, of course, with Bonhoeffer we need to acknowledge the paradoxical nature of dialogical encounter. We come to the "other" with Christ, and yet it is precisely the "other" who shows us who Christ is.

8. Cambridge: Cambridge University Press, 2001.

9. Theodore A. Gill, "Barth and Mozart," *Theology Today* 43, no. 3 (October 1986): 405.

In All Its Richness . . .

We begin with the essay of Jeremy Begbie, in which Calvin's impact on theological dialogue with music is explored. This is an appropriate starting point as Begbie brings together a number of related themes, setting the tone for what follows both in terms of the arts and of the book. Among these is his acknowledgment of John's interest in the arts as a part of his theological engagement. Then the fact that the essay focuses on Calvin and the Reformed tradition is appropriate in terms of John's own Reformed position. Andreas Pangritz follows with his discussion of the dimension that music, that of Heinrich Schütz and Johann Sebastian Bach in particular, played in Dietrich Bonhoeffer's theological thought. Finally in this section, Thomas Ulrich explores the Catholic element in the work of Karlheinz Stockhausen. Here we are given an idea as to how the starting-point of dialogue can begin with the arts, as a religious element in the music — through theological interpretation — comes to be understood in a new light.

Michael Welker reflects on the possibilities of a constructive dialogue between the sciences and theology in the fields of eschatology and the common good. By means of a *via negationis* Welker demonstrates six traps of past discourse with science that need first to be discovered and then sprung. In this way he contributes to a theoretical basis for dialogue. Bonhoeffer provides the inspiration for Larry Rasmussen's essay on the relationship between the Christian faith and ecological responsibility, in which he argues the imperative that love for God be expressed as love for the earth.

Clifford Green's contribution points to the variety of implications that from a theological perspective are at stake when we enter into dialogue with the humanities. This essay also opens up the many fields into which we are led through the humanities. Three of the essays focus on dimensions of theological engagement with the public sphere. As a political theorist Jean Bethke Elshtain offers her perspective on the debate as to who we — Christians as citizens — are in relation to the wider socio-political worlds of which we are a part. Writing in the wake of the September 11 attacks in the United States, Jim Cochrane asks whether religion (still) has a positive role to play in public life in the twenty-first century, while Steve de Gruchy reflects critically and from a theological perspective on the complex issue of development.

Our next grouping comprises three essays, representing as many different perspectives, that reflect on the interaction between religion, theology, and socio-cultural and political reality. Chirevo Kwenda is a black African theologian, also a tribal chief. Jaap Durand's background is that of a theologically and politically dissenting white Afrikaner, while Graham Ward, from his European (British) vantage point, deals with these phenomena within the framework of globalism, with specific reference to the electronic media.

Victoria Barnett introduces our final grouping of essays with her reflections on the political power of the theological imagination, which, developed positively, evokes the kind of creativity that can lead to transformation. In the essays that follow hers we see the outworking of theological imagination with reference to one particular theme, reconciliation — both facilitating and undergirded by discourse in a number of areas including ethics, exegesis, politics, and sociology. This is indeed appropriate, given South Africa's position at this point in her history, in the wake of apartheid and facing the challenge of implementing the recommendations of the Truth and Reconciliation Commission (TRC). Charles Villa-Vicencio, who was head of research for the TRC, explores the notion of metaphor for both a political and a theological use of the term "reconciliation." Cilliers Breytenbach, as a result of exegetical Pauline studies, shows some reserve about a political appropriation of the term, while Ralf Wüstenberg attempts a reconstruction of the theological doctrine of reconciliation within politics.

The volume concludes with Dirkie Smit's essay on "prayer and politics," taking up John de Gruchy's contention that Christian piety at its best has made a significant contribution to the social transformation of the world. The particular poignancy of this essay, as a fitting way to end this volume, lies in its demonstration that John's life and work are essentially grounded in the church of Christ.

We offer this book in honor of John, in gratitude for what he has given and meant to us personally, and in the hope that these essays will inspire us and others as to theology's direction in the years ahead of us.

Laudatio of John W. de Gruchy

Wolfgang Huber

What could make a South African theologian choose to enter into dialogue with Dietrich Bonhoeffer and Karl Barth, the Confessing Church, and the Barmen Theological Declaration as decisive partners? In John de Gruchy's case the answer has a name — it is Eberhard Bethge.

Paying tribute to John de Gruchy as winner of the Karl Barth Prize today therefore implies evoking the memory of Eberhard Bethge. Together with us, Eberhard would have rejoiced at John de Gruchy's being awarded the Karl Barth Prize. And he would equally have enjoyed the VIII International Bonhoeffer Congress meeting here in Berlin. Eberhard Bethge is no longer among us in person. He does, however, remain vivid in our memories. Beginning this speech by referring to Eberhard Bethge when we are looking at John de Gruchy is an inner necessity, not an arbitrary act.

As John de Gruchy reports, in 1960 Eberhard Bethge was invited to deliver the Alden Tuthill Lectures in Chicago on the significance of Dietrich Bonhoeffer's life and theology. In a side remark, Bethge pointed out that Bonhoeffer's intense 1934 struggle with the Faith and Order Movement was not mentioned at all in the standard description

This Laudatio of John W. de Gruchy was delivered on the occasion of his Karl Barth Prize award ceremony, August 20, 2000, in the Berlin Cathedral. It has been translated by Frau Irene Tröster (Berlin).

of the history of the ecumenical movement by Rouse and Neill. Bethge
added: Nevertheless, knowledge of this struggle would immensely help
in evaluating the then topical struggle within the South African
churches, and the crisis between the South African churches and the
WCC. That was a casual statement in 1960 — the year of Sharpeville and
Cottesloe. On 21 March 1960 in the township of Sharpeville, Transvaal,
the police had, with utmost brutality, put an end to a peaceful demonstration. Sixty-nine blacks, mainly women, lost their lives in the hail of
bullets. According to official reports, another 186 were injured. Quite a
few of the dead had been shot from behind. In the state of emergency
that followed, thousands of blacks were arrested, and a great number
of them were banned for a long period of time. The Sharpeville Massa-
cre triggered a dramatic turn in worldwide opinion on the apartheid
regime whose inhumanity had been revealed by the events of 21 March.

What conclusions did the churches draw from this event? Weren't
they all compelled to openly acknowledge the unacceptability of the
apartheid regime and disavow all forms of cooperation with it? Was
not common rejection of the apartheid regime in words and action a
precondition for ecumenical relations among the churches? That was
the issue of the Cottesloe Consultation, held as early as December 1960.
Cottesloe is a Johannesburg suburb. The consultation failed in results,
as the Nederlandse Gereformeerde Kerk (NGK) was not ready to accept
its decisions.

Such was the situation about which, according to Eberhard
Bethge, the German theologian from distant Chicago, much could be
learned from Dietrich Bonhoeffer. For one man at least this hint was
productive: it was John de Gruchy, an English-speaking white South
African theologian. At that time he was age 24, and for him the path of
his theological studies was determined. Dietrich Bonhoeffer and the
Confessing Church in Germany, Karl Barth and the Barmen Theological Declaration became the crucial points of his theological thought
and engagement.

I

John de Gruchy is a Reformed theologian; his home church is the relatively small United Congregational Church of Southern Africa. As he

may say occasionally, the Reformed tradition is not at home only in the churches bearing the Reformed name. As a young man of 22, in 1961, he was ordained by that church, and subsequently ministered in Durban and Johannesburg. At 29, in 1968, he became Director of Studies and Communication in the South African Council of Churches (SACC). During this period of office, he finished the thesis triggered by Eberhard Bethge's impulse. It was a comparative study of the ecclesiologies of Karl Barth and Dietrich Bonhoeffer. Particular stress was laid on the issue of its consequences for the church situation in South Africa. The young theologian's impetus can be felt when reading the title of this unfortunately unpublished thesis: "The Dynamic Structure of the Church: A Comparative Analysis of the Ecclesiologies of Karl Barth and Dietrich Bonhoeffer."

During de Gruchy's period in office, the "Message to the People of South Africa" was published by the South African Council of Churches (SACC) in 1968, thereby publicly expressing the question smoldering since 1960: Was South Africa in a Status Confessionis? Was it necessary to constitute a "Confessing Church"?

For John de Gruchy South Africa was in a situation of confession, and he was ready to respond in the spirit of a Christian pacifism quoting both Dietrich Bonhoeffer and John Howard Yoder alike. But he was also conscious of the dilemma burnt into the conscience of the public worldwide: Whoever pleaded for nonviolent resistance in the case of South Africa knew and had to know that he was referring to a situation full of violence, most murderous violence. The dilemma Dietrich Bonhoeffer had faced during the conspiracy was a dilemma in South Africa, too.

In 1973 Eberhard and Renate Bethge accepted an invitation by John de Gruchy, that is, an invitation by the SACC, to visit South Africa. After the journey, Eberhard Bethge published an essay in Germany titled "Confessing Church in South Africa?" which begins as follows: "Are we involved in a 'church struggle' like that in the Third Reich, and do we have to create a 'Confessing Church' as you did in Germany?" Virtually no discussion takes place in which this question is not being posed. Indeed, "Confessing Church" is circulating as a catchword in South Africa, stimulating and appalling friend and foe. Some circles think that the time of the Status Confessionis has come.

Whether the notion of Confessing Church was appropriate for

South Africa or not, and although the differences between the thirties in Germany and the seventies in South Africa might demand utmost caution, Bethge expressed one point of correspondence. He suggested that the Kirchenkampf parallels were only adequately applied when equal attention was given to two crucial elements: renouncing any form of religious ideology that replaces Jesus Christ as the one Word of God by a humanly chosen revelation in history, and the insight that Christians are not allowed to withdraw from the political consequences of what they have learned by faith.

Eberhard Bethge's report was published in 1973. In the same year John de Gruchy changed his area of work and took up academic teaching at the University of Cape Town, where he is still teaching, that is, when he is not holding one of the guest professorships that, by now, have added up to a considerable number. Having a great deal of in-depth professional experience in spite of his youth, he took up the task of teaching. Soon after, at 37, he was awarded the venerable-sounding title of Senior Lecturer. A variety of academic titles were bestowed upon him in Cape Town — or is it better to say that they were invented for him? In 1992 he became the Robert Selby Taylor Professor of Christian Studies.

But the continuity of his academic path has always been related to the radical transformations and turning points, conflicts and transitions in his own society and in the situation of his own church. Some catchwords for the changing challenges John de Gruchy engaged in are: the church as accomplice of the apartheid regime; the struggle against the violation of elementary human rights only hesitantly and incompletely fought during South Africa's period of "separate development"; the impact of the early nineties shift; the church's modified responsibility in a situation of transition; and the transformation from an allegedly Christian State to a "rainbow nation." These are issues that illustrate the changing challenges John de Gruchy was ready to face in his theological work. The unique Proprium of this theology is manifested by two basic foundations linked inextricably: loyalty towards the earth — in this case loyalty towards the situation of the people in South Africa, and loyalty towards Jesus Christ as the One Word of God.

Being related to the context is not the same as being confined by the context. De Gruchy's theology covers immense horizons as shown on the international level. John de Gruchy makes the voice of South African theology heard both in America and in China, in New Zealand

and in Norway. He is one of the most distinguished figures in the International Bonhoeffer Society, and since 1976 he has missed none of the International Bonhoeffer Congresses which take place every four years. He is co-responsible for the English edition of Dietrich Bonhoeffer Werke, and by the publication of the *Making of Modern Theology* series he has also contributed to making or rather remaking nineteenth- and twentieth-century German theology accessible for English-language students of theology. Interconnection of contexts is a meaningful task for a theology that is, in a reflective sense, contextual.

II

John de Gruchy's work covers a wide range of themes in a high degree of complexity. For me three particular publications with a systematic character have been his major works so far. Although their objective is not to explain or display the theological legacies of Barth and Bonhoeffer, or those of the Confessing Church or the Barmen Declaration, it is all the more interesting to be aware of how this legacy is given significance in the three major works. The titles are: *The Church Struggle in South Africa; Liberating Reformed Theology; Christianity and Democracy*.

The Church Struggle in South Africa was first published in 1979 and re-edited in 1986.[1] More than any other book it allows us access to the position taken by the various South African churches towards the task of contributing to peace and justice in their country. No trace of self-indulgence and arrogance can be found in these conclusions. Yet they foster clear theological judgment and subsequent readiness to shoulder the necessary consequences. The formation of theological judgment, however, is clearly and unmistakably informed by Barth and Bonhoeffer.

From Barth, for instance, de Gruchy adopts criticism of a doctrine of election that breaks free from Christology. Predestination was one of the principal issues of both Afrikaner theology and Deutsche Christen theology alike. But as Barth had already pointed out, isolated from its theological context, such a predestination doctrine leads to a misguided belief in one's own history as endorsed by the "Almighty."

---

1. Grand Rapids: Eerdmans.

Adolf Hitler provides a notorious example of this. As Barth showed, such an understanding of predestination proves its inadequacy particularly in times of historical crises, when it is either too optimistic or too fatalistic. It cannot stand the test of reality.

From Bonhoeffer, however, de Gruchy adopts the differentiation between the Ultimate and the Penultimate. He appreciates the confessional character of commitment to justice and peace in South Africa and underlines its necessity. But he denies any ideas that equate overcoming apartheid with the establishment of the kingdom of God. It is not a matter of the historical materialization of utopian visions, but that of preparing the way for the Lord who will come solely of his own free will, and who can never be forced to come by any form of human action.

Liberating Reformed Theology was published in 1991 as a "South African contribution to an ecumenical debate";[2] the German translation was published in 1995. Reformed theology as a particular manifestation of Reformation theology itself needs liberation before it can develop its liberating force, as it has undoubtedly collaborated in legitimizing oppression. In dialogue with present representations of liberation theology de Gruchy seeks to understand Reformed theology as a liberating theology that is "Catholic in essence, Protestant in principle, engaged in society, and prophetic in witness."

But linking such a project with Karl Barth means giving the meaning of liberation theology an unmistakable turn, by anchoring the idea of the liberation of humankind in the doctrine of election. As God's unconditional grace must be acknowledged and respected as ground for the salvation of humankind, so God's freedom is likewise the sole ground for the liberation of humankind.

Both from Barth and from Bonhoeffer de Gruchy adopts a particular view on God's commandments. The law as understood in the light of the gospel may not be misinterpreted as a legalistic instrument of oppression, but contains a mandate for humanizing and liberating action; in this sense it is the foundation of the struggle for human rights. De Gruchy not only refers to Barth's definition of the relation between the gospel and the law, but equally to Bonhoeffer's differentiation between "cheap grace" and "costly grace," and the avowal of guilt by the

2. Grand Rapids: Eerdmans and Cape Town: David Philip.

churches in Bonhoeffer's manuscripts on ethics. It is this avowal of guilt that reflects where the Ten Commandments, as the epitome of biblical directives (as "Signposts to Freedom" in the words of J. M. Lochmann), could lead the church: namely to contributing to the flourishing of life by sticking to the law claiming justice.

Christianity and Democracy is the title of de Gruchy's third major work to be mentioned here. Published in 1995,[3] it is a reflection on the transitions both in South Africa, leading to the 1994 Constitution with Nelson Mandela as President in the same year, and in Germany and Eastern Europe. De Gruchy is one of the few authors to have examined the inner connection between the two transformation processes. Therefore his book contains a case study not only on South Africa, but also on Eastern Germany. The churches here are called "midwives of democracy." Firsthand participants may think that the aspects of the German development presented by de Gruchy may be somewhat over-emphasized. Yet it is undoubtedly correct that we should make stronger use of our ecumenical interrelations as a possibility of broadening and intensifying our mutual learning about the role and testimony of the church in such transformation processes.

The point of departure for de Gruchy's reflections is the idea that the Christian faith cannot be identified with any particular form of State. The impulses he took from Bonhoeffer and even more from Barth prevented him from equating the Christian faith and any form of State. The predominant issue in the book is Barth's question concerning the affinity between the Christian society and the character of a civil society where people can live freely. Bonhoeffer's view of human freedom, sociality, and justice and his participation in the resistance movement gave impulses with a far-reaching impact on democracy, even though de Gruchy thinks that he was not a liberal democrat. From Barth and from Bonhoeffer we may learn that a church willing to contribute to freedom as a maxim of living and to its political counterpart, democracy based on liberty, cannot afford to neglect examining its own order in the light of these principles. This is so since the most important contribution a church can make towards shaping the civil society resides in constituting the shape of the Christian congregation.

Thus it can be felt that in the third book, too, with its truly ambi-

3. Cambridge: Cambridge University Press.

tious subtitle, *A Theology for a World Order,* the key principles are influenced by the partners with whom the young de Gruchy had once chosen to be in dialogue: Dietrich Bonhoeffer and Karl Barth, the Confessing Church, and the Barmen Theological Declaration. He is an independent partner in this dialogue, independent on his path in theology. But he has never ceased to be grateful to the theological teachers he chose.

He deserves our gratitude. The Karl Barth Prize is a worthy expression of that gratitude, I believe.

THEOLOGY AND MUSIC

Music, Word, and Theology Today: Learning from John Calvin

Jeremy Begbie

Calvin is not renowned for his generosity towards music. In this respect he is often contrasted with Martin Luther, whose apparently boundless enthusiasm, it is presumed, meets its opposite in Calvin's suspicious antagonism.[1] The shallowness of this kind of judgment, however, is not hard to demonstrate. Not only does it hide the many-sidedness of Luther's own position, it grossly oversimplifies Calvin's views, too easily aligning him with Zwingli, and disregards the sizable musical legacy to the church. Moreover, it overlooks the particular theological interests and emphases lying behind Calvin and Luther's estimate of music.

In this article, we examine something of the shape of Calvin's approach to music. My purpose is not to provide a comprehensive picture,[2] but to focus on one aspect, the way he conceives the relation be-

---

1. Cf. e.g., W. E. Buszin, "Luther on Music," *The Musical Quarterly* 32 (1946): 80-97. Buszin speaks of "Calvin's indifference, or rather hostility, to music," p. 80.

2. The most important secondary sources for understanding Calvin's theology of music are Charles Garside, "The Origins of Calvin's Theology of Music: 1536-1543," *Transactions of the American Philosophical Society* 69 (1979): 4-35, and Jeffrey T. VanderWilt, "John Calvin's Theology of Liturgical Song," *Christian Scholar's Review* 25, no. 1 (1995): 63-82. These surpass earlier works by Walter Blankenburg, "Calvin," in *Die Musik in Geschichte und Gegenwart,* vol. 2 (Kassel und Basel: Bärenreiter-Verlag, 1952), pp. 653-66, and Oskar Söhngen, "Fundamental Considerations for a Theology of Music," in Theodore Hoelty-Nickel, ed., *The Musical Heritage of the Church,* vol. 4 (St. Louis: Concordia, 1954), pp. 7-16.

tween music and words, and to set this in counterpoint with some of his controlling theological concerns. Such a study provokes hard but important questions about the way theology comes to terms (or fails to come to terms) with a nonverbal phenomenon such as music. These are questions being pressed with special force today. In a highly aesthetic "postmodern" climate, theology is being forced to engage more deeply than ever with practices like music, practices that are undeniably coherent and meaningful but irreducibly distinct from those of spoken and written language. It is, moreover, especially appropriate to be considering this kind of engagement in a Festschrift to John de Gruchy, whose recent sustained conversation with the arts, not least the nonverbal arts, has provided a much-needed source of stimulation for theological endeavor.

Throughout we need to bear in mind that, like Luther, Calvin's interest in music is essentially a practical one. Most of his comments on music arise from a resolute concern for adequate musical provision in his churches, specifically in worship. (Indeed, he rarely considers music independently of its role in public worship.) And it is worth underlining that the main practical outcome in Calvin's case, the Genevan Psalter, had a quite astonishing impact. Selling tens of thousands of copies in his lifetime, few other liturgical volumes have left such an indelible mark on Protestant worship. Therefore, although something of the shape of what we might call "a theology of music" emerges, it does so only in the midst of these very down-to-earth practicalities.

Music, Words, and the Word: From Tolerance to Endorsement

An especially instructive place to begin to open up Calvin's thinking on music is with a marked shift in his thinking, highlighted in a classic study by Charles Garside.[3] In the first (1536) edition of the *Institutio,* we are given a brief comment on the subject of music in the context of a discussion of private prayer. Prominent at this time was Calvin's deep concern for the interiority of prayer as over against empty, outward

---

3. Garside, "Origins."

4

forms: authentic prayer is lodged within the "heart." Overt acts, in order to be of value, must issue from this center. He writes: "it is fully evident that unless voice and song, if interposed in prayer, spring from deep feeling of heart, neither has any value or profit in the least with God."[4] Later he refers to public singing, something well established in Basel (where he completed this edition of the *Institutio*). At the Lord's Supper, after the minister has prayed that the congregation receive the sacrament with due faith and gratitude, and that they might be made worthy of such a feast, Calvin stipulates that if the congregation are to sing they should sing psalms. And at the end of the Supper, praises should be sung *(laudes Deo canerentur).*[5]

Little else is said about music in this edition of the *Institutio*. A year later, the contrast is striking. Writing the 1537 Articles for the organization of the church in Geneva, he now states that singing is to be made integral to public worship:

> it is a thing most expedient for the edification of the church to sing some psalms in the form of public prayers by which one prays to God or sings his praises so that the hearts of all may be aroused and stimulated to make similar prayers and to render similar praises and thanks to God with a common love.[6]

He urges that the psalms alone are to be sung, for only in this way will the heart be appropriately stimulated. We also find an appeal to history — psalmody was an apostolic practice that now needs to be restored in the vernacular, after centuries in which liturgical music had rendered the Word of God largely unintelligible to worshipers. The singing of psalms is thus intrinsically linked to Calvin's program of restoring the face of the ancient church.

All Calvin's later writings on church music develop these points. Garside underlines the significance of Calvin's change of attitude, looking ahead to the first edition of the Genevan Psalter:

4. W. Baum, E. Cunitz, and E. Reuss, eds., *Iioannis Calvini Opera Quae Supersunt Omnia* (Braunschweig: Schwetschke, 1863-1900), henceforth ICO, I, p. 88.

5. ICO, I, p. 29. It is impossible to tell what kind of music Calvin had in mind at this time, though we know that collections of songs for private devotion were available.

6. ICO, X, p. 6.

on the basis of what [Calvin] published in 1536 the possibility of a Calvinist liturgy employing music to any considerable degree seemed at best remote. Seven years later, however, he revealed himself as a determined, although by no means uncritical, advocate of psalmody and superintending editor as well of what eventually would be one of the most influential psalters ever created for Christian worship.[7]

What accounts for this shift? Garside traces it to the influence of Martin Bucer, whose own views on church music can be seen to correspond very closely to Calvin's in the Articles,[8] and to Calvin's pastoral experience, which undoubtedly had a large part to play. He assumed pastoral responsibilities in Geneva for the first time in 1536. Farel's worship was devoid of music, following Zwingli's example, and Calvin found the situation intolerable: "Certainly at present the prayers of the faithful are so cold that we should be greatly ashamed and confused."[9] He would probably have recalled reports of congregational singing from Roussel and other French evangelicals. In addition, there was his own experience in Basel. In any case, the remedy for Geneva's "cold" prayer is psalm-singing: "The psalms can stimulate us to raise our hearts to God and arouse us to an ardour in invoking as well as in exalting with praises, the glory of his name."[10]

Whatever the reasons, we should not miss the significance of what has happened. Calvin has come to realize the contribution music can make to the appropriation of words (in this case, the words of Scripture), a contribution at once distinctive and, it would seem, integral to public worship. And he does this without any hint of weakening his commitment to the authoritative primacy of the written Word —

7. Garside, "Origins," pp. 6-7.

8. Garside lists the points in common: prayer (sung or spoken) must originate in the heart; liturgy (including songs) must be in the vernacular; what is said and sung must be derived exclusively from Scripture; use of singing must rest securely on the evidence of Scripture and of early church practice; liturgical reform must be geared towards a recovery of the early church's worship. Garside, "Origins," pp. 10-14.

9. ICO, X, p. 12.

10. ICO, X, p. 12. VanderWilt wrongly cites this passage from the Articles as a quotation from the 1536 *Institutio* ("John Calvin's Theology," p. 67). This is a serious error, given that Garside's persuasive argument hinges on this being written a year later, by which time Calvin's attitude to music had changed markedly.

indeed, he explicitly justifies his attitude to music by reference to Scripture.

Music and Emotion

But precisely what is music's distinctive contribution? The heart of the matter is indicated in Calvin's contrast between prayer that is "cold" and prayer where the heart is stimulated by song. More significant than anything else for Calvin is music's strong emotional power. When sung, psalms can assume a quality that greatly intensifies communal prayer and praise, appealing directly to the worshiper's heart. In the passage just quoted above, Calvin's language is strongly affective — singing psalms has the power to arouse *(esmouyer)* and stimulate *(inciter)* our hearts, so they can be raised to ardor *(ardeur)*. In his 1543 Preface to the Psalter, he writes: "we know by experience that song has great force and vigor to move *(d'esmouvoir)* and inflame *(enflamber)* the hearts of men to invoke and praise God with a more vehement and ardent zeal *(zele)*."[11] In Calvin's view, then, texts are appropriated with a greater intensity when combined with music, the conjunction of text and music in singing enabling an especially potent conjunction of mind and emotion. And this should be understood in a thoroughly corporate sense: his overarching interest is in building up the church, and it is the emotional effect of communal singing that left such a marked impression on him. The "experience" he refers to in the Psalter Preface — which should convince his readers of the power of song — is the experience of corporate singing (very probably he has his pastorate

---

11. John Calvin, "Genevan Psalter: Foreword," in Oliver Strunk, ed., *Source Readings in Music History: From Classical Antiquity through the Romantic Era* (New York: Norton, 1950), p. 346. It is notable that here he speaks of "song," and does not explicitly mention texts. This may signal an even stronger sense of the peculiar potency of music than he had had in 1537. His firsthand experience of hearing the psalms sung in the vernacular in Strasbourg — where he was pastor from 1538-1541 — would likely have had a decisive impact upon him. It was probably a major factor in provoking him to produce the Strasbourg Psalter of 1539, and the Genevan Psalter of 1542. Cf. Garside, "Origins," pp. 17ff. Notably, in the 1537 Articles Calvin remarks that "we were not able to estimate the benefit and edification which will derive from this [psalmody] until after having experienced it." ICO, X, p. 12.

in Strasbourg in mind). We recall the statement quoted earlier: through song, "the hearts of all may be aroused and stimulated to make similar prayers and to render similar praises and thanks to God with a common love."[12]

Delights and Dangers

However, as with all good gifts of God, music has its shadow side. Along with many writers of the ancient world, he seems to have believed that music bypasses the mind, appealing to the heart directly through emotional stimulation. Therein lies its power to shape a person's moral character, for when the heart is changed, our everyday life is inevitably transformed.[13]

Like Luther, Calvin holds that music was an original gift of God, but, unlike Luther, he does not directly link this to the grand Pythagorean tradition that sees music as an embodiment of cosmic order. (For Luther, music is regarded among other things, as an expression of the God-given harmony of the cosmos, and as such a means of preserving creation over against the forces of dissolution.)[14] Rather, Calvin traces it to Jubal in Genesis 4:21,[15] describing it as one of the *"luculenta divinae*

12. ICO, X, p. 6.

13. *Institutes of the Christian Religion,* ed. John T. McNeill (Philadelphia: Westminster Press, 1975), III:6:4. "Heart," for Calvin appears to denote something akin to the very center of the personality. He distinguishes between brain (cerebrum) and heart (cor), insisting that knowledge of God, and faith, do not merely "flit" in the brain but take root in the heart. (*Inst.* I:5:9 — with regard to knowledge of God, and, in exact parallel, with regard to faith — *Inst.* III:2:36. Cp. *Inst.* III:2:8; III:2:33.) Hence his attack on "trifling Sophists who are content to roll the Gospel on the tips of their tongues when its efficacy ought to penetrate the inmost affections of the heart, take its seat in the soul, and affect the whole man a hundred times more deeply than the cool exhortations of the philosophers!" *Inst.* III:6:4. On the complex notion of the "soul" in Calvin, cf. Mary Potter Engel, *John Calvin's Perspectival Anthropology* (Atlanta: Scholars Press, 1988), pp. 42ff. and ch. 5.

14. Cf. Joyce L. Irwin, *Neither Voice Nor Heart Alone: German Lutheran Theology of Music in the Age of the Baroque* (New York: Peter Lang, 1993), p. 4; Brian L. Horne, "A Civitas of Sound: On Luther and Music," *Theology* 88 (1985): 21-28. See below, n. 54.

15. "[Jabal's] brother's name was Jubal; he was the ancestor of all those who play the lyre and pipe."

bonitatis testimonia,"[16] one of the "bright sparkling remnants of glory" that has survived the fall as an enduring testimony to the goodness of God. It has been given for our recreation and pleasure. To be more specific, it has been given for our "spiritual joy," that we might rejoice and delight in God, which is our "true end."[17] Music thus gains high approval from Calvin:

> Just as our nature, then, draws us and induces us to seek all means of foolish and vicious rejoicing, so, to the contrary, our Lord, to distract us and withdraw us from the enticements of the flesh and the world, presents to us all possible means in order to occupy us in that spiritual joy which he so much recommends to us. Now among the other things proper to recreate man and give him pleasure, music is either the first or one of the principal, and we must think that it is a gift of God deputed to that purpose.[18]

Calvin is much more cautious than Luther about ascribing powers to music that might detract from the unique agency of God. For example, while fully prepared to speak of the power of music to influence the soul, either to a good or bad end, unlike many of the humanists, Calvin was not prepared to say that music can drive away evil spirits. Commenting on the story in 1 Samuel 16 where David plays his lyre to comfort Saul ("and the evil spirit would depart from him"), Calvin refuses to link the departure of the spirit with the music, roundly attacking those who see anything in this other than a manifestation of the divine will. Music did indeed soothe Saul, but God drove out the spirit in his sovereign freedom.[19]

Calvin differs even more markedly from Luther in underlining repeatedly what he sees as the severe postlapsarian hazards of music. Spiritual joy, of which music can be a reminder, was part of our endowment prior to the fall. But the catastrophe of sin has turned music into an ambivalent gift — it is able to poison and disfigure the heart as

16. ICO, XXIII, p. 100.

17. Calvin, "Genevan Psalter," p. 346.

18. Calvin, "Genevan Psalter," p. 347.

19. ICO, XX, pp. 181-ff. Contrast Luther's comments on the same passage, in Ulrich S. Leupold and Helmut T. Lehmann, eds., *Luther's Works* (Philadelphia: Fortress Press, 1965), vol. 53, p. 323.

much as uplift it, and this in turn issues in disastrous moral effects. In drawing out this ambivalence, Calvin follows Plato closely, elaborating memorable metaphors like that of a funnel: "It is true that every bad word (as St. Paul said) perverts good character, but when the melody is added, that word pierces the heart much more strongly and enters within. Just as wine is poured into the vessel through a funnel, likewise venom and corruption are exuded down into the very depths of the heart through melody."[20] Typical of the sixteenth-century humanist, Calvin appeals to Plato: "there is hardly anything in the world with more power [than music] to turn or bend, this way and that, the morals of men, as Plato has prudently considered."[21]

Alert to what he sees as the colossal powers of music with their attendant dangers, Calvin is acutely concerned that music is turned to good effect. Critical to this is a proper attitude of heart. From Calvin's first musings on music in worship to his last, this concern never left him. Even a fine song, with proper text and music, can be sung to evil purpose if it does not issue from a regenerate heart. Without claiming that this is the only relevant factor in ensuring beneficial music in worship, Calvin never tires of stressing that inward disposition and outward practice must conform. He writes:

> unless voice and song, if interposed in prayer, spring from deep feeling of heart, neither has any value or profit in the least with God. But they arouse his wrath against us if they come only from the tip of the lips and from the throat, seeing that this is to abuse his most holy name and to hold his majesty in derision. . . . Yet we do not here condemn speaking and singing but strongly commend them, provided they are associated with the heart's affection.[22]

20. Calvin, "Genevan Psalter," p. 347.

21. Calvin, "Genevan Psalter," p. 347. On Plato and music, cf. Wayne D. Bowman, *Philosophical Perspectives on Music* (Oxford: Oxford University Press, 1988), pp. 20-44.

22. *Inst.* III:20:31. In the Foreword to the Genevan Psalter, he writes: "we must remember what Saint Paul says — that spiritual songs cannot be well sung save with the heart." Calvin, "Genevan Psalter," p. 346. The same stress lies behind his remarks in his commentary on Ephesians, on Eph. 5:18. According to Calvin, where Paul writes "singing in your hearts, it is as if he had said, 'From the heart and not only on the tongue, like hypocrites.'" John Calvin, *The Epistles of the Apostle Paul to the Galatians, Ephesians, Philippians and Colossians*, trans. T. H. L. Parker (Grand Rapids: Eerdmans,

Along with this emphasis on the rightly oriented heart, we find a repeated accent on the participation of the whole church in worship, and (something we have already noted) on "understanding (intelligence)." Again we are reminded of a corporate strain running through all Calvin's thinking about music for worship. The whole church must sing (no specially trained choirs are to be allowed), and if worship is to edify the whole congregation it is imperative that all singing be in the vernacular. If we are to sing with the heart, Calvin argues,

> the heart requires the intelligence, and therein, says Augustine, lies the difference between the singing of men and of birds. For a linnet, a nightingale, a parrot will sing well, but it will be without understanding. Now the peculiar gift of man is to sing knowing what he is saying. After the intelligence must follow the heart and the affection, which cannot be unless we have the hymn imprinted on our memory, in order never to cease singing.[23]

By implication, it is also crucial that text and music relate properly. Central here is the principle of "moderation." Music is to be tempered, shaped to a text.[24] It is crucial that we be "diligent in ruling [music] in such a manner that it may be useful to us and in no way pernicious."[25] This notion of moderation first appeared in the 1543 *Institutio* and was carried forward in subsequent editions. Calvin's logic, applied to music in worship, is not hard to follow:

> surely, if the singing is to be tempered to that gravity which is fitting in the sight of God and the angels, it both lends dignity and grace to sacred actions and has the greatest value in kindling our hearts to a true zeal and eagerness to pray. Yet we should be careful

---

1980), p. 203. Compare his comments on Colossians 3 ("in your hearts sing psalms . . ."): "as we ought to stir up others, so also we ought to sing from the heart, that there may not be merely an outward sound with the mouth. Yet we must not understand it as though [Paul] is telling everyone to sing inwardly to himself, but he wants both to be conjoined, provided the heart precedes the tongue." Calvin, *Epistles*, p. 353.

23. Calvin, "Genevan Psalter," p. 348.

24. On this concept of "moderation," cf. Léon Wencelius, "L'idée de modération dans la pensée de Calvin," *Evangelical Quarterly* 7 (1935): 87-94, 295-317.

25. Calvin, "Genevan Psalter," p. 347.

that our ears be not more attentive to the melody than our minds to the spiritual meaning of the words.[26]

Calvin goes on to allude to Augustine's *Confessions,* specifically to where the early Father speaks of the danger of being more moved by singing than what is sung, and where he writes of his wish that he could restore the custom of instructing the reader to veer closer to speaking than singing, so that the music might serve the words. Calvin continues: "when this moderation is maintained, it is without doubt a most holy and salutary practice."[27] Without such moderation, music is liable to debase and contaminate us, leading to our condemnation.[28] Music appropriate to the Word of God may indeed be able to amplify the Word for us, but "frivolous" or "vain" music threatens to render the text impotent to convey its impact; it undermines and subverts the authority of God in the human heart. Hence "such songs as have been composed only for sweetness and delight of the ear are unbecoming to the majesty of the Church and cannot but displease God in the highest degree."[29]

Psalms and Melodies

It is the need for moderation that determines Calvin's restriction of sung texts to the Psalms — though from the 1539 Strasbourg Psalter onward, he was prepared also to include sung versions of other biblical material (the song of Simeon, the Ten Commandments, the Creed, and, from 1562, two table songs).[30] This, and the authorization of only certain kinds of melody, were designed to arrest the negative dynamics of sin and ensure music's positive use. We can consider each in turn.

26. *Inst.* III:20:32.

27. *Inst.* III:20:32.

28. Calvin, "Genevan Psalter," p. 347.

29. *Inst.* III:20:32.

30. In the Strasbourg Psalter (1539), Calvin included a sung Creed (the words are arranged by Calvin himself). However, this is omitted in the 1542 edition. I have been unable to find any writing of Calvin's that justifies singing the Creed, as in the 1539 Psalter: its inclusion is unusual in that it is not biblical, and the overriding argument is that the words provided by God — the Bible — must be used, because anything else is inevitably inferior.

Why such a concentration on the Psalms? Because they are the words God gave us to praise him, and nothing could "moderate" music better. Given our fallen nature, left to ourselves, we are prone to produce poor and damaging words, and (as we have noted) Calvin believes music can multiply the harmful effects of bad words. So we ought to make every effort to ensure that the words are of the very best, and the Psalms of David, being provided by God, simply cannot be surpassed. Again, Calvin draws on Augustine:

> what Augustine says is true — that no one can sing things worthy of God save what he has received from him. Wherefore, although we look far and wide and search on every hand, we shall not find better songs nor songs better suited to that end than the Psalms of David which the Holy Spirit made and uttered through him. And for this reason when we sing them we may be certain that God puts the words in our mouths as if he himself sang in us to exalt his glory.[31]

Nevertheless, in addition, every effort must be made to use appropriate music. Here we find Calvin eager that all is done in a manner that honors God's dignity and sovereignty. Accordingly, "It must always be looked to that the song be not light and frivolous but have weight *(pois)* and majesty *(maiesté)*."[32] Calvin seems less concerned that the music should fit a particular text than that it should be fitting in general: that it should have a gravitas appropriate to the worship of the one true God of the scriptures.

---

31. Calvin, "Genevan Psalter," p. 348. The citing of Augustine was also important for supporting his case about bringing practice into line with the early church. Cf. *Inst.* III:20:32. What remains unclear here, however, is why he appears to see no need to justify this restriction in the face of the wider categories of song that seem to be referred to in Colossians 3:16 and Ephesians 5:18 (cf. Calvin, *Epistles*, pp. 203, 353). Noting that it is hard to distinguish the three types of song cited in these verses — psalms, hymns, and spiritual songs/odes — he seems prepared to accept the "commonly" held view that "psalms" refers to songs accompanied by some instrument, and "hymns" to songs that may or may not be so accompanied. Even more remarkably, he makes no attempt to argue that Paul is thinking of sung psalms. Indeed, the incongruity between his exegesis of these verses and his own convictions about music in church does not seem to perturb him in the least.

32. Calvin, "Genevan Psalter," p. 346.

There is no doubt at all, then, that Calvin is recommending a specific style, to be sharply distinguished from secular genres that risk trivializing the divine presence. Again calling on Augustine, he argues that there is "a great difference between the music one makes to entertain men at table and in their homes, and the Psalms which are sung in the Church in the presence of God and his angels."[33] Secular melodies are not to be used — a prohibition that marks a decisive break both with Calvin's past, and, of course, with Luther. Moreover, Calvin looks to the replacement of all secular vocal music with singing the Psalms. (We should not be misled by Calvin's warm recommendation in the Preface to the Psalter to sing in "homes" and "fields."[34] What might appear to be an endorsement of "secular" song is in fact nothing of the sort: the context makes it clear that he has psalm-singing in mind.) One of Calvin's motivations here seems to have been a concern to exclude even the possibility of certain types of obscene song finding a place in church or in society.[35] At any rate, as far as worship is concerned, his free paraphrase of Colossians 3:16 makes his intentions very clear:

> Leave to unbelievers that foolish delight which they get from ludicrous and frivolous jests and witticisms. Let your words, not merely those that are serious, but those also that are joyful and cheerful, contain something profitable. In place of their obscene, or at least barely modest and decent, songs, it becomes you to sing hymns and songs that sound forth God's praise.[36]

For similar reasons, harmony is shunned, and instrumental accompaniment disallowed (though instruments are permitted in homes and schools).[37] In addition to the need for a style of sufficient weight

33. Calvin, "Genevan Psalter," p. 346.
34. Calvin, "Genevan Psalter," p. 346.
35. Garside, "Origins," pp. 24f.
36. Calvin, *Epistles,* p. 353.
37. Instrumental music, as Calvin saw it, belonged to the dispensation of the old covenant, and should thus be disallowed in church worship. It was instituted for those "yet tender, like children" being trained under the law; in contrast "the voice of man . . . assuredly excels all inanimate instruments of music." Purely instrumental music is like the "unknown tongue" that Paul shuns in 1 Corinthians 14. "Genevan Psalter," p. 346. What, then, of the references to instruments in worship in the Old Testament? Interestingly, Calvin's responses are based on the tacit assumption of the

and gravity, it is the principle of the intelligibility of the text that explains the ban on instruments: in some medieval practice, it would seem that instruments had come to play an excessively prominent part, obscuring the words.[38]

Calvin was not a skilled musician, in contrast to Luther (and in even greater contrast to Zwingli), and did not write any of the melodies. However, in addition to contributing Psalm paraphrases of his own, he had a considerable influence on the various editions of the Psalters. Not surprisingly, the characteristics of the Genevan psalm tunes bear out Calvin's desires. They are monophonic (without harmony), unaccompanied, generally syllabic (one note to each syllable), and rarely exceed an octave in range (thus easily singable).[39] The sense of dignity Calvin so longed for was achieved not so much through slow tempi as through the simplicity of the melodies, their uncluttered accessibility. Again, running through this is a corporate concern: that the whole church may participate fully in the act of singing, and thus be built up.

It is sometimes assumed that the musical austerity of the Psalter was an innovation, dramatically out of line with the progress of late medieval and Renaissance music (and thus another example of the church impeding the development of music!). In fact, the Psalter is thoroughly in line with much in humanist music theory and prac-

---

moral force of music. He regards it as God's concession to infirmity — the Jews needed every incitement to spirituality possible. But, unlike the contemporary Roman Church, instruments were employed in a pious, godly way. The crucial point, however, is that the Jews were in religious infancy: with the coming of Christ, all such "external" aids are rendered unnecessary, and are more likely to impede rather than assist access to God. Cf. H. P. Clive, "The Calvinist Attitude to Music," *Bibliothèque d'Humanisme et Renaissance* 19 (1957): 91-94.

38. Cf. Clive, "Calvinist Attitude," pp. 90ff.

39. Most of the melodies have their origin in existing models. Many have argued that the roots of the Genevan melodies are in medieval church songs (the older theory that they derive from secular folk-songs finds much less support today). The more immediate models are hard to determine. As far as the first Strasbourg Psalter (1539) is concerned, it seems that a number originate in Strasbourg, especially in the work of the musician Matthäus Greitter. Cf. Ford Lewis Battles, *The Piety of John Calvin* (Grand Rapids: Baker, 1978), pp. 144-65. The most influential musician on the 1562 edition — the first complete version — was Louis Bourgeois, who arrived in Geneva in 1545. Cf. Walter Blankenburg, "Church Music in Reformed Europe," in Friedrich Blume, ed., *Protestant Church Music* (New York: Norton, 1974), pp. 519ff.

tice.[40] The strong impact of humanism on the Reformer has never been doubted, though we do not know how well versed he was in its music theory. In any case, his views on the word-text relation are highly congruent with the mainstream of humanist writing. The matching of music to word was of central importance to the humanists;[41] they recommended curtailment of melismatic writing for the sake of a more syllabic delivery, acute attention to the accentuation of words and their proper arrangement, and, in general, a "simplification of musical means and clarification of textual content, a concern ... with audibility, with intelligibility."[42] The sixteenth-century treatises of Lanfranco, Vincentino, Zarlino, and Stocker bear all this out, and, moreover, it has been suggested that such ideas were widely promoted in the fifteenth century also.[43] The motivation, of course, was differently focused than in Calvin. The humanists were intent on recovering the marriage of word and music that had been extolled in ancient literature: "the fundamental purpose of the revival of [the humanist] word-text ideal was to reproduce what the Italians called the maravigliosi effetti of ancient music ... all agreed that the best way to do so was to emphasize the text rather than the music."[44] For Calvin, as we have seen, the primary thrust was theological; music was to accord with the text to ensure that it truly was the power of God's Word that would take hold of the church and enable it to worship God from the heart.

40. Charles Garside, "Calvin's Preface to the Psalter: A Re-appraisal," *Musical Quarterly* 37 (1951): 575-76.

41. Don Hárran, *Word-Tone Relations in Musical Thought from Antiquity to the Seventeenth Century* (Neuhausen-Stuttgart: American Institute of Musicology and Hänssler-Verlag, 1986). Hárran asserts that "Renaissance humanism and its vitalising effect on all areas of cultural endeavour mark the Great Divide between the incidental treatment of text in the early theoretical writings and its more methodological treatment in the later ones: the codification of the rules that govern the alignment of notes and syllables is at root a humanist enterprise" (p. 10). Cf. also D. P. Walker, "Musical Humanism in the Sixteenth and Early Seventeenth Centuries," *The Music Review* 2 (1941): 1-13, 111-21, 220-27, 288-308; 3 (1942): 55-71.

42. Hárran, *Word-Tone Relations*, p. 82. Indeed, Walker speaks of a situation in which "the text completely dominates its setting" (p. 289).

43. Honey Meconi, "Is Underlay Necessary?" in T. Knighton and D. Fallow, eds., *Companion to Medieval and Renaissance Music* (New York: Schirmer, 1992), pp. 284-91.

44. Garside, "Calvin's Preface," p. 576, et passim. Cf. Walker, "Musical Humanism," p. 226.

Hugging the Words?

Having said this, despite Calvin's rhetoric of the conformity of music to text, owing much to the humanists, the practice by no means wholly matches the theory. Calvin, it might reasonably be thought, would authorize melodies following speech in every respect, "hugging the contours of language," to use Daniel Chua's metaphor.[45] But matters are not so simple. The melodies show a distinct rhythmic independence from the words they carry, giving them a character quite distinct from, say, the songs of the German Reformed regions. The rhythmic structures of the Genevan tunes follow one of two models (both from Strasbourg). However, within certain clear parameters, much variation could be and was attempted (as some editions of the Psalter show).[46] From one point of view these new rhythmic patterns can be seen as the product of a certain rationalizing tendency (common also in the humanists, who are undoubtedly in the background here), but from another they signal a certain distance between words and music, words being accommodated to a musical-rhythmic grid neither derived from nor directly associated with the words. Walter Blankenburg writes: "The intimate interweaving of text and melody, typical for other regions of Reform song, is replaced here by a goal of rhythmic construction, i.e. by a certain measure of musical autonomy. There is no other feature in church music as typically Calvinist as this one."[47]

Comments and Questions

Scripture's Primacy

Even from this relatively cursory outline of Calvin's account of music, what is perhaps most immediately apparent throughout is a resolute desire to be solidly focused on, and faithful to the texts of Old and New Testament. As Garside rightly points out, all the dimensions of Calvin's

45. Daniel Chua, *Absolute Music and the Construction of Meaning* (Cambridge: Cambridge University Press, 1999), p. 34.
46. Blankenburg, "Calvin," p. 528.
47. Blankenburg, "Calvin," p. 529.

approach to music — pastoral, historical, Augustinian, and humanistic — are ultimately "fused . . . and made indissolubly one in Scripture."[48]

There are at least three senses in which his convictions about music and its use in worship show a sense of the primacy of Scripture. First, at a fairly obvious level, he is attempting a reform of worship in accordance with the simplicity he believed it possessed in apostolic times — as testified in Scripture. Music must be deployed in accordance with apostolic practice. Scripture therefore has a programmatic priority in his account of music; it informs us of the customary practice of the earliest Christian communities to which contemporary practice must conform. Second, Scripture also has primacy in that no other texts could possibly excel the scriptural text for the purpose of singing in worship, and the most obvious texts to use are the Psalms, the church's divinely provided songbook. Third, Calvin is obviously pressing for scriptural primacy in another sense, namely that in worship (and, it would seem, beyond worship) sung music is to be subservient to the scriptural text (in this case, preeminently the Psalm texts). Music must be moderated or tempered by the text. This is understood at the lexical level (Calvin clearly approves of the music following the temporal structure of the words as closely as possible), but also at the semantic level: even though he does not speak of each melody matching each Psalm or each part of a Psalm, he wants the ethos of all music in worship to be one of weight and majesty, as befits the God with whom the Psalms (and all the elements of worship) engage. Crucial to this is that music must allow the words to be audible and intelligible. The relative simplicity of the music, its lack of harmony, and the absence of instruments not only safeguard a sense of weight and majesty, but help to render the words audible and comprehensible, so that the church can attend to their "spiritual meaning." To quote Garside again,

> Calvin's vernacular psalmody in the last analysis is nothing other than a formulation, in uniquely musical terms, of the Reformation principle of sola scriptura. Thus from its inception Calvin's theology of music in its textual dimension was scriptural. The Psalter was conceived, and always would be considered by him, as an indis-

48. Garside, "Origins," p. 29.

pensable instrument for the prosecution of his ministry of the Word of God to the city of Geneva and the wider world beyond.[49]

Qualifications

Notwithstanding the importance of Calvin's desire to situate music within a theological milieu that gives priority to the sacred texts, two qualifications are in order. First, we drew attention earlier to a conspicuous change in Calvin's attitude to music, from little more than forbearance to enthusiastic endorsement, from treating it as a minor (and dispensable?) component to regarding it as an intrinsic part of worship's practice and character. Calvin discovered, it would seem, and in an apparently unforgettable way, music's affective power for a community. He was keen to harness this power in order that the church might praise God more fully, with more zeal. Put differently, he came to realize that music had irreducible capacities of its own, which could be brought into interaction with words. This, then, is quite different from believing that music is lifeless without words, or that it will automatically buckle down and reproduce the shape and meaning of any words that happen to be put with it. Calvin's caution about music arises from his vigorous respect for music's particular and potent eloquencies.

Second, Calvin's notion of the preeminence of Scripture in relation to music can only be properly understood when set against much broader horizons in his theology. Prima facie, the subordination of music to the text of Scripture might sound somewhat arbitrary and unduly restrictive. But when approached in the light of his understanding of the dynamics of revelation and salvation, and the place of Scripture's words in these dynamics, whatever our final estimation might be, Calvin's concerns become much more intelligible. The heart of the matter is that Scripture is not an end in itself, a terminus or object of faith, but rather serves the mediation of the salvific knowledge (*cognitio*) of God. Through divine "accommodation" to our capacity, the words of Scripture serve the trinitarian dynamic of salvation. Scripture functions (in different ways) as the primary means through which

---

49. Garside, "Origins," p. 29.

humans discover a saving union, initiated and sustained by the Spirit, with Christ — the one in whom all parts of our salvation are contained, in whose humanity our humanity has found its telos in relation to the Father. Human language, and decisively the language of Scripture, though weak in itself, is thus for Calvin intrinsic to the triune God's saving work among us.[50]

When we bear this in mind, together with Calvin's theological construal of corporate worship (especially his trinitarian theology of the Lord's Supper),[51] we have good reason to follow Jeffrey VanderWilt when he writes: "The project of the psalms was but a correlative extension into music of that famous, Calvinist principle of sacramental theology, his curiously compelling interpretation of the Sursum corda:

> 'Therefore, lift up your hearts on high, seeking the heavenly things in heaven, where Jesus Christ is seated at the right hand of the Father; and do not fix your eyes on the visible signs which are corrupted through usage. In joy of heart, in brotherly union, come, everyone, partake of our Lord's Table, giving thanks unto him for the very great love which he has shown us. Have the death of this good Saviour graven on your hearts in eternal remembrance so that you are set afire, so also that you incite others to love God and follow his holy Word.'"[52]

In this light, it is perhaps no accident that Calvin makes one of his most theologically telling comments about music in worship in a context where the focus is resolutely on the risen High Priest at the right hand of the Father. He is discussing Hebrew 2:12, a verse in which

---

50. The secondary literature on Calvin's soteriological doctrine of Scripture is vast, but cf. e.g., T. F. Torrance, *The Hermeneutics of John Calvin* (Edinburgh: Scottish Academic Press, 1988); "Knowledge of God and Speech about Him according to John Calvin," in *Theology in Reconstruction* (London: SCM, 1965), pp. 76-98; B. A. Gerrish, *Grace and Gratitude: The Eucharistic Theology of John Calvin* (Minneapolis: Fortress Press, 1993), pp. 76ff.; T. H. L. Parker, *The Doctrine of the Knowledge of God: A Study in the Theology of John Calvin* (Edinburgh: Oliver and Boyd, 1952); David L. Puckett, *John Calvin's Exegesis of the Old Testament* (Louisville: Westminster/John Knox Press, 1995); Ronald S. Wallace, *Calvin's Doctrine of the Word and Sacrament* (Edinburgh: Oliver and Boyd, 1953).
51. Gerrish, *Grace and Gratitude*.
52. VanderWilt, "John Calvin's Theology," p. 77. VanderWilt is quoting *La Forme des prières et chantz ecclésiastiques.*

words from Psalm 22 are put on the lips of Jesus: "I will proclaim your name to my brothers and sisters, in the midst of the congregation I will praise you." In our public song, Calvin comments, "Christ heeds our praise, and is the chief Conductor of our hymns."[53]

What I have tried to indicate here is that Calvin's commitment to the subservience of music to text (the Psalms) in worship is motivated by a profound commitment to the irreplaceable and determinative place of Scripture in the mediation of the triune God's reconciling work. Calvin believes that the media of human words are intrinsic to the way in which God draws us into union and communion with Christ through the Spirit, and thus into Christ's eternal communion with the Father. By the same token, whatever proximate meanings of the text we may sing in worship, the ultimate semantic dimension is precisely this dynamic or a variant on it. Thus when Calvin speaks of psalm-singing as enhancing and enriching the experience of worship, through intensifying our emotional engagement with specific texts, it is implicitly with the Sursum Corda in mind — the "lifting of our hearts" in the power of the Spirit to Jesus Christ at the right hand of the Father, who is in our midst "conducting" our hymns.

Cosmology and Music

We have seen something of how Calvin's convictions about music are highly congruent with his prime theological tenets concerning Scripture, the trinitarian dynamic of salvation and worship. Nevertheless, there may be points where even those sympathetic to Calvin's wider schema may be uneasy with aspects of his treatment of music, and uneasy for theological reasons.

Intriguingly, Calvin makes no overt attempt to speak of music in terms of the "cosmic" tradition that had imbued music theory for centuries. The notion that musical sound, especially musical harmony, coincides with and gives expression to cosmic order derives preeminently from Pythagoras, finding its entry into Western literature through Book X of Plato's *Republic*, and passing into music theory through

---

53. *The Epistle of Paul the Apostle to the Hebrews and the First and Second Epistles of Peter*, trans. William B. Johnston (Edinburgh: Oliver and Boyd, 1963), p. 27.

Boethius in his concept of *musica mundana*.[54] Yet, although Calvin was undoubtedly familiar with this stream, and was happy to speak about music as one of the "bright sparkling remnants of glory," the notion that music "sounds" the order of the universe plays no substantial part in his reflections on music. The contrast with Luther is noteworthy. For Luther the "cosmic" tradition played a pivotal part in his writings on music, grounding his views about music's ethical power. Indeed, Brian Horne contends that Luther's extraordinarily high regard for music was due primarily to its ability to grant an embodiment of divine order, holding chaos at bay and reminding us of the fundamental harmony that God confers upon the world.[55] For Calvin, God holds chaos at bay, and although Calvin presumably believes that music, as a "remnant" of primal glory, retains traces of God's creative power, it is treated largely as a rhetorical tool — albeit a wonderful, God-provided one. Further, though a gift of God, Calvin approaches music primarily as a human practice, vulnerable to the effects of the fall. It is possible that Calvin's concern that *finitum non est capax infiniti* had a significant part to play here — he may well have believed that the ancient musical

54. For a concise survey of this tradition, cf. Bowman, *Philosophical Perspectives*, pp. 19-68. See also the entertaining account given in Jamie James, *The Music of the Spheres: Music, Science and the Natural Order of the Universe* (New York: Copernicus, Springer-Verlag, 1993). As Daniel Chua puts it, the music Pythagoras bequeathed to humanity was not so much a music to be composed as a music that composed the world (*Absolute Music*, p. 15). Boethius, mediating this tradition, probably did more than anyone else to shape the musical mind of the medieval age. He designated the four mathematical disciplines within the liberal arts the quadrivium — geometry, arithmetic, astronomy, and music. Music's source lies in the divine realm of unchanging numbers, so its essence is in numerical proportions, the proportions that give harmony and unity to things. *Musica mundana* — cosmic music — emanates from the forms and motions of the spheres, sonorous yet inaudible on earth. *Musica humana* is the music of the human soul and body, and entails the blending of the soul's higher and lower parts. *Musica instrumentalis* is music as actually heard; it is a first step towards comprehending proportion, harmony, and balance in their higher versions. As Henry Chadwick explains, "Arithmetic directs the mind towards immutable truths unaffected by the contingencies of time and space. But music advances even further towards that 'summit of perfection' for which the quadrivium is a prerequisite. The theory of music is a penetration of the very heart of providence's ordering of things . . . a central clue to the interpretation of the hidden harmony of God and nature." Henry Chadwick, *Boethius* (Oxford: Clarendon Press, 1981), p. 101.
55. Horne, "A Civitas of Sound."

cosmology did not pay sufficient heed to the Creator/creature distinction.[56] It is also possible that he feared that locating music's center of gravity in an ontology of creation at large would run the risk of giving unwarranted divine sanction to an activity highly vulnerable to the distortions of human sin.

Daniel Chua and others have drawn attention to the weighty significance of the collapse of the medieval vision of music, especially for the way music and word are related in the early modern and Enlightenment periods, and for the way music is treated in modernity, not least by the church.[57] Simplifying drastically: from the sixteenth century, modernity began to lose confidence in the grand "cosmic" musical scenario, and by the early eighteenth century the ancient vision had been largely abandoned. Chua comments: "at certain imperceptible points in the seventeenth century, music was tugged out of its cosmological structure like a loose thread and was made to reformulate itself in a new epistemological space that focused on its existence while undermining the very ability of music to justify itself."[58] Consonant with this, as early as the sixteenth century some theorists proposed a transfer of music from the ancient quadrivium (in which music was grouped with geometry, arithmetic, and astronomy) to the trivium (rhetoric, grammar, and dialectics). This, according to Chua, "signals a modern ontology"[59] in which music is construed as first and foremost a tool of the human, rhetorical will.

Not surprisingly, it was instrumental music that was hardest to validate in early modernity; vocal music at least had words to anchor it in extra-musical reality, giving the notes something to "refer" to, a stability of reference and thus a certain legitimacy. But without the medieval musical cosmology in place, it was increasingly hard to find ways of underwriting wordless music. Typically, instrumental music comes

56. Carlos Eire notes that the two commonest phrases used to sum up Calvin's theology of worship are *soli Deo gloria* (to God alone be the glory) and *finitum non est capax infiniti* (the finite cannot contain the infinite). Carlos M. N. Eire, *War Against the Idols: The Reformation of Worship from Erasmus to Calvin* (Cambridge: Cambridge University Press, 1986), p. 197. See the whole of ch. 6 for a very illuminating discussion of Calvin and idolatry.

57. Chua, *Absolute Music.*

58. Chua, *Absolute Music,* p. 76.

59. Chua, *Absolute Music,* p. 76.

to be seen as something radically different from — and potentially inferior to — vocal music. A suspicion of instrumental music is very evident in much Reformation writing, and the tussles in music-theory between vocal and instrumental music in the succeeding decades and centuries proliferate.

Various strategies for dealing with instrumental music's waywardness were offered — most involved the attempt to ground music in speech in some manner. Some writers went to great lengths to show that instrumental music was an elaborate form of speech, using figures akin to those of spoken rhetoric *(Figurenlehre)*. In some forms of early Enlightenment thought, the problem of grounding instrumental music was answered in terms of physics and physiology (Jean-Philippe Rameau's work is the prime example here). What was once explained in terms of medieval metaphysics could now be accounted for, some thought, in terms of Newtonian science. This gave rise to a number of elaborate explanations of the effects of music on the body and, through the body, on our emotions. But without an ontology (or, we might say, a doctrine of creation) capable of embracing human and extra-human, vocal and instrumental music (as in the ancient medieval vision), it is not surprising that some of the attempts to reunify music and words were widely regarded as highly strained and artificial, and had a relatively short shelf-life.[60]

The burgeoning of instrumental music in the seventeenth and eighteenth centuries and the development of its new auditorium, the concert hall; the development of the concept that Richard Wagner was much later to dub "absolute music"; the prominence of the notion of a "work" encoded supremely in a score, and supposedly free of any "outside" connection (especially with words) — all of these are part of that complex narrative that one writer has called "the emancipation of music from language."[61] The eventual divinization of "pure" music by the early Romantics (and later by Schopenhauer) can usefully be read as an

---

60. For treatments of these developments, cf. John Hollander, *The Untuning of the Sky: Ideas of Music in English Poetry, 1500-1700* (Princeton: Princeton University Press, 1961); John Neubauer, *The Emancipation of Music from Language: Departure from Mimesis in Eighteenth-Century Aesthetics* (New Haven: Yale University Press, 1986); Mark Evan Bonds, *Wordless Rhetoric: Musical Form and the Metaphor of the Oration* (Cambridge, Mass.: Harvard University Press, 1991).

61. Neubauer, *Emancipation*.

attempt to recover a glimpse of the ancient medieval vision. (Some of the early Romantics were quite explicit that this is just what they were seeking to do.) Music returns with a vengeance to reclaim its long-lost theological status.[62]

We should not miss the way in which the Christian church became caught up in these currents and cross-currents of discourse. Especially instructive, for example, is Joyce Irwin's painstaking account of Lutheran battles over music in the period between Luther and Bach.[63] The trends she charts are thoroughly in line with Chua's analysis. Luther's own belief in linking music to God's created order was taken up by a number of writers, yet with the emergence of Pietism in the late seventeenth century, together with its associated controversies, we find the ancient cosmological vision being sidelined, and vocal and instrumental music often being treated as essentially separate and antagonistic to each other. Some argued for a radical assimilation of music to words, others for a robust recognition of music's ability to glorify God quite apart from words — a polarity itself deeply symptomatic of an inability to theorize the music-word relation adequately. Of special interest is Irwin's observation of the paucity of theology in many of the church debates in the early eighteenth century: a heavy reliance on physics, physiology, and psychology, but with at best a thin theological veneer.[64]

Conclusion

Of course, I am far from wishing to suggest that the blame for any or all of these problematics can simply be pinned on Calvin. There is at least room to wonder, however, whether Calvin's explication of the word-music relation aligns rather too easily with those in early modernity who, in an eagerness to "de-sacralize" music and sever it from one type of doctrine of creation, are unable to offer an alternative, integrally theological vision of the world in which to situate it. Calvin's constant reiteration of the rhetoric of conformity (music must con-

---

62. Chua, *Absolute Music,* Part 3.
63. Irwin, *Neither Voice Nor Heart Alone.*
64. Irwin, *Neither Voice Nor Heart Alone,* ch. 12.

form to words), without setting music within a wider ontology of creation (as in Luther), risks driving music into a functionalism in which the links between music and the natural order are bypassed in favor of the efficient utility of its sounds, directly harnessed (clamped?) to particular words.

We are bound to question whether Calvin's way of construing the music-word relation allows sufficient room for music's distinctive and particular capacities, and thus for developing an account of music and words that can do justice both to music's resonances with language and its irreducible differences.[65] It is highly significant that Calvin's theory and practice are at odds. As we have seen, even the music he authorizes does not "hug" the rhythmic and metrical contours of language in all respects, nor is there an attempt to ensure a complete one-to-one match between the melodies and the meaning of the words of each Psalm. In other words, even here, in one of the most rigorous projects ever undertaken to align music to words, complete with heavy theological backing for the text's priority, music stubbornly resists complete assimilation to words. Music is permitted — indeed, encouraged — to do its own kind of work in its own kind of ways.

Over many decades, John de Gruchy has engaged intensively as a theologian with a huge range of practices and disciplines. In recent years he has given assiduous attention to the arts, especially the nonverbal visual arts. His example in this respect, and our brief study of Calvin, I would suggest, both push us in a very similar direction. They compel us to ask at least two critical questions. First, to what extent can a contemporary theology make "room" for a practice like music? More fully: To what extent can theology account for the kind of rationality or coherence of a nonverbal practice like music, a coherence at one and the same time grounded in the creational order of sound and in the order of human making and culture, a coherence that has many affinities with verbal language and yet cannot be reduced to the rationality of words? Second, is contemporary theology prepared to learn from and draw upon the distinctive powers of a phenomenon such as music in order to do its job more effectively?[66] I submit that a responsible theology today

65. Cf. Jeremy Begbie, *Music, Word and the Future of Theology* (forthcoming).
66. Cf. Jeremy Begbie, *Theology, Music and Time* (Cambridge: Cambridge University Press, 2000).

cannot afford to ignore these two questions (whether they are asked specifically of music or of any other nonverbal art form), and this is especially so in the so-called "postmodern" sensibility, with its high sensitivity to all things aesthetic. In his most recent professional work, John has pointed to a way ahead; it is time that many others followed his lead.

Point and Counterpoint —
Resistance and Submission:
Dietrich Bonhoeffer on Theology and Music
in Times of War and Social Crisis

Andreas Pangritz

Introduction

From its beginning Christian theology has been conceived in close relationship to music. Theological dogmatics describing the content of
Christian faith was originally rooted in "doxology" — the glorification
of God's glory *(doxa)*, the human answer in praise and mourning to
God's word. Only later the meaning of dogmatics changed, emphasizing primarily the aspect of doctrine — authoritative teaching of the
church rather than revolutionary singing of the "dogma."

There are theological thinkers who in their dogmatic work express the relationship between theology and music, dogma and doxology more than others. It follows therefore to ask if in their case musical allusions can be taken seriously as parables interpreting the
theological content of the texts as well. The example of Karl Barth is
well known. Barth's predilection for Mozart's music sheds light on
central concepts of his *Church Dogmatics*.[1] Another example is Dietrich
Bonhoeffer. As a theologian of Lutheran descent he was familiar with
Luther's conviction that music deserved the first position after theol-

---

1. Cf. Andreas Pangritz, "'Freie Zuneigung': Über Karl Barths Verhältnis zu Mozart,'" in Ute Gniewoß et al., eds., *Störenfriedels Zeddelkasten: Geschenkpapiere zum 60.
Geburtstag von Friedrich-Wilhelm Marquardt* (1988) (Berlin: Alektor, 1991), pp. 178-202.

ogy. According to Luther music, as God's gift, was invoked to chase the devil away.[2]

Bonhoeffer's *Letters and Papers from Prison*[3] contain a series of musical reflections that seem to have crucial significance for his latest theological thinking. Most of these allusions appear in letters prior to the formulation of the theological theme — the question as to "what Christianity really is, or indeed who Christ really is, for us today."[4] Reflections on music prepare for and interpret Bonhoeffer's latest theological thinking and can thus be of help in understanding the revolutionary "new formulas." Finally, Bonhoeffer employs the musical formula of "polyphony of life" to describe the contrapuntal interplay between spiritual and secular love as the essence of nonreligious Christianity:

> What I mean is that God wants us to love him eternally with our whole hearts — not in such a way as to injure or weaken our earthly love, but to provide a kind of *cantus firmus* to which the other melodies of life provide the counterpoint. One of these contrapuntal themes . . . is earthly affection. Even in the Bible we have the Song of Songs. . . . Where the *cantus firmus* is clear and plain, the counterpoint can be developed to its limits. The two are "undivided and yet distinct," in the words of the Chalcedonian Definition, like Christ in his divine and human natures. May not the attraction and importance of polyphony in music consist in its being a musical reflection of this Christological fact and therefore of our *vita christiana?*[5]

---

2. Martin Luther, *"Perì tês mousikês"* (1530), in *WA* 30, no. 2, p. 696. Luther's musical advisor Johann Walther even believed that music was wrapped up and hidden in theology (cf. Oskar Söhngen, *Theologie der Musik* [Kassel: Johannes Stauda, 1967], p. 81).

3. Dietrich Bonhoeffer, *Letters and Papers from Prison,* The Enlarged Edition (New York: Macmillan, 1972). Cf. Bonhoeffer, *Widerstand und Ergebung: Briefe und Aufzeichnungen aus der Haft,* ed. Chr. Gremmels et al. (Gütersloh: Chr. Kaiser/ Gütersloher Verlagshaus, 1998) (Dietrich Bonhoeffer Werke [DBW], vol. 8).

4. Bonhoeffer, *Letters,* 30 April 1944, p. 279.

5. Bonhoeffer, *Letters,* 20 May 1944, p. 303. Cf. the letters to Eberhard Bethge, 21 May 1944: "The image of polyphony is still pursuing me . . . ," p. 305; 29 May 1944, p. 311.

ANDREAS PANGRITZ

Heinrich Schütz and the "Restoration of all Things"

A great deal of Bonhoeffer's musical allusions in *Letters and Papers from Prison* refer to Heinrich Schütz, the "father of German music" in the seventeenth century. Bonhoeffer had become acquainted with Schütz's music through Eberhard Bethge during the Finkenwalde period. On 4 February 1941 he thanked Bethge in a letter from Ettal monastery for a birthday gift, Hans Joachim Moser's biography of Heinrich Schütz: "I owe Heinrich Schütz to you, and with him a whole rich world. I would like to accompany you singing 'Make haste, O God, to deliver me . . .', which — by the help of the attached notes — I hummed away to myself. It is not by chance that it was you, by whom Schütz has approached me."[6]

It is likely that the relevance of Schütz's *Kleine Geistliche Konzerte*, which Bethge, Bonhoeffer, and many others felt especially during World War II, refers to a correspondence of situations. Schütz had composed these settings during the Thirty Years War in Germany (1618-1648). Written for small ensembles, these concerts formed Schütz's musical protest against the war and its consequences. As Schütz writes in the dedication of the first volume of his *Kleine Geistliche Konzerte* (1636): "It is obvious for many observers, in which way the laudable music among other liberal arts has severely declined and at some places even been destroyed by the ongoing dangerous events of war in our beloved Fatherland of German nation." Or in the dedication of the second volume (1639):

> I am ashamed to appear in the face of His Serenity with such small and simple works. But the wickedness of the present times is unfavourable for the liberal arts and does not permit my other works, which I have at hand without any glory, to appear in public. At the moment there was no other choice, therefore, than this poor work. But should the arts, which have nearly been suffocated and trodden into the mud by the arms now, be elevated again to their former dignity and value by the mercy of God, I will not forget to appear

6. Dietrich Bonhoeffer, *Konspiration und Haft 1940-1945,* ed. J. Glenthøj et al. (Gütersloh: Chr. Kaiser/Gütersloher Verlagshaus, 1996) (Dietrich Bonhoeffer Werke, vol. 16), p. 129.

according to my duty in the face of His Princely Serenity with a richer pledge.[7]

In *Letters and Papers from Prison* these concerts are meaningful for Bonhoeffer, especially through the close relationship between music and (mostly biblical) text. More than once Bonhoeffer mentions Psalm 70 ("Make haste, O God, to deliver me") in Schütz's setting.[8] Other compositions by Schütz, mentioned by Bonhoeffer, are the settings of Psalms 3:6-9; 27:4; and 47.[9]

This selection of texts from the book of Psalms permits an insight into Bonhoeffer's spiritual life as a prisoner, reflected in the "Prayerbook of the Bible."[10] We listen to him praying for help against his enemies (Psalms 3 and 70) and expressing his hope that God might show himself as "frightening" to the "Gentiles," and that he might elect "the glory of Jacob, whom he loves" (Psalm 47).[11]

---

7. Heinrich Schütz's dedications quoted from Wilhelm Ehmann, "Vorwort," in *Heinrich Schütz, Neue Ausgabe sämtlicher Werke*, vol. 10 (Kassel: Bärenreiter, 1963), p. vii (my translation).

8. Cf. Schütz, "Eile mich, Gott, zu erretten . . ." (Schütz-Werke-Verzeichnis [SWV] 282), in Schütz, *Neue Ausgabe*, vol. 10, *Erster Theil Kleiner Geistlicher Concerten*, No. 1, pp. 1ff.; mentioned by Bonhoeffer four times: Letters to his parents, 15 May 1943 (*Letters*, p. 40); to Eberhard Bethge, 20 November 1943 (*Letters*, p. 134); Advent IV 1943 (*Letters*, p. 171); and 21 May 1944 (*Letters*, p. 306 [cf. DBW 8, p. 446, note 23]).

9. Cf. the compositions "Ich liege und schlafe . . ." (SWV 310), in Schütz, *Neue Ausgabe*, vol. 10, *Anderer Theil Kleiner Geistlichen Concerten*, No. 5, pp. 96ff.; mentioned by Bonhoeffer in the letter to his parents, 15 May 1943 (*Letters*, p. 40), and in the letter to Eberhard Bethge, 21 May 1944 (*Letters*, p. 306 [cf. DBW 8, p. 446, note 23]); "Eins bitte ich von dem Herren . . ." (SWV 294), in Schütz, *Neue Ausgabe*, vol. 10, *Erster Theil*, No. 13, pp. 100ff.; mentioned by Bonhoeffer in the letter to Eberhard Bethge, Advent IV 1943 (*Letters*, p. 171); and "Frohlocket mit Händen . . ." (SWV 349), in Schütz, *Neue Ausgabe*, vol. 15: *Symphoniae Sacrae Secunda Pars*, pp. 82ff.; mentioned by Bonhoeffer in the letter to his parents, 15 May 1943 (*Letters*, p. 40), and in the letters to Eberhard Bethge, 20 November 1943 (*Letters*, p. 134), and 21 May 1944 (*Letters*, p. 306 [cf. DBW 8, p. 446, note 23]).

10. Cf. Dietrich Bonhoeffer, *Das Gebetbuch der Bibel: Eine Einführung in die Psalmen* (1940), ed. G. L. Müller (München: Chr. Kaiser, 1987 [DBW 5]).

11. Especially the text of the concert "Make haste, O God, to deliver me" (Psalm 70) seems to be meaningful regarding Bonhoeffer's situation as a prisoner. "Make haste, O God, to deliver me; to help me, O Lord./Let them be ashamed and confounded, that seek after my soul;/let them be turned backward and put to confusion,

Bonhoeffer cannot read these Psalms any longer without hearing them in the settings by Heinrich Schütz,[12] where the Word of God is expressed, interpreted, and intensified through musical "figures." Some examples: in the setting of Psalm 3 the line "I laid me down and slept," descending to the extreme depth and contrasted by rapidly ascending melodic leaps on "I awakened"; in the same setting the fiercely dentated melodic figure on "thou hast broken the teeth of the ungodly"; in Psalm 70 the threefold repetition of the derisive "Aha, Aha" of the enemies; and in the same setting the expressive ascension of the melodic line to the most extreme altitude on "O Lord, make no tarrying." Remarkable as well is the artificial setting of the "Selah," mysterious in its meaning, in the settings of Psalms 3 and 47.

In one of the letters to Eberhard Bethge, on Advent IV 1943, Bonhoeffer cites from his memory not only the text but also the notes of a "Geistliches Konzert." In this case the text is not a biblical Psalm, but a hymn on Christ by St. Augustine: "O sweet, o kindly,/O good Lord Jesus Christ."[13] Bonhoeffer cites the ascending melodic figure of seven notes on occasion of the exclamation "o," languishing for union with Christ, in the line "o how my soul longs for you." In Schütz's setting the melismatic figure on "o" is repeated four times, each time a fifth higher (*e flat–b flat, b flat–f, f-c, c-g*), so that the musical expression is intensified in an extraordinary measure. Moser underscores the fact that by means of transposed repetition of the melismatic motif, the "ecstatic cry of longing" forms the "center and climax" of the composition. In addition he points out that there is a certain affinity between this figure and the melismatic "o" in Schütz's motet on the Song of Songs: "O, quam tu pulchra es. . . ."[14] And it is true that the language of

---

that desire my hurt./Let them be turned back for a reward of their shame, that say 'Aha, Aha',/Let those who seek thee and love thy salvation rejoice and be glad,/and say always: Praise God on high!/But I am poor and needy;/make haste unto me, O God:/thou art my help and deliverer,/O Lord, make no tarrying."

12. Bonhoeffer, *Letters*, p. 40.

13. Cf. Heinrich Schütz, "O süßer, o freundlicher, o gütiger Herr Jesu Christe . . ." (SWV 285), in Schütz, *Neue Ausgabe*, vol. 10, *Erster Theil . . .*, No. 4, pp. 83ff.

14. Cf. Hans Joachim Moser, *Heinrich Schütz: Sein Leben und Werk* (1936), 2nd ed. (Kassel: Bärenreiter, 1954), pp. 436f. Cf. Heinrich Schütz, "O quam tu pulchra es, amica mea/Veni de Libano, amica mea" (double motet; SWV 265/66), in Schütz, *Neue Ausgabe*, vol. 13, *Symphoniae Sacrae*, pp. 72ff.

the Augustinian hymn is colored by erotic associations, when it continues, "My helper, you have ensnared my heart/With your love,/That I yearn for you without end. . . ."

In a formulation resembling Moser's phrasing, Bonhoeffer comments that he now and then thinks of the "o" from the Augustinian hymn "O bone Jesu" in Schütz's setting. "Doesn't this passage in its ecstatic longing combined with pure devotion, suggest the 'bringing back' of all earthly desire?"[15] It seems that here Bonhoeffer's Christological interest has already found its full intensity and intimacy in musical concepts before the essential theological question, "who Christ really is, for us today,"[16] appears in *Letters and Papers from Prison*. In close connection with the hymn "O bone Jesu" Bonhoeffer quotes also the Paul Gerhardt[17] hymn "Beside thy cradle here I stand," which he characterizes by "a slight flavor of the monastery and mysticism," mentioning also the "Imitation of Christ" by Thomas à Kempis.[18] Thus it seems legitimate even to speak of a tendency to mysticism in connection with Christ in this context.

It is important to realize on the other hand that Bonhoeffer, after having mentioned the ecstatic "o" in Schütz's setting, continues quite soberly: "'Bringing back' mustn't, of course, be confused with 'sublimation'. . . ."[19] "Bringing back" or "recapitulation" *(anakephalaíōsis)*, the restoration of all things, is the theme of the whole paragraph we are dealing with.

The immediate cause of Bonhoeffer's chain of thought is another verse by Paul Gerhardt — the fifth stanza of the Christmas hymn "All my heart this night rejoices . . . (Fröhlich soll mein Herze springen . . .)." Bonhoeffer writes that "For this last week or so these lines have kept on running through my head: 'Brethren, from all ills that grieve you/You are freed; All you need/I will surely give you (= bring back to you).' What does this 'I'll bring back' mean? It means that nothing is lost, that everything is in good hands, kept safe in Christ, although it is transformed, made transparent, clear, and free from all selfish de-

15. Bonhoeffer, *Letters*, p. 170. Translation altered.
16. Bonhoeffer, *Letters*, 30 April 1944, p. 179.
17. The famous Lutheran theologian and poet of the seventeenth century.
18. Bonhoeffer, *Letters*, p. 170.
19. Bonhoeffer, *Letters*, p. 170. Translation altered.

sire."[20] Bonhoeffer alludes here to the doctrine of recapitulation or restoration of all things by the anti-Gnostic church father Irenaeus (second century), characterizing it as "a magnificent conception, full of
comfort."[21] Referring to the biblical roots of the doctrine in Ecclesiastes 3:15 ("God seeks again what is past"), it seems to Bonhoeffer that
this doctrine is the appropriate answer to our "longing for the past,"
which may seize us "when we least expect it."[22] It is Bonhoeffer's own
experience that "nothing tortures us more than longing," and during
the months in prison he was sometimes terribly homesick.[23]

Bonhoeffer would not be satisfied by any substitute for what he
had lost and was longing for:

> Substitutes repel us; we simply have to wait and wait; we have to
> suffer unspeakably from the separation, and feel the longing till it
> almost makes us ill. That is the only way, although it is a very pain
> ful one, in which we can preserve unimpaired our relationship with
> our loved ones. . . . There is nothing worse in such times than to try
> to find a substitute for the irreplaceable.[24]

Bonhoeffer seeks instead to find "the strength to overcome the
tension" in "full concentration on the cause of longing," and he is convinced that Christ will "restore all this as God originally intended it to
be, without the distortion resulting from our sins."[25]

Obviously Bonhoeffer understands Irenaeus's doctrine of recapitulation in its anti-Gnostic historical or rather eschatological perspective
as restoration or bringing back of all things by Christ in the moment
when he descends from heaven to earth. Only in this understanding of
recapitulation does the musical allusion to the ecstatic "o" in Schütz's
setting make sense.

20. Bonhoeffer, *Letters*, Advent IV 1943, pp. 169-70. Translation of Paul Gerhardt altered.

21. Bonhoeffer, *Letters*, p. 170. Cf. Irenaeus of Lyon, *Adversus haereses* I.10.1: Christ will come back from the heavens in the glory of the Father "in order to restore everything *(epì tò anakephalaiôsasthai tà pánta)*" and to resurrect the flesh of the whole humanity.

22. Bonhoeffer, *Letters*, 18 December 1943, p. 169.

23. Bonhoeffer, *Letters*, p. 167.

24. Bonhoeffer, *Letters*, p. 167.

25. Bonhoeffer, *Letters*, pp. 168-70. Translation altered.

On the Theological Status of Music

The close relationship between music and word, as demonstrated in Schütz's settings, has yet another consequence in Bonhoeffer's *Letters and Papers from Prison*. Music achieves an unexpected freedom just by its foundation in the word of Christ. In this context Bonhoeffer is ready even to introduce an important correction concerning the doctrine of the mandates in his *Ethics*. As he writes in his letter to Renate and Eberhard Bethge, 23 January 1944: "Who is there, for instance, in our times, who can devote himself with an easy mind to music, friendship, games, or happiness? Surely not the 'ethical' person, but only the Christian."[26] What is the meaning of this phrasing?

In an insertion probably made in 1941 to the chapter "Christ, Reality and Good (Christ, the Church and the World)" of his *Ethics,* Bonhoeffer had described the relatedness of the world to Christ in the four concrete "mandates: labor, marriage, government, and the church."[27] In this context, music, as a "creation of Cain," had been counted among the various aspects of the mandate of labor.[28] In the recently mentioned letter from prison (January 1944) Bonhoeffer counts music, together with friendship (the letter's primary concern), among the various aspects of culture and education. But now he does not want to classify culture and education any longer under labor, "however tempting that might be in many ways." Still, he insists that "marriage, work, state, and church all have their definite, divine mandate,"[29] but in contrast to *Ethics* he introduces a "broad area of free play, which surrounds" the "sphere of obedience" regulated by the mandates.[30] Full

---

26. Bonhoeffer, *Letters,* p. 193. Translation altered.

27. Cf. Dietrich Bonhoeffer, *Ethics* (New York: Macmillan/Collier Books, 1986), p. 207.

28. Cf. Bonhoeffer, *Ethics,* p. 209: "The first creation of Cain was the city, the earthly counterpart of the city of God. There follows the invention of the fiddles and flutes, which afford to us on earth a foretaste of the music of heaven. . . . Through the divine mandate of labour there is to come into being a world which, knowingly or not, is waiting for Christ, is designed for Christ, is open to Christ, serves Him and glorifies Him."

29. Bonhoeffer, *Letters,* p. 192.

30. The usual translation of *"Spielraum der Freiheit"* by "sphere of freedom" does not cover the aspect of "play" in the German term *Spielraum.*

humanity, according to Bonhoeffer's new insight, embraces more than the four mandates: "Our 'Protestant' (not Lutheran) Prussian world has been so dominated by the four mandates that the sphere of free play has receded into the background." Now music is regarded as belonging to the sphere of free play, which "must be confidently defended against all the disapproving frowns of 'ethical' existences, though without claiming for it the *necessitas* of a divine decree, but only the *necessitas* of *freedom*."[31] But exactly in this necessity of freedom music forms — like friendship — a necessary aspect of full humanity, something *"sui generis,"* belonging to the mandates "as the cornflower belongs to the cornfield."[32]

The new theological status of music, belonging to the sphere of free play rather than to the mandate of labor, has consequences with respect to the relationship between music and word. In the settings by Schütz the art of music has to serve the word of Christ, which according to Bonhoeffer's earlier view bestows music with ethical dignity as an aspect of the mandate of culture or labor. As an aspect of the sphere of free play, surrounding the ethical sphere, music (together with other aspects of culture and education) gains a new freedom with respect to the word. In its aesthetic autonomy it can be regarded as justified, even if the free play does not simply "serve" the word.

The Art of Fugue and the Conspiracy

The new theological concept of music seems to recur one month later, when Bonhoeffer, in a letter to Eberhard Bethge, refers to *The Art of Fugue* by Johann Sebastian Bach: "For really, there are some fragments . . . whose importance lasts for centuries, because their completion can only be a matter for God, and so they are fragments that must be frag-

---

31. Bonhoeffer, *Letters,* p. 193. Translation altered. Still, it seems to be uncertain as to which way Bonhoeffer will ground this "sphere of freedom" in Christology. Thus after "freedom" he adds in paranthesis "of the Christian . . . !?" In some respect the "sphere of free play" seems to be connected with the mandate of the church particularly. On the other hand the "sphere of free play" surrounds the whole "world of mandates." It is obvious that Bonhoeffer's thinking here is in experimental flux.

32. The image of cornflower and cornfield will reappear in Bonhoeffer's poem "The Friend" (*Letters,* pp. 388-91).

ments — I'm thinking, e.g., of the *Art of Fugue*."[33] Bonhoeffer sees the fragmentariness of *The Art of Fugue* in analogy to the social situation of his generation: "The longer we are uprooted from our professional activities and our private lives, the more we feel how fragmentary our lives are, compared with those of our parents."[34] According to Bonhoeffer the times of the polyhistor or polymath, even the times of the specialist have gone, and "our cultural life remains a torso. The important thing today is that we should be able to discern from the fragment of our life how the whole was arranged and planned, and what material it consists of."[35]

Speaking of fragmentariness Bonhoeffer does not refer to the fragment as genre, praised by some romantic theories of art in contrast to the classical ideal of perfection. Bonhoeffer speaks of the lives of a whole generation, which have, by the pressure of outward events, been "split . . . into fragments, like bombs falling on houses."[36] The reference to Jeremiah 45, following the reflection on the correspondence between *The Art of Fugue* and "the fragmentariness of our lives," is telling in this context. "I can never get away from Jeremiah 45," writes Bonhoeffer. "Here, too, is a necessary fragment of life — 'but I will give you your life as a prize of war'."[37]

It is a matter of fact that Bach's *Art of Fugue* remained uncompleted.[38] On the other hand, *The Art of Fugue* is, in its scientific construction, an exemplary masterpiece of the times of the polymath. Bach's music, and particularly his later speculative works, claimed to be

33. Bonhoeffer, *Letters,* 23 February 1944, p. 219. Together with Bonhoeffer Bethge had bought the edition *Die Kunst der Fuge,* für zwei Klaviere gesetzt von Erich Schwebsch, nach der Neuordnung von Wolfgang Graeser (Wolfenbüttel and Berlin, 1937). Now and then they had tried to play together single movements of the work (cf. E. Bethge, letter to the author of this essay, 12 August 1984).

34. Bonhoeffer, *Letters,* p. 219. Cf. Bonhoeffer's letter to his parents only three days earlier: "Our generation cannot now lay claim to such a life as was possible in yours. . . . But this fragmentariness may, in fact, point towards a fulfilment beyond the limits of human achievement . . ." (p. 215).

35. Bonhoeffer, *Letters,* p. 219.

36. Bonhoeffer, *Letters,* p. 215.

37. Bonhoeffer, *Letters,* p. 219.

38. At the end of the manuscript, where the "Fuga a 3 soggetti" breaks off, we find the following entry by the hand of Carl Ph. E. Bach: "Over this Fugue, where the name BACH is used in the countersubject, the author died."

expressions of musical erudition comparable with scientific scholarship. One may hesitate, therefore, to compare the fragmentary character of *The Art of Fugue* with such forced "fragments of life" as Bonhoeffer observes them in Jeremiah and in the lives of his own generation. The fact, however, should be taken into account that the time of Bach's life was not free from social conflicts either. On the contrary, it was characterized by a severe crisis of the culture of the Reformation, reflected in Bach's musical language. Theodor W. Adorno regarded Bach as a "genius of remembering." The archaic traits, particularly in Bach's later works, indicated the resistance to the beginning commercialization of music, "which together with the increasing subjectivism inevitably was carried through" in his times, until music assumed the "character of merchandise" like everything else.[39] In other words, *The Art of Fugue* forms a stumbling block rather than representing the musical style of the time, a pièce de résistance against the growing influence of capitalism in musical culture. Thus, it is not only by chance that this work remained uncompleted. Bach was regarded as conservative in *The Art of Fugue* particularly. But precisely this retirement into stylistic isolation can be interpreted as a protest against the enlightened absolutism of the princes who, in Bach's view, alongside with their support of the "gallant style" in music, betrayed the original intentions of the Reformation. In some respect the social isolation of the later Bach can be compared with the isolation of contemporary music in Germany already before the time of National Socialism.[40]

Historically, then, Bonhoeffer's comparison between the situation of his generation and the fragmentariness of *The Art of Fugue* makes sense. Theologically, *The Art of Fugue* seems to him to be relevant to the present situation of war because of its fragmentariness especially. For "If our life is but the remotest reflection of such a frag-

39. Cf. Theodor W. Adorno, "Bach gegen seine Liebhaber verteidigt" (Bach defended against his admirers; 1951), in Theodor W. Adorno, *Kulturkritik und Gesellschaft I: Prismen. Ohne Leitbild*, Gesammelte Schriften, vol. 10/1 (Frankfurt am Main: Suhrkamp, 1977), pp. 142 and 146.

40. Concerning the fragmentary character of Schoenberg's and Berg's operas Adorno suggested accordingly that "in the present situation every important product in art and philosophy was condemned to fragmentariness" (Theodor W. Adorno, *Dissonanzen: Einleitung in die Musiksoziologie*, Gesammelte Schriften, vol. 14 [Frankfurt am Main: Suhrkamp, 1973], p. 260).

ment, if we accumulate, at least for a short time, a wealth of themes and weld them into a harmony in which the great counterpoint is maintained from start to finish, so that at last, when it breaks off abruptly, we can sing no more than the chorale, 'I come before thy throne', we will not bemoan the fragmentariness of our lives, but rather rejoice in it."[41]

Only two days earlier Bonhoeffer had thought about the "boundaries between necessary resistance to 'fate', and equally necessary 'submission'."[42] He had come to the conclusion that "we must confront fate . . . as resolutely as we submit to it at the right time. One can speak of 'guidance' only on the other side of that twofold process, with God meeting us no longer as 'Thou', but also 'disguised' in the 'It'; so in the last resort my question is how we are to find the 'Thou' in this 'it' (i.e. fate), or, in other words, how does 'fate' really become 'guidance'?"[43] — a guidance, in which God himself takes on the resistance already given up by human beings. With this reflection in mind every false appeasement by the entry of the final chorale is excluded; rather, that chorale underlines once more the irreconcilability with the powers of death, pointing towards the God of life who, on the other side of the human turn from "penultimate" resistance into "ultimate" submission, takes on his own resistance against death.

The historical question, how it happened that *The Art of Fugue* was handed down with the chorale as a conclusion, is not part of Bonhoeffer's interest.[44] For him the theological perspective is decisive. If on the other side of the silence enforced by the violence of death "we can sing no more than the chorale,"[45] then this singing may serve as an

---

41. Bonhoeffer, *Letters*, p. 219.

42. Bonhoeffer, *Letters*, 21 February 1944, p. 217. Translation altered.

43. Bonhoeffer, *Letters*, p. 217.

44. According to the edition by E. Schwebsch, used by Bonhoeffer and Bethge, the chorale does not belong to the original work, although it is tolerated as a concluding gesture of reconciliation: "Without any external connection with the 'Art of Fugue', even in a different tune, a voice is heard, expressing humbly what should have been pronounced in metaphysical greatness by the final harmony of this work or rather of the life's work: 'I come before thy throne'" (E. Schwebsch, Vorwort; cited from Walter Kolneder, *Die Kunst der Fuge,* vol. 3 [Wilhelmshaven: Heinrichshofen, 1977], p. 330).

45. Bonhoeffer, *Letters*, p. 219.

indication of "fulfilment beyond the limits of human achievement" of the "fragment of our life."[46]

In this context a recollection by Winfried Maechler seems to be worth mentioning. According to Maechler, Bonhoeffer wrote to his friends at the military front about the progress of the resistance movement, "as if it were a performance of the 'Art of Fugue' to which he had listened in Berlin."[47] Maechler remembers: "I myself met him the last time on a holiday in Berlin, when he was just about to visit a concert with the 'Art of Fugue' in Charlottenburg castle. He promised to write me now and then about the progress of the planned plot, as if it was the performance of a concert. I received a card only once and it read: 'Unfortunately the performance had to be postponed, because some artists had to cancel their participation'." And Maechler comments further that "when the performance finally took place, it was already too late."[48] The Art of Fugue as indication of the progress of the resistance movement, or the plot as performance of The Art of Fugue — the comparison gives a lot to think about. The fact that The Art of Fugue remained uncompleted, that it ends abruptly before reaching the goal, gives a fateful undertone to this comparison with respect to the military conspiracy. Where is the "fulfilment beyond the limits of human achievement" of this fragment of human history?

Conclusion

We have seen that Bonhoeffer understands the complexity of the "free play" with contrapuntal structures in Bach's Art of Fugue as a sign pointing to the "Word" in the chorale. At the same time he underlines the status of music hovering between its "being tied to the Word" and its liberation to "true worldliness" in the "sphere of free play" sur-

46. Bonhoeffer, Letters, p. 215.
47. Winfried Maechler, "Vom Pazifisten zum Widerstandskämpfer: Bonhoeffers Kampf für die Entrechteten," in Die Mündige Welt (I), 3rd edition (München: Chr. Kaiser, 1959), p. 90.
48. Winfried Maechler, "Bonhoeffers Fanøer Friedenspredigt als Appell an die Christenheit heute," in Dietrich Bonhoeffer und die Kirche in der modernen Welt (epd-Dokumentation, Nr. 2-3/1981), p. 104.

rounding Christ and his commandment in the "sphere of obedience" structured by the "mandates."

In some respects this theological concept of music resembles Karl Barth's view, according to which the essence of music is "playing." Whereas Bonhoeffer refers primarily to Bach, Barth refers to the music of Wolfgang Amadeus Mozart in order to demonstrate the playful character of music: "One aspect of the daily bread is playing. . . . But playing is a thing demanding mastery; it is therefore a high and austere thing. Listening to Mozart I perceive an art of playing, which I do not hear in any other music."[49] According to Barth this refers to Mozart's church music as well as to his secular music:

> It is true that Mozart did not comply with the well-known pro-
> gramme according to which the tone has to serve and interpret the
> word only. . . . But is this the only possible programme of sacred
> music? . . . His tone seems to be — in his church music as well as in
> his other music — a free counterpart to each given word. . . . Here
> and there, he listens, he respects the word in its special content and
> character, but then he adds music to it, here and there, his music, —
> a thing tied to the word, but in this bond free in its own nature.[50]

Likewise Bonhoeffer regards *The Art of Fugue* in its contrapuntal structure as an example of "free play." This music takes up the "material," by which "our lives" have been constructed, in order to process it, to play with it, and finally to bring it — as a "fragment" — before the throne of the Lord. Perhaps this indication of a "fulfilment beyond the limits of human achievement" may include the expectation of recapitulation or restoration of all things. In Walter Benjamin's thesis "On the Concept of History" this expectation is represented by the "angel of history." In the face of "the catastrophe, piling up fragments upon fragments incessantly," he wishes to dwell on the ruins, in order to "resurrect the dead and to mend the smashed."[51]

49. Karl Barth, *Wolfgang Amadeus Mozart* (Zürich: Theologischer Verlag, 1956), p. 8 (my translation).

50. Barth, *Mozart,* pp. 26f.; cf. also Barth's essay "Mozarts Freiheit," in Barth, *Mozart,* pp. 31ff.

51. Walter Benjamin, "Über den Begriff der Geschichte," in Benjamin, *Gesammelte Schriften,* vol. I/2 (Frankfurt am Main: Suhrkamp, 1974), p. 697.

Likewise the notion of "polyphony of life," conceived by Bonhoeffer as a musical description of a Christian life, does not mean harmony without conflict or dissonance. Rather it includes the perception of light and shadow, of love and suffering, of longing and passion amidst social crisis and catastrophe. In other words, it contains both aspects of hope: hopeful resistance against fate and submission to God's will, full of hope as well.

Spiritual Unity and the Subject of the Composer: The Catholic Element in the Work of Stockhausen

Thomas Ulrich

I

Karlheinz Stockhausen, born 1928, is no doubt one of today's most important and influential composers. Since the early 1950s, together with Pierre Boulez and Luigi Nono he has formed part of the "troika" of avant-garde music. He was and still is a pioneer of electronic music. At the World's Fair in Osaka, Japan, in 1970 the Federal Republic of Germany built for Stockhausen a special concert hall where Stockhausen together with twenty other musicians performed his works for half a year, with approximately one million people attending. In 1976 Stockhausen's composition *Sirius* was commissioned by the government of the Federal Republic of Germany for the American Bicentennial celebration. Since 1977 Stockhausen has composed *Licht* ("Light"), a cycle of seven operas, six of which have been completed and performed at La Scala in Milan and the Royal Opera House at Covent Garden in London. Stockhausen's oeuvre consists of 230 works and ten volumes of texts, partly translated into English: a unique life-work. His self-understanding is that of a composer of spiritual music. It makes sense therefore to try to interpret his oeuvre from a theological point of view.

This essay was translated by Renate M. Low and Carol Graham-Harrison.

The thesis of this essay is that the work of Stockhausen as a whole stems from a "catholic" impulse. Stockhausen comes from a background of Rheinish Catholicism; this had a deep impact on him. But he has left it behind. Therefore I use the word "catholic" not in a narrow Christian-denominational sense, but in a very broad sense oriented to the literal meaning of the word; we can then refer it back to the Catholicism of Christianity. The word "catholic" comes from the Greek; we can recognize its meaning from Plato's *Menon* 77a. Here it means "in general," i.e., to comprehend what is general about an object from examples, from individual cases — not to break up, not to disintegrate a totality, but to rise to that universal totality which is evident in every individual thing.

II

The all-embracing, the universal is certainly a main feature in the work of Stockhausen. *Telemusik* combines music from all over the world; *Hymnen* works with the national anthems of nations of both hemispheres; *Kurzwellen* opens to the sounds of the radio waves that embrace the planet; and, beyond that, the view is directed towards cosmic regions as in *Sirius*, in which the music is "connected with the rhythms of the stars,"[1] or as in *Sternklang*, which opens our minds to cosmic totality. In the technique of composition the emphasis on space, which is composed and designed artistically *(Gruppen, Carré, Oktophonie)*, corresponds to the view into infinite physical space. And equally a universal outlook: a view on the variety of traditions, of spiritual and musical styles used as musical material. Corresponding to space is time, which Stockhausen forms from millennium *(Jahreslauf)* down to the (planned) second and which he puts in cosmic context *(Tierkreis, Sirius)*. Finally, Stockhausen's work evinces an all-embracing productivity, directed not only towards the traditional parameters of music, but also to space, movement, colors, and scents.

1. *Sirius*. Elektronische Musik und Trompete, Sopran, Bassklarinette, Bass (1975-77), in *Texte* IV, p. 301.

III

Thus everything is integrated. Stockhausen is guided by an impulse that goes beyond boundaries. This impulse towards new dimensions, towards the unheard, the dynamic of the progression that transcends all that we are accustomed to — is responsible for much of the fascination of his work. This is no minor master cultivating his narrow patch. In every new piece of music he goes full-out, taking all the risks implicit in departure towards the unknown.

But a transcending impulse towards universal dimensions is not enough to characterize something as "catholic" in the basic meaning of the word; there must also be a synthesizing power of unification that identifies the One, the Universal in the multiplicity. This is in fact the core of Stockhausen's work; in his musical thinking relationships are thematic: how the abundance of complexity can come into being from one basic impulse. Even in his earliest works an extreme intellectual punctualism serves an organic idea of form (for instance *Klavierstück* III) — in *Gesang der Jünglinge* the natural sounds of wind, fire, and ice are mediated with synthetically produced electronic sounds; in *Studie* I a serial organization of the musical material that embraces every single event is unified with the subjective reaction of the composer to a personal experience (the birth of one of his daughters); in *Kontrakte* taped music is united with live music; and above all, in the technique of formula-composition of the greatest virtuosity, there operates a so-to-speak "alchemistic" impulse that changes one thing into another: rhythm changes into pitch, form into sound, melody into larger form. In this way a grand musical universe like the cycle of seven operas, *Licht,* can emerge from a "super-formula": form, the specific sound of particular scenes, the number of actors, the scenic details.

IV

Thus, in the thought and work of Stockhausen everything is related, every specific detail stems from one basis; also, all his seemingly separate works are in fact just parts of one oeuvre, parts of a larger form in which everything is connected with everything else. The impulse that goes out towards the universal equally turns back into the creative ego, into Stockhausen himself. He is the master of everything that happens in his compositions. He is free in the handling of musical material; Adorno's criticism of the serial music of the 1950s[2] — that he idolized his musical material — could not touch even the young Stockhausen, let alone the creator of the formula-compositions who rejected as narrow-minded the attempt to derive every detail of *Licht* from the super-formula. On the contrary, for many listeners, strangely enough, it is Stockhausen's personal subjectivity that is most apparent, for instance in the very private love poems of *Stimmung,* and in some of the witticisms and quirky ideas of the *Licht*-cycle. Even more so: the difficulties marking Stockhausen's present reception can be traced back to the same point. The criticisms, to put them briefly, are: his private mythology, his exaggerated sense of his own importance, his sense of modern music as a family business. These criticisms are beside the point. It may, however, be possible to understand them better than they were intended as they point to a profound insight.

V

The drive to the cosmic, the universal, the all-embracing, and the emphasis on the creative subjectivity of the person, the individual — these stand in sharp contrast to each other — there is no obvious connection between them. Yet it is commonly known that this highly unlikely structure is the basis of "catholic," even of Christian, biblical thinking: the universality of creation and the fact that the Creator and Redeemer is a single person and, linked to this, that humankind is made in God's image and, as individuals, we are not only part of creation but also face the world in a shaping and preserving action: "For I will consider thy heavens, even the works of thy fingers: the moon and the stars, which thou hast ordained. What is man, that thou art mindful of him. . . . Thou makest him to have dominion over the works of thy hands" (Psalm 8:3, 4, 6).

In Christian thinking, however, man[3] is understood as creature,

2. Theodor W. Adorno, *Klangfiguren.* Musikalische Schriften I (Frankfurt: Suhrkamp-Verlag, 1959), p. 265.

3. *Editors' note:* This article has been translated from German where the word "mensch," here written as "man," is gender-inclusive. There is no English parallel.

as dependent, as hearing and receptive. This motif is very important for Stockhausen's understanding of himself. Already at the beginning of his path through life he conceived of himself as "servant of God," as being in the service of the Unconditional and dependent on it. As music for Stockhausen is a "fast aeroplane to God," so music itself comes from "above," not only from Sirius, but from the sphere of God himself. That is the region inspiration comes from; the composer must search for it, be open to it. And that is not just an idea, but in a real sense determines the creative process. Again and again Stockhausen reports that a completed work has appeared to him in a dream; the only task for the composer is to write it down — consciously to elaborate what in a way already exists. And that is also important for the performer: with the works of his intuitive music Stockhausen's instructions essentially try to bring about a state of receptivity and openness in the musicians so that the narrow ego becomes permeable to the stream that comes from "above." That stream the musicians must seize and give creative form to.

VI

Thus Stockhausen composes within a system of coordinates that determines the tradition of Western Christianity as a whole and is characterized by fundamental relationships: the relation of the all-embracing, the universal, and the cosmic to the individual, to personality and subjectivity; and, to put it in terms of activity, the relationship of receptivity to productivity, of receptivity to the individual's own creative work. My thesis is that these relationships are not artificial, attached to Stockhausen's work by a certain interpretation, but they fundamentally determine his oeuvre and account for its epoch-making position. Stockhausen's work is not just this attempt to develop musical material, to open unknown spaces of sound, to test new forms, and so on, i.e., to solve single problems in music. His work, rather, actualizes the basic relationship of Western Christianity for our time and in the language of our time — that is the content and aim of his oeuvre and that is the reason for understanding all his works as "spiritual" music.

This thesis leads us to deeper investigation: How are the poles of this basic relationship connected to one another in a real way? The answer to this question is controversial and points to the conflicts of the Reformation that broke up Europe. These conflicts of long ago have led to the development of fundamental structures of thinking that even today determine the way life is experienced, and have the power to open realms of experience, not only for religious people. Therefore I think it is helpful to refer to this language of the past.

My contention, further, is that Stockhausen's answer corresponds to traditional Catholic thinking. Nature and grace are related in a positive way: I feel in myself the impulse to the Infinite, the Absolute Reality. The stream that comes from it purifies me, elevates me, and enables me to use my abilities in a creative manner. Thus the composer, turning to that which is "above," allows himself to be enriched, to be elevated to a cosmic consciousness that carries him beyond the ordinary narrow limits. Inspired in this way, the ego can now take possession of this gift of grace in order to give it shape, to elaborate it, and to produce a work of beauty instead of a merely ordinary, ugly, shapeless piece of work. The extraordinary complexity of Stockhausen's work stems from this impulse. This is the origin of the way he elaborates in sounds: the permanent impulse to go beyond what is familiar, to press forward to new dimensions, to include and to give form to all realms of sensual experience — in short, to create in abundance is the main feature of his work, which is totally devoid of ascetic overtones.

VII

What do we gain by relating Stockhausen's oeuvre to this system of concepts from the past? We discern a basic impulse from which every individual element derives, revealing the spiritual claim of his work. Also, we are given a means of criticism that does not come from outside, but points to the inner complexities of this basic impulse. Let us then, in conclusion, attempt some constructive explanations.

In Protestant thinking, the Catholic way to relate God and Man, the Individual and the Absolute, Nature and Grace, was characterized as "theologia gloriae" in contrast to the concept of "theologia crucis": to put it briefly, the recognition, the experience that we can talk about God only in contradiction to that which is readily apparent, easily accessible and obvious. Nothing we make can in any way do justice to

God; the actor, however much educated and trained, will still always only stay within his own sphere, capable only of celebrating himself. Once the actor appears as ego, inevitably he establishes himself as a being centered in himself (even if honestly acting in attitudes of humility); he separates himself, thus entering into opposition to God. The emergence of the ego in its self-constitution — and every action stemming from this origin — then becomes an act of sin and is in a specific way inadequate to its object. How is it possible then for human action (in our case for artistic activity) to take that into consideration? This can be answered only in the sense that the limitation and ambiguity of all human activity is revealed in the work of art itself. In this sense it is not a question of greater and improved productivity but of showing works that also incorporate the central meaning of receiving, the receptivity of listening into the process of the creative act — works that present themselves as fragments; works that, in the destruction of form, point to a reality, the overwhelming complexity of which cannot possibly be gathered into a limited form; works in which the subjectivity of the composer, with his individual intentions, are held back. Such works, it can be said, correspond to the spirit of Reformation in today's climate when the notion of subject and work of art has become altered. The creative work of John Cage — even if fed to a considerable extent from Eastern sources — points in that direction and in my opinion has fundamental importance for the idea of a spiritual music of today. Furthermore, with the work of such a commanding artistic personality as Karlheinz Stockhausen one can now ask the question: Can the subjectivity of a creative person (even as richly gifted and impressive as Stockhausen) mirror this complex and strange world and reveal its truth (this is his intention),[4] or does this person just multiply himself and stay alone in his creative genius? To put it less provocatively and more as an open question in order to point the analysis of Stockhausen's work in a certain direction, one could ask: What significance has receptivity as such, not only in Stockhausen's thinking, but in the actual process of composition and in the shape of his works?

4. Cf. Rudolf Frisius, *Karlheinz Stockhausen*, p. 254.

VIII

However, music is not religion, nor is it theology, nor philosophy of religion. Even when musicians fight aesthetic wars, the listening to music does not require a final existential decision supported by the condemnation of others. Creative success, beauty, and the impression left by a vibrant piece of artistic work do not merely depend on a consequent realization of a theoretical idea, even if this idea is perfectly ingenious and ideologically "correct." The extensive claim Stockhausen makes with his life's work nevertheless provokes in the thoughtful listener the question how he or she should see the world and respond to it. This in my opinion is the true spiritual character of Stockhausen's music. It does not rest in this or that answer which his work may give — no matter if one understands it in an esoteric or multireligious way, in a Catholic way or in the sense of a personal and private religion. In whichever way one responds — and even if one does not want to answer in a "catholic" way — each piece of music in its own way brings about joy and surprise, consolation and strong emotions, consternation and serenity — as all great music does.

THEOLOGY IN DIALOGUE
WITH SCIENCE

Springing Cultural Traps:
The Science-and-Theology Discourse
on Eschatology and the Common Good

Michael Welker

There are many different definitions and theories of culture. The period between the late fifties and the late sixties saw intensive debates in the social and cultural sciences concerning the possibility of gaining a theoretically founded common concept of "culture." Theories and definitions by Parsons, Kroeber, White, and others seem to share a certain helplessness with respect to their subject. This helplessness is best grasped in the tendency to proffer summarizing formulae for what a culture really is: we get many listings, from the symbolic foundations of human action to the most important human artifacts.[1] But all the definitions and theories of culture seem to agree explicitly or implicitly on the fact that cultures serve the communication of human beings via memories and expectations. With the help of our culture we develop astounding abilities to connect and disconnect, to share and to differentiate our memories and our expectations. We anticipate, reproduce, and reconstruct in our memories and imaginations what others remember, anticipate, and expect. Moving in the realms of memory and imagination we attune our emotions, thoughts, and practices in very powerful ways. We do not have to talk to each other, to see each other, and to touch each other all the time. We can, so to speak, manage most of our communication by flying above physical reality, with only occa-

1. Kathryn Tanner, *Theories of Culture: A New Agenda for Theology* (Minneapolis: Fortress Press, 1997), chapter 1.

sionally illustrative landings. The complex entity "culture," which one sociologist has called the "brain of the society," makes this possible.

Part of the particular power of our current cultures is that they provide high degrees of secure common memories and expectations, although they can host very different sets of values and virtues. We can put ourselves into others' shoes although we in fact do not share exactly the same hierarchy of values and virtues. This ability is greatly enhanced and cultivated in late modern pluralistic societies and cultures. Different "societal systems," as sociologists say, operate with different symbol-systems and rationalities: law, politics, the market, the sciences, education, the arts, religion — they do not follow one common code. And most of these systems or spheres are highly differentiated in themselves. We see it, for example, in the sciences and the humanities, the differentiated market systems, the highly patterned world of media and information, and at the ecumene of the Christian churches and the orbit of the religions. We live in a complex world that does not exhibit a one-hierarchy order, but rather a multihierarchical texture. And our cultures allow us to navigate in this world with some trust and some success.

But the powers of our cultures to allow for an attunement or at least a clear differentiation of shared memories and expectations seem to be limited. The relation of theology and science seems to reveal some of these limits. The interesting question now is whether these limits are grounded in a reality "out there" — or whether these limits are due to the texture of our culture. Are we even trapped by our culture, blinded, led into systemic distortions? We do know that our cultures are no innocent entities. On a second order level of thinking, we rightly give high praises to a culture as such. Most people associate culture automatically with "goodness," and they do the same with "morals," "the ethos" and many, too, with "religion." Although human beings can not live without cultures and morals and at least latent forms of religion, on a first order level all these indispensable forms of ordering, shaping, and freeing human life can become partially or totally corrupted. We have, for example, seen racist, fascist, stalinist cultures and have seen cultures with an ecological brutality that today seems simply astounding to us. Is the seemingly widening gap or even split between science and theology in our otherwise so hospitable cultures a sign of such a distortion, a minor distortion at least? Are we somehow trapped by our culture?

In what follows I would like first to speak briefly about the gap between science and theology in our culture and how the majority in science and theology seem to cope with it. Second, I will speak about various endeavors in the twentieth century to bridge the gap. In the third and last part I will show how a science and theology discourse that dared to deal with a genuinely theological topic led to the discovery of several "cultural traps" that made the discourse so difficult and fruitless for such a long time.

The Gap between Science and Theology and How Most of the Academy Has Historically Coped with It

We have been told time and again that modernity brought us a continually widening gap between natural science and theology. To be sure, modern common sense was becoming steadily distanced from the world of mathematical sciences on the one hand and to the religious world on the other hand. Many tried to help themselves out of this by attributing religion to the "strange world of the past" and the sciences to the equally "strange world of the future." At the same time they profited both from religion's powers to shape aesthetics, morals, and mentalities, and from the predictabilities and technological benefits science brought with it. Somehow the powers of the so-called past world and of the so-called future world both came together in the present.

The more or less lazy but comfortable double ignorance of modern common sense between natural science and religion (respective theology) is not the whole story. Even acomplished scholars seem to have great difficulty in bridging the gap. The complexities of an adequate scholarly treatment both of religious topics and natural-scientific topics are so demanding and seem so incompatible with each other, that only very few human beings on this planet are able to join meaningfully in the academic discourse in these areas. A human life seems not long enough and a human brain seems not potent enough to become truly familiar with both worlds. The times of the "universal geniuses" are long gone. What priests and healers in some remote parts of our planet are able to embrace in the life-worlds of their tribes, seems absolutely impossible in a world which witnesses or at least believes in its market-, media-, and technology-driven "globalization."

Modern science and modern theology have not, of course, simply submitted to resignation in the face of this development. They have not simply given up the belief in the one world, the one reality, the unity of knowledge, the unity of truth. Many modern scientists became, as Carl Friedrich von Weizsäcker once put it: "agnostic, but open" toward religion. Although some reacted quite aggressively to religion and theology, assigning it to the realms of other-worldliness, of hyper- and virtual reality, of personal feeling and a mere certainty that is not able to sustain truth claims, many scientists honored this so-called realm of meaning or the existential realm. And not a few theologians specialized in the realms of meaning and existence, often moving into all sorts of moralism, lay therapy, and entertainment. The more academically oriented theologians and scientists, however, resisted this development by claiming that at least the history of the past, the interest in past worlds and past truth-claims should keep theology in the common academic orbit.

But this type of resistance also had its price. The good news always seemed to be yesterday's news. Academic theology became obsessed with history of religion and with itself, its own history. Doing good jobs in interpreting and reinterpreting past worlds and its own classics, theology only seldom risked an analytical theological view of the societal and cultural reality of today. Only in times of trial and trouble did a truly systematic theology come alive. Those, however, who did risk addressing issues of the present and the future, seemed to move toward the boundaries of their academic disciplines or even across the border. Very often they became morally active speakers for specific causes. In this case, those theologians who, for example, were ecologically concerned met scientists who shared similar concerns. But the commonality in the moral agenda did not — or at least: not yet — provide a commonality that could be transported back into the academic orbit and stimulate interdisciplinary research. The gain of a moral commonality was in most cases at the cost of an estrangement from the academic environment.

The final approach with which some academic theologians tried to react against the widening gap between theology and science was a move toward radical abstraction or toward a transcendentalization of all religious topics. Speaking of God simply as "the ultimate point of reference" or of faith as a trusting relation to the other side of my inner self-reference, they tried to offer ultimate forms that no reasonable person could resist accepting. The price of these offers of theology and religion "in a nutshell" was finally self-secularization and self-banalization of theological discourse. While some scientists accepted this needle-point theology as an attempt toward academic honesty, most of them chose to find it simply boring. "Are you merely interested in everything, or also in something specific?" This laconic question of Samuel Beckett was for some modern scientists right on target over against the "ultimate point of reference" or the subjectivist "inner other." For a growing number of people, however, who do not feel at home with the metaphysics of the ultimate point or with post-Cartesian subjectivity any longer, these theological offerings are nothing but declarations of bankruptcy: the lust to control everything by one construct or one thought alone. A naive confusion of the unity of reality and truth with one simple thought or idea — if this is all theology has to offer, we had better get rid of this pretentious enterprise. In the midst of all these not very inviting and convincing general moves to set things straight again, we have, however, seen more promising and more illuminating moves between science and theology.

Specific Endeavors to Cross the Borders between Science and Theology and the Limits of External Approaches

Among the most visible and influential attempts to bridge the gap between science and theology in the twentieth century are the short and snappy statements of genius scientists about God and creation.

"I believe in Spinoza's God, revealed in the harmony of all that is." This confession of Albert Einstein's has been quoted frequently. Even more frequently have we heard and read his famous objection against quantum theory with the words: "Der Alte würfelt nicht!" "The Old Guy does not throw dice!" We owe many thought-stimulating and thought-provoking remarks to great scientists, who used and still use religious language and metaphors to express their fundamental convictions. These remarks turned into golden words, entering the orbit of world-famous quotations. Some of these remarks had quite an impact on theological work and thinking. Alfred North Whitehead's statement: "God is the fellow-sufferer, who understands," is one of these.

Not only great scientists of past times with clearly different worldviews from ours, like Newton, Faraday, and Maxwell, but also leading natural scientists of the twentieth century provided us with such golden words about God and creation in the perspective of a scientist.

Among these famous quotes, however, are also many skeptical and agnostic ones. Steven Weinberg's "The more I looked at the universe, the more I found it pointless," was used by him and by others with strong anti-religious and anti-theological twists. Carl Sagan cited Stephen Hawking's world-bestseller, *A Brief History of Time: From the Big Bang to Black Holes*,[2] for strong agnostic propaganda on its first pages: "This is also a book about God — or perhaps about the absence of God."[3] The word "God" fills these pages. Hawking embarks on a quest to answer Einstein's famous question about whether God had any choice in creating the universe. Hawking is attempting, as he explicitly states, to understand the mind of God. And this makes all the more unexpected the conclusion of the effort, at least so far: a universe with no edge in space, no beginning or end in time, and nothing for a Creator to do."[4]

"Nothing for a Creator to do"? If we look more closely at Hawking's own complex argumentation — probably with only a minority of his readers — we encounter quite a different story. In an intriguing way we see that the mind of a great cosmologist can become somewhat confused theologically. Hawking is playing with three concepts of God. The first concept is based on Hubble's discovery that the distant galaxies are moving away from us. Hawking states: "An expanding universe does not preclude a creator, but it does place limits on when he might have carried out his job!"[5] This is the God of the Big Bang or the God of the first second. This concept, according to Hawking, could be questioned if we found a unified theory that would connect quantum mechanics and the general theory of relativity, and that could describe the universe as "completely self-contained, with no singularities or boundaries."[6] The question then would be: "What place, then, for a cre-

2. Toronto: Bantam Books, 1988.
3. Stephen Hawking, *A Brief History of Time*, p. x.
4. For a detailed discussion see M. Welker, "Creation: Big Bang or the Work of Seven Days?" *Theology Today* 52 (1995): 173-87.
5. Hawking, *A Brief History of Time*, p. 9.
6. Hawking, *A Brief History of Time*, p. 174.

ator?"[7] And this is the question that Sagan picks up for his provocative blurb.

But Hawking himself does not only play with agnosticism. He rather states: This would be "the ultimate triumph of human reason — for then we would know the mind of God."[8] A titanic cosmic piety, God's mind and human mind united, could also be the second concept. Only in one perspective, it seems as if now the first second is also to be taken away from God, as if God were to disappear with the removal of the absolute beginning. In another perspective, that which is supposed to then become clear is described in religious, indeed doxological forms: "we would know the mind of God"!

Hawking, however, finally hints that the merely cognitive triumph and victory through insight into God's plan and mind would still be deficient: "Even if there is only one possible unified theory, it is just a set of rules and equations. What is it that breathes fire into the equations and makes a universe for them to describe? . . . Is the unified theory so compelling that it brings about its own existence? Or does it need a creator, and, if so, does he have any other effect on the universe?"[9]

There is little risk in assuming that the dominant common sense in the contemporary Western world also moves back and forth between these three positions. In an instructive and analytically helpful way Hawking is mapping a religiously confused contemporary common sense. So it pays to listen carefully to a great scientist who addresses with some continuity religious issues, even when the theological outcome is quite poor. In other cases, when a mathematician and natural scientist takes the contents of religious traditions seriously, the outcome can become much more promising. Alfred North Whitehead was a mathematician and natural scientist who took the contents of the Jewish-Christian traditions seriously. In a much more comprehensive way John Polkinghorne does so in our days. We cannot go into details in dealing with these theologically fruitful endeavors in this context. But one can, by way of example, show that Whitehead was able to give shape to a whole theological movement, so-called "process theology,"

---

7. Hawking, *A Brief History of Time*, p. 141.
8. Hawking, *A Brief History of Time*, p. 175.
9. Hawking, *A Brief History of Time*, p. 174.

because he took biblical wisdom-traditions seriously, with their specific realism and rationalities. He analyzed processes of universalization and individualization and the co-evolution of these processes: "Religion is world-loyalty" and "Religion is what the individual does with his own solitariness."[10]

As impressive as Whitehead's abilities are to give religion a place in his metaphysics and his theory of culture, one should also clearly see the limits of his approach. A theologian who is not blinded by Whitehead's sophisticated metaphysics and by his even more stimulating theory of modern culture will see that Whitehead engages only a small spectrum of the canonic biblical traditions, grown over more than a thousand years. He engages the wisdom traditions, in Job, in some of the Psalms, in the book of Wisdom and in some parts of the New Testament, particularly of the gospels. This limited but serious and thought-shaping contact with grand religious traditions already leads to very powerful statements about religious issues.

But in the twentieth century we have not only seen the movement of the geniuses between science and theology. To this movement most of us could respond with admiration, regarding it with a slight skepticism, or by adopting from it stimulating quotations and new patterns of thinking. We have also seen a lot of broad academic step by step work, and a lot of investment from the side of individual common sense on this topic, particularly in the last third of the century. In all sorts of schools and classes, in groups and centers for continuing education, in retreat centers and societies, in first rate academic consultations, and in popular books and journals, the topic of science and theology has been treated in various ways. The strong investment of the John Templeton Foundation has stimulated the installation of several hundred courses in "Science and Theology" or "Science and Religion" in colleges, mostly in the English-speaking world. In several parts of the world centers have been built for the academic exchange between science and theology. I mention only Robert Russell's initiative in Berkeley, Arthur Peacocke's in Oxford, the cooperation of John Polkinghorne, Janet Soskice, and Fraser Watts in Cambridge, and the Vatican observatory research group in Tucson, Arizona, and Castel Gundolfo.

10. Alfred North Whitehead, *Religion in the Making* (New York: Macmillan, 1960), p. 59 and pp. 16 and 58.

The first chairs and lecturer positions have been created. In many parts of the world colleagues have started multi-year interdisciplinary dialogues and consultations, the two consultations at the Center of Theological Inquiry in Princeton among them. Finally, the last twenty years have brought a broad flow of academic and semi-academic literature in this field. A whole academic sub-culture has emerged.

It would be risky to say that the impact of all these activities on the gap between science and theology has been breathtaking. To be sure, a long period of mutual disinterest and ignorance has come to an end. But the basic constellation I described earlier has remained very much the same. In the light of consultations we had in Princeton we were able to hazard some good guesses as to why this is still the case.[11] The vast majority of the discourses and activities remained external to theology and science. They remained on an observer-level. Many dealt with the history of science and theology. Some dealt with moral issues that scientists and theologians should raise, particularly with burning questions of natural ecology. Some dealt with the important issue of methodologies, but rarely putting the methods to the specific test. Finally, some discourses were searching for bridge-theories or discussing classic theories like those of Aristotle, Teilhard, Polanyi, Lonergan, and Whitehead as candidates to facilitate the dialogue. But most of these discourses, although they were helpful and engendered insight and trust, did not touch on the cultural configuration we are in. They did not lead to the discovery of cultural traps that limit and even block the discourse between science and theology. This was different with an enterprise which dared to work on a theological content and topic.

Discovering and Springing Cultural Traps for the Common Good

The discovery that an interdisciplinary discourse on the topic of eschatology can maintain a critical and nuanced realism while dealing with cultural and religious issues provided excitement in our interdisciplin-

---

11. For the documentation of these consultations see John Polkinghorne and Michael Welker, eds., *The End of the World and the Ends of God: Science and Theology on Eschatology* (Harrisburg, Pa.: Trinity Press, 2000).

ary discourse. We saw why most eschatological statements are quite inaccessible to present-day common sense. We saw why these statements remain simply extravagant as a way of thinking and experiencing caught in a reductive materialism and a scientific naturalism. Do these statements not belong in the realm of fantasy, dreams, or pathological phenomena? Or is there a possibility of making the reality characterized by these eschatological imaginations, symbols, rationalities, and rhetorics accessible to common sense that is caught within the boundaries of naturalism?

The answer given by the natural and cultural scientists and the theologians was, "Yes, there is such a possibility." However, it means that scientific naturalism has to be opened up. Without attempting to jump into another world, a hyper-real world or a virtual world, the boundaries of naturalism have to be grasped and cautiously extended. Both continuity and discontinuity with the natural world have to be conceived with regard to the eschatological realm. If we want to make this clear to common sense that is estranged from religious thought and feeling and tied up in naturalism, we will first have to show that eschatological topics deal with cultural and historical events. We will then have to discriminate religious events from merely cultural and historical ones.

The excitement that accompanied the common move into realities unseen but yet real was even enhanced by the discovery that we were able to question a whole set of mostly latent presuppositions that had governed and restricted much of our own previous thinking and certainly also the thinking of other theories we used to work with. We discovered these restrictions as cultural traps which reinforced each other.

The first trap can be called the *modernist trap*. This is the illusion that we can and must reach a universal perspective that can integrate all the different cultural spheres or disciplines with a simple epistemic move. For the science-and-theology discourse that meant that we just have to establish a methodological, metaphysical, or transcendental level, we have to reach a level of a meta-discourse, in order to bridge the gap between them. Without denying the value and importance of such strivings, we became aware that this attempt easily loses contact with both sides, playing in a realm of a philosophical or quasi-philosophical theory, which develops icons and ideals of science and philosophy accessible to common sense, but does not do justice to either one of them. Instead of encountering and enduring the differences and looking for both continuities and discontinuities between their realms of experience, it tends to smooth and to idealize both commonalities and differences.

The second trap easily goes together with the first one, but is not identical with it. It is the *trap of reductionism,* signaling us that we should minimize or avoid content and that such avoidance of content might be necessary in order to establish a bridge between science and theology. This reductionism can happen on one side or the other. We have often seen discourses in which science entered with all its complexity and glory, while theology only came up with such reductionist and boring ideas as the "ultimate point of reference" or a transcendental inwardness named "faith," or a realm of the numinous that reduces us to silence. But we have also, although more rarely, seen the other reductionism, where science was ciphered as a representative of a certain concept of nature, a specific understanding of reality or of "the law" that happened to fit into a certain theology. Its own complexity was taken away. It was simply reduced to a sparring partner of theology.

The first two traps could reinforce each other, adding plausibility to each other, creating systematic and systemic distortions. Although we certainly cannot avoid employing selection and the reduction of complexity, and although we have to work with typifying modes of thought and leading abstractions, radical reductionism leads to a self-banalization that is not helpful at all for the science-and-theology discourse.

The third trap could be called the *dualistic worldview trap.* It also fits neatly with the two previous traps, which can recommend themselves as great aids in escaping dualistic turmoil. Of course we cannot and should not avoid dualities, differences, contrasts, and even conflicts in our life and thinking. But we should not freeze them into a dualism. We do have to face many differences, creative differences, form-giving differences, differences that are hard to bear and even distortive and demonic differences. The differences between science and theology can become fruitful as long as we avoid the great frozen dualisms.

We have to become aware that science is in itself highly differentiated and that the differentiations and differences between theologies in one religion, not to speak of the differences between theologies of different religions, are considerable. So we have to work with provisional, tentative, topic-centered differentiations and dualities. We have to avoid the danger of being frozen by procedures that are overly generalized and lose touch with the topic, leading us from one trap to the next. First we create a helpless situation by fixing absolute dichotomies, and then we move into reductionism or into the modernist trap in order to get out of this mess. Discovering and disabling this trap, we see that we belong to different truth-seeking communities, with different primary topical fields and certainly different modes and methods. But the fact that we all belong to truth-seeking communities means we have to explore commonalities, analogies, and differences in their procedures. We cannot do this once and for all, but instead must do it with a clear awareness of the topics at issue and of the contexts of the partners in discourse.

The fourth trap we discovered can be closely related to the dualistic worldview trap. It can be called the *cliché trap*. The cliché trap picks up characteristics of either theology or science or both of them and overgeneralizes and overstates these. For example: science deals with facts — theology deals with meanings or even just fictions. When such a trap combined two clichés in a popular dualism, it was particularly difficult to spring. Even if one felt that there was only truth to the characterization of the one side, there was still the other side to be respected. And the other side was all too often protected by what I like to call the Frederick-the-Great syndrome.

Frederick the Great, King of Prussia, loved to play and compose music, and he loved to write poems. It is said that the poets used to say: His poetry is awkward, but he is a great musician! And the musicians are reported to have said: His music is hard to bear, but his poems are outstanding! The Frederick-the-Great syndrome is a shadow on every interdisciplinary work. It is certainly a real danger to every interdisciplinary agenda. But it is also a denunciation, ready to hand. Beyond that, the Frederick-the-Great syndrome can stabilize distortive dualistic clichés. For example the dualistic cliché: science deals with facts — theology deals with meaning; science deals with objectivity — theology deals with individual feeling. When theologians and scientists encounter these dualities individually, they might want to protest the description of their own side. But then, there is the other side and the somehow, somewhat plausible contrast, that finally leads to swallowing the dissatisfaction.

The science-and-theology discourse on eschatology challenged several clichés, including dualistic clichés such as: science deals with visible reality — theology, with invisible virtuality or hyper-reality, whatever this might be. Both disciplines, this became very clear, deal with both visible and invisible reality. As we have elaborated in the introduction to the book *The End of the World and the Ends of God*, after quantum cosmology we can not save science from the burden of dealing with unseen reality. On the other hand, it became clear that the unseen reality with which theology must deal is not a soft element that allows for all sorts of vague guesses and a speculative "anything goes." We have *standards of intelligibility* in both disciplines to disclose the realm of the unseen. And one of the most exciting tasks of the science-and-theology discourse is to discover, disclose, and reshape these standards in conversation on a specific topic, which might indeed lead to a clear differentiation of their tasks. A subtle, critical, and self-critical adjustment of this differentiation and difference needs to be aware of the cliché trap, the dualistic worldview trap, and their mutual reinforcement.

The fifth and sixth trap we discovered (without making this as explicit as I am about to do) were specific clichés on both sides that seemed to propose and to sponsor a specific dualism. The trap on the side of theology was that theological eschatology deals with the future, and with an open future after all. Although some of us supported this perspective to some degree, for most of the group it became more and more clear that theological eschatology also deals with past and present realities. There is a richness in biblical eschatological symbols that we should not lose in a modernist worldview that tells us that our past is fixed and our future is open. Christian theological eschatology deals in specific ways with the different modes of time, the theology of hope being one of these ways. Coming to faith, living in love, becoming justified by God, being sanctified, being enlivened and ennobled by God's Spirit, living in Christ, being the body of Christ, being a new creation, being transformed from glory to glory, being saved for the day of the Lord, entering God's reign, gaining eternal life — all these eschatological symbols focus on different aspects and dimensions of life before God, with God, and in God that the Jewish-Christian traditions envision and try to explore. All these different symbols are not just the same soft rhetoric for a vague future transformation that one can't really know anything about. These eschatological symbols, strange and even polluted terms in an environment that has secularized itself to the degree of public religious illiteracy, focus on dimensions of our life that we at least partially have to retrieve into the realms of experience, if we do not want to live with reductionistic and even distortive views of reality.

The sixth trap we discovered is the cousin or even the twin of the fifth one. Let us name the fifth trap the *"religion deals with vague future"* *trap.* The sixth then can be named the *"science deals with reality and reality is only material nature" trap.* As you see, a lot of complicated presuppositions come together in this trap. It shapes and reduces reality to that with which natural sciences are said be concerned. It then generalizes this reality to all reality. In one stroke it seems to give great power to the sciences — but in fact limits their potential to deal with a reductionistic materialism and a very limited understanding of nature. Strangely enough, this *scientific* concept of nature and reality needs the cousin or twin of the fifth trap, or at least an equivalent, to dump all the dimensions of reality that do not make sense to it. Our discourse saw this bad alliance and tried to spring this trap in order to reach a more comprehensive and more truthful picture and understanding of reality, and to open at least a small window between the different approaches.

The discovery of cultural traps and the attempt to spring these cultural traps is not just a luxury, a pleasure for some academics with strange curiosities and too much time for adventurous ideas. The discovery and the attempt to spring these cultural traps deals not only with boundaries and distortions in our individual academic disciplines. It deals with boundaries and distortions in our culture, our worldview, our focus on religion, and our focus on deeper dimensions of our experiences and longings. The discovery of cultural traps and the attempt to spring them does not satisfy all of those longings. It does not give automatic fulfillment to our search to expand our experiences and give them fuller expression. But it can open doors and windows. It can give us some access to an unseen reality that we have blocked out.

In his powerful book *Science and the Modern World,* Alfred North Whitehead describes our culture as latently structured by the interplay of scientific, ethical, aesthetic, and religious paradigms. Modernity has greatly strengthened the scientific paradigm. This has had many positive repercussions, particularly for the academy, for the exponential development of technology, and for the market. It has also had repercussions on dimensions of ethics, aesthetics, and religion that are difficult to measure. Even the discovery of these paradigm shifts is blocked by powerful cultural factors that might be cultural traps. What we begin to see with some clarity is that the rise of the sciences was accompanied by severe distortions in the realm of religion. Whitehead contends that modernity has lost God, and that it is seeking God. The science-and-theology discourse on eschatology did not work toward divine revelation. It was an academic, not a religious enterprise. But we would not deny, I guess, that our discovery of cultural traps and the invitation to spring them might bear positive repercussions for many sides. A more fruitful interdisciplinary academic discourse might not be the only outcome. Ethics, aesthetics, and religion will certainly develop differently when we are freed from the traps that our discourse on eschatology was able to see.

The Whole of Earthly Life

Larry Rasmussen

In *Christianity, Art and Transformation*, John de Gruchy writes of "restoring broken themes of praise" in ways that draw from Dietrich Bonhoeffer's aesthetic sensibilities. By the time the discussion concludes, new insights into Bonhoeffer's life and theology emerge and a new dimension of Bonhoeffer studies is uncovered. Granted, that is not the purpose or goal of de Gruchy's volume. "Theological aesthetics in the struggle for justice" is.[1] The discussion nonetheless is a testimony to the vitality of Bonhoeffer's fragments. It is also testimony to the range and vitality of de Gruchy's work.

What follows here is another tribute to Bonhoeffer's capacity to meet us anew; in this case precisely as we face compelling issues of transition. As de Gruchy finds Bonhoeffer fruitful for "the recovery of 'aesthetic existence' within the life of the church" in and for a world with little solid ground under its feet, I find Bonhoeffer fruitful for a world in which Christian faith must express love of God as fidelity to Earth if Christianity is to contribute to sustainability in a humanly dominated and jeopardized biosphere.

What is more, there is a deep connection between Bonhoeffer's aesthetic and his love of the earth. Bonhoeffer says so straightforwardly

1. The subtitle of John W. de Gruchy, *Christianity, Art and Transformation* (Cambridge: Cambridge University Press, 2001).

in one of the prison letters that we usually pass over but de Gruchy recovers for close attention.

> Take, for example, Brueghel or Velasquez, or even Hans Thoma, Leopold Kalkreuth, or the French impressionists. There we have a beauty which is neither classical nor demonic, but simply earthy, though it has its own proper place. For myself, I must say that it's the only kind of beauty that really appeals to me.[2]

This belongs to the consistent affirmation of earth and the sensual in Bonhoeffer. Indeed, together with the *cantus firmus* of the love of God, passion for earthly existence is the rhythm of the Christian life itself. Belief in a new world and the resurrection itself come only to those who "love life and the earth so much that without them everything seems to be over."[3] Little wonder that Bonhoeffer, for whom "the whole of earthly life"[4] is to be savored as the blessing of God, is drawn to the Song of Songs and its erotic delight in both human love and the rest of creation's. For Bonhoeffer a Christian aesthetic is profoundly earthy and the Christian life utterly worldly.

The ecclesial vocation follows. For times with little ground under our feet, when a future must be fashioned that is quite different from the past that formed us, the church is a zone of freedom for polyphonous cultural renewal. It is a place where in Christ the "broken themes of praise are restored"[5] and new life explored. This includes new institutional forms and practices.

With this link to Bonhoeffer's aesthetic *via* de Gruchy's discussion, we turn to the main theme of this essay: thinking *from* Bonhoeffer as well as *with* him about Christianity as an Earth faith. Not least the search is for churches already alive as zones of Earth-affirming freedom, places and spaces where "all Christian thinking, speaking, and organizing [are being] born anew out of . . . prayer and [righteous] ac-

---

2. Dietrich Bonhoeffer, *Letters and Papers from Prison* (New York: Macmillan, 1972), p. 239. See pp. 152-53 of de Gruchy's *Christianity, Art and Transformation.*

3. Bonhoeffer, *Letters,* p. 157.

4. Bonhoeffer, *Letters,* p. 74.

5. The source of de Gruchy's title for this chapter of *Christianity, Art and Transformation,* p. 167.

tion,"[6] where aesthetic existence already displays elements of needed transformation.

One of Bonhoeffer's references to the "Song of Songs" has already been made — the earthy little book of the Hebrew Bible he writes of from prison, with its sensuous love between human beings, as voiced by a woman, a man, and a group of women, and the sensuous love of these passionate souls for the land and its life.

There is another reference. It is from Bonhoeffer's 1928 Barcelona address on "the foundations of Christian ethics." Included is a remarkable sentence: "the earth remains our mother, just as God remains our Father, and our mother will only lay in the Father's arms those who remain true to her. Earth and its distress — that is the Christian's Song of Songs."[7]

Which is to say: fidelity to God is properly lived as fidelity to Earth. Christianity is judged by its contribution to Earth's care and redemption. If Christianity is not, in its practices, an Earth-honoring, Earth-positive faith in which the whole Community of Life — the societal, the biophysical, even the geoplanetary — has moral and religious standing, then it is not truly faithful. If Christianity is not an utterly "this-worldly" faith[8] in which eternity "is revealed only through the depths of earth,"[9] and if we are not wholly immersed "in life's duties, problems, successes and failures, experiences and perplexities"[10] as the place of God's own sufferings for the life of the world ("Earth's distress"), then we have missed what it means to have faith.

Song of Songs means, then, for Bonhoeffer and for us, living life to the fullest, embracing Earth and its distress as the way of embracing God and being embraced by God. It means both saving life and savoring life.

Let me state this in language appropriate to Christian ethics in our era. "Earth and its distress" as the Christian's "Song of Songs" means justice-centered Christianity. Yet it is justice with a particular

6. Bonhoeffer, *Letters*, p. 300.

7. Dietrich Bonhoeffer, "Grundfragen einer christlichen Ethik," *Gesammelte Schriften* (Munich: Kaiser, 1966), 3:56; translation mine.

8. Bonhoeffer, *Letters*, pp. 369-70.

9. Bonhoeffer, "Grundfragen einer christlichen Ethik," *Gesammelte Schriften* 3:56; translation mine.

10. Bonhoeffer, *Letters*, p. 370.

range. The proper subject of justice is not "the environment." It is not even "society." It is "creation" as a whole in a humanly dominated biosphere. It is the human and the more-than-human, together. Creation's well-being — the socio-communal, the biophysical, the geoplanetary — is at the center of Christian moral responsibility and practices, liturgical and contemplative practices included. The terms for adequate moral theory in twenty-first-century Christianity are an inclusive sense of creation and a correlative notion of justice. The theological line of thought is not God-Church-World but God-Cosmos-Earth-Church.

Were there world enough and time, we could talk about the particular ethical issues that belong to "Earth and its distress" in an era of planetary transition under the impact of globalization. "The ecological question" would certainly be added to what Weber, Troeltsch, Marx, and the Social Gospel called "the social question." And Bonhoeffer's conviction, echoing W. E. B. Dubois, that racism and the "color line" was *the* problem of the twentieth century would need to be extended another century to echo James Cone's conclusion in "White Theology Revisited." "The challenge for black theology in the twenty-first century," he writes, "is to develop an enduring race critique that is so comprehensively woven into Christian understanding that no one will be able to forget the horrible crimes of white supremacy in the modern world."[11] The perpetual plague of "we/they," morality and "the other," whether in racial/ethnic, class, or gender form, culture or nature, belongs to and even defines "Earth's distress." When will we learn that "they" do not live here anymore? It is only "we," together, for better or worse.

Fidelity to God lived as fidelity to Earth is Bonhoeffer's first contribution to viable Christianity for us. The second is his insight into living amidst historical transition with little solid ground beneath our feet, yet full historical responsibility before us. It is full, collective responsibility in the form of a comprehensive this-worldly ethic with an

---

11. James Cone, "White Theology Revisited," *Risks of Faith: The Emergence of a Black Theology of Liberation, 1968-1998* (Boston: Beacon, 1999), p. 137. Incidentally, Cone's famous essay of 1968, "Christianity and Black Power," shows Bonhoeffer's influence. It ends thusly: "The Church includes not only the Black Power community but all men who view their humanity as inextricably related to every man. It is that grouping with a demonstrated willingness to die for the prevention of the torture of others, saying with Bonhoeffer, 'when Christ calls a man, he bids him come and die.'" *Risks of Faith,* p. 12.

eye to consequences for future generations. Claiming Christ for a (postmodern) world coming of age was Bonhoeffer's way of thinking about this. It included a stock-taking and renewal of Christianity and society together. Fifty and more years later, we might view and state the transition and task somewhat differently. I will use Thomas Berry's *The Great Work: Our Way into the Future.*

Each epoch has what in retrospect is its "great work." The great work of Israel was to convey a new and dramatically influential experience of the divine in human affairs. The great work of the classical Greek world was to forge a profound understanding of the human mind and create a strong Western humanist tradition. The great work of Rome was to gather Mediterranean peoples and those of Europe into a civilizational "oikumene." The great work of India was to lead human thought into subtle and perhaps unsurpassed philosophical and religious experiences of time and eternity. And the great work of the Native peoples of the Americas was to establish a rapport with the natural powers of those continents in ways that effected integral relationships with these powers. Berry's thesis is that we now stand between the great work of the modern epoch — manifest in the dramatic achievements of science, technology, industry, commerce, and finance — and another era, one demanding a different "great work." The reason is a crisis of sufficient magnitude to warrant that the great work of modernity be superseded. The crisis is that "commercial-industrial obsessions" now threaten indispensable life systems in such degree that life as we have come to live it is unsustainable on modernity's terms. The crisis is that the same comprehensive progress that yielded modernity's enormous benefits now threatens the future. Industrial society's successful domination of nature now jeopardizes it on a global scale.

Modernity has brought us, in different words, both the enduring social question, now gone global, *and* a critical ecological one, also gone global. And they are tied together from the inside out. The great work ahead, then, is to effect the transition from a period of "the human devastation of Earth to a period when humans [are] present to [the rest of] the planet in a mutually beneficial manner."[12]

As Bonhoeffer himself already sensed in the baptismal sermon for

12. Thomas Berry, *The Great Work: Our Way into the Future* (New York: Bell Tower, 1999), p. 3.

Dietrich Bethge and in the outline for a new book, this means changed cosmologies and changed theologies and moral universes, together with altered institutions and different habits. It means different inner disciplines as well as outward arrangements, different languages of understanding, as well as a different play of religious, cultural, and moral imagination. Like past "great works," this one's creation will also be decades-long, perhaps centuries-long. Yet whatever the duration, this-worldly spiritual-moral formation of a kind appropriate to humans as "present to the [rest of the] planet in a mutually beneficial manner" must of needs be near the heart of twenty-first-century Christianity and decisive for the shape of ecumenism. Our common task now is an ecumenical and interfaith ethic of "sustainable community" for the whole Community of Life, a genuine Earth faith for Earth community.

There are no pristine Christian traditions for this task. Of that Bonhoeffer was painfully aware. Conversions to Earth on the part of Christianity itself are therefore crucial to Christianity's place in the ecumenical, interreligious, and pan-human vocation of twenty-first-century Earthkeeping. "Conversion" here means what it has commonly meant in religious experience, including Bonhoeffer's: namely, both a break with the past and yet a preservation of essential trajectories; both a rupture and new direction yet a sense that the new place is also "home" or "truly home"; both a rejection of elements of tradition yet the making of new tradition in fulfillment of the old; both difference from what has gone before and solidarity with it. Substantively, "conversion to Earth" means measuring all Christian ecumenical impulses by one stringent criterion: their contribution to Earth's well-being.

Such conversion happens in the manner Bonhoeffer hinted at in the baptismal sermon: namely, a dialectic of prayer (or arcane discipline and spirituality) and doing justice (or renewed practices and institutions). We could state the dialectic in this way for our moment in time. At one pole there are revisions of the deep traditions of Christian faith. (This might even include, as Bonhoeffer says in the Outline for a Book, "the question of revising the creeds" themselves.[13]) At the other pole, there is learning this-worldly, Earth-honoring faith in common secular engagement in a humanly dominated biosphere, an engagement where Earth itself is the shared "Commons."

---

13. Bonhoeffer, "Outline for a Book," *Letters*, p. 383.

All of this means a valorizing of Christian pluralism that is both necessary and ecumenically desirable. Christian traditions are many, they are often wildly different from one another, even in the same family, and they ought to be treated in ways that honor their genealogy and merit the respect and recognition of their devotees. "Catholicity" is the name for the nature of the church as the community of churches, present and past, that manifest the ecumenical range of historically incarnate faiths lived across two millennia on most of Earth's continents. Such catholicity and ecumenicity are inherently plural; they can only exist as internally diverse.

Valorizing ecumenical Christian pluralism is also in order because the great work before us is comprehensive of nature and culture together. No one tradition, religious or secular, and certainly no one theology and set of Christian practices, can satisfactorily address the full range of matters that require attention. It is mandatory to think ecologically about ecumenism and ecumenically about ecological well-being. The genius of biodiversity as the basic strategy for creativity and survival has a counterpart in the genius of religious and cultural diversity.

Thus we draw upon two stimuli from Bonhoeffer for "the great work" we are embarked upon: Earth and its distress as the Christian's "Song of Songs" and our age as an epochal moment lived responsibly toward the future even though we have little ground under our feet and even ask ourselves whether we "are of any use."[14] With these in mind I will finish with visits to Christian communities already doing the great work. In their practices and theology they are already demonstrating conversion to Earth and renewing and transforming the deep traditions they draw upon. They all give Christian traditions a strong voice but not a veto. And they were chosen precisely because they represent a diversity of confessional and cultural traditions as well as different geographical settings, and racial/ethnic, class, and gender membership. I add, in light of de Gruchy's own most recent work, that in all of them the arts are integral to the struggles for justice.

"Orthodox Alaska" is the first stop. I went to investigate two matters relevant to Christianity as a rooted, Earth-honoring faith. The ma-

14. The reference is to Bonhoeffer's own question in the essay, "After Ten Years," written as a gift for fellow conspirators at the turn of the year 1943; see *Letters,* pp. 16-17.

jority of the Orthodox Church in Alaska are Native Alaskan and have been ever since the Russians sold Czarist America to the United States in the 1860s. I wanted first to investigate the synthesis of shamanistic Native Alaskan cosmologies of land, sea, and sky with Orthodoxy's rich creation-filled trinitarian theology as led by monks and priests who, in haunting chanted liturgies, sacramental practices, and community pastoral care, functioned much as the shamans did. That synthesis, now deeply internalized, is beautifully captured in a favorite saying of Orthodox Alaska: "Earth is the icon that hangs 'round God's neck." And indeed iconography itself was the second reason to visit Orthodox Alaska. As the native iconographer Daniel Ogan told me, every icon is both mystical and theo-ecological. An icon is a sort of pinhole entry into the mysteries of God and creation, a meditative way by which to peer into the heart of the real and eternal. To effect this, the icon as an art form is a microcosm hinting, in every detail, of macrocosmic dimensions. For example, on the royal doors in the Chapel of St. Herman in Kodiak, behind which the priests consecrate the elements for Eucharist, one of the icons is a salmon, a second is an otter, a third a raven, a fourth a rose, all of them totems of Orthodox Aleuts, Yupik, Tlingit, and Athabaskan peoples. When you gaze upon the salmon, for example, you see stars and galaxies inside, and as, its body. That salmon is at home in the universe and the universe is at home in that salmon. Indeed, "Earth itself is the icon that hangs 'round God's neck." In a word, here is ancient liturgy and ancient craft among ancient peoples who carry on the creation-filled pan-en-theism of the Orthodox communions.

A second community demonstrating "the great work" in process is the Maryknoll Ecological Sanctuary in Baguio, Luzon, the Philippines. Nuns no longer live in convents, it seems, but in bio-shelters. At least they do here. Here they also express the great tradition of Catholic sacramentalism as "the hymn of the universe"[15] itself. Here all thirteen to fifteen billion years of the universe story is expressed in fourteen stations of the cosmic journey, as these are laid out with remarkable artistic creativity around the mountaintop in the sanctuary. Here the tale of

---

15. An allusion to the writing of Teilhard de Chardin, the inspiration of this recapturing as well as revising, now in an evolutionary context, of Catholic sacramentalism.

evolution, including the evolution of cultures and religions, is told as the universe story flowing forth from the heart of God. And here justice-centered Christianity encompasses the whole Community of Life as expressed in the life of the community. Concretely that means Maryknollers working with tribal communities on mining and timbering issues in which together they oppose the practices of international corporations that are destroying communal lands. It also means Maryknollers hosting and joining advocacy groups that address the wrenching problems of the urban poor of Baguio. All in all, the great tradition of Catholic sacramental communion is rendered in a distinctively Filipino way that incorporates the common creation story science has provided us. At the same time this revised sacramentalism issues in a justice mission for the region.

A third visit was to the Association of African Earthkeeping Churches of Masvingo Province, Zimbabwe. Unfinished liberationist struggles encompass the social, biophysical, and geoplanetary together here, as independent African churches seek "to regain the lost lands and reclothe the Earth."[16] When Eucharist is celebrated, trees are planted, or seeds dedicated, or first fruits gathered as part of a festival of booths. The fate of the people and the fate of the land are inextricable, and their well-being is joined at every point in liturgical practices that are simultaneously social justice/ecological practices.

In South Africa itself there is the Khanya Programme of the Methodist Church of Southern Africa and the D. T. Hudson Christian Ecovillage Trust, both in the Eastern Cape near East London. The planned arrangement of sacred space in new churches in both locales reflects a cosmology inclusive of the whole Community of Life. Three rondavels, the traditional round homes of the Xhosa peoples, are used as the basic form. They overlap to form a tri-circle church. People enter one rondavel as the nave; the second, visible to the people in assembly, is the granary where seeds and produce of the church gardens are kept; and the third rondavel is the cattle kraal, where animals are sheltered. All three are equally and together "church." The altar as the *axis mundi* rests at the center where the three circles overlap; in the back is a large tank of water, for the gardens, for the cattle, and for baptism.

The ascetic tradition of greening the desert in the manner lived at

16. This is the Shona phrase often used in the AAEC.

the Coptic Monastery of the Holy Virgin Mary in Wadi-al-Natrun in the Great Western Desert of Egypt was yet another example of "the great work" underway. In the tradition of the desert fathers and mothers the desert greened is variously rendered. It is a patch of Eden regained, or new creation, even resurrection from the dead on the home turf of death itself. Creation-honoring, Earth-restoring, anti-consumerist strains of asceticism exist, and this is one of them.

Earth-rich Christian spiritualities of place also exist. Consider Iona, an isle of the Inner Hebrides, Scotland. Here Celtic, Benedictine, and Reformed Christianities have communicated the gospel through common Earthly concerns tied to the topography of the western Hebrides. These concerns have been expressed in culturally specific liturgical language and art forms grounded in common Earth. Take, for example, St. Martin's Cross. Sculpted from local stone in the tradition of High Irish Crosses, it was fashioned at Iona in the eighth or ninth century and has stood there the subsequent twelve centuries. On one side of this three-meter-tall cross are carved the local flora and fauna. On the other side are presented the favored stories of scriptures, along with biblical flora and fauna. God is thus revealed in two great books — nature and holy writ. Or listen to the text of St. Patrick's breastplate hymn, also from these Celtic lands. It is typical in its sense of the immediately surrounding world as sacred space. "In the strong name of the Trinity, I bind unto myself today, the virtues of the starlit heaven, the glorious sun's life-giving ray, the whiteness of the moon at even, the flashing of the lightning free, the whirling wind's tempestuous shocks, the stable earth, the deep salt sea, around the old eternal rocks."

These and other communities have begun the socio-ecological and ecumenical reformation of the churches. Their uses of the arts for transformation are apparent and critical. And their practices and reflection have begun the necessary "re-reading" of the deep traditions of varied Christianities in an Earth-honoring and Earth-inclusive way. That re-reading means, for example, an asceticism that loves the Earth fiercely in a simple way of life and as a counterworld to the consumerist materialism that is destroying us. It means a sacramentalism that sings the hymn of the universe itself as our own story, with all else as kin and this cosmos as our true and common home. It means Christian mysticism and contemplation in which carefully listening to the heart of this world lets us hear the heartbeat of God. And it means prophetic/

liberative practices where power is shared for the saving and savoring of all life.

To conclude. "Earth and its distress" *is* the Christian's "Song of Songs." It is a song of many songs. May fidelity to God as fidelity to Earth be the common ecumenical orientation across what are wildly diverse local expressions of Christian faiths drawing from multiple deep and rich traditions.[17]

17. This essay is a reworking of two others and draws from them in significant ways. One is the introductory chapter in Dieter Hessel and Larry Rasmussen, eds., *Habitat Earth: Eco-Injustice and the Church's Response* (Minneapolis: Fortress Press, 2001). The other is a plenary address given at the International Bonhoeffer Congress in Berlin, 2000, on "The Shape of Christianity in the 21st Century and the Future of Ecumenism." I also draw, although not directly, on my book, *Earth Community, Earth Ethics* (Maryknoll, N.Y.: Orbis Books, 1996).

THEOLOGICAL ENGAGEMENT
WITH THE PUBLIC SPHERE

Freedom for Humanity: Karl Barth, Ecclesial Theology, and Public Life

Clifford Green

Since the days of his doctoral dissertation on ecclesiology, two theologians have particularly stimulated and informed the work of John de Gruchy as a theologian, teacher, and minister of the church: Karl Barth and Dietrich Bonhoeffer. If Bonhoeffer's name has appeared more frequently in his writings than Barth's, that does not mean that Berlin overshadowed Basel. On the contrary, de Gruchy regards their theology as complementary, not competitive — in this showing a better understanding of both than those who would play off one against the other. De Gruchy's work in theology, church, and public life — above all, in the anti-apartheid struggle — was so obviously in the tradition of Barth and Barmen that the German Evangelical Church of the Union awarded him the Barth Prize in 2000. In tribute to this friend of many years I offer this essay on Barth. Like Barth, de Gruchy believes that Christian theology is simultaneously rooted in the church while actively engaged with society and politics, that it is simultaneously "dogmatic" and contextual, historically anchored and contemporary. In other words, ecclesial theology and public theology are two sides of the one activity, as are dogmatics and ethics. Accordingly this essay will consider some ways that Barth provokes the ecclesia in North America in its theological reflection about public life at the beginning of a new century.

On his first and only visit to the United States in 1962, Karl Barth was asked about the future of American theology. Fixing his eye on Lady Liberty in New York Harbor, he astutely remarked that she needed a good deal of demythologizing. Nevertheless, she could also be the symbol of a true American theology of freedom. Such a theology, and the church that embraced it, would, according to Barth, be "marked by freedom from fear of communism, Russia, inevitable nuclear war and . . . [all other] principalities and powers. Freedom *for* which you stand would be freedom *for* — I like to say a single word — humanity, . . . that freedom to which the Son frees us, and which, as his gift, is the one real human freedom."[1]

Freedom for humanity, which is simultaneously *freedom for life*, is the theme in Barth's politics that I will highlight. The threefold emphasis of the World Council of Churches on "justice, peace, and the integrity of creation" coincides with Barth's own priorities to a considerable degree, so I will use it to shape this essay.

Basic Perspectives

I. Anybody thinking in Barth's spirit must immediately take the recent phrase "new world order" not only with a grain of salt, but *cum maximo grano salis*. To be sure, the geopolitical situation has changed in the last decade from what it had been since the mid-twentieth century. Precisely because Barth fixed his eyes on God's kingdom and God's righteousness, he dealt with human affairs as a great relativizer, and he was certainly a skeptic about all inflated and self-serving claims. He would not encourage churches in the West to join in an orgy of self-congratulation at the demise of the communist Soviet Union and the triumph of capitalism. Rather he would encourage us, as he did in his essay on "The Church between East and West,"[2] to cast a self-critical eye on ourselves, particularly on the injustices of our capitalism and the defects of our democracy.[3] Nor would he encourage us to remain stuck in the dualistic para-

---

1. *How I Changed My Mind* (Richmond: John Knox, 1966), p. 79. Note that in 1949 Barth had said that both West and East, in their different ways, "seem to be concerned with 'humanity'"; see Clifford Green, ed., *Karl Barth: Theologian of Freedom* (Minneapolis: Fortress Press, 1991), p. 316.

2. Green, *Karl Barth*, pp. 301-18. It is worth noting, incidentally, that nearly everybody in the early 1940s was talking about a "new world order." It quickly turned into the Cold War.

3. Barth's critique is similar to Michael Walzer's analysis, in his *Spheres of Justice:*

digm of the Cold War, only substituting Islam now in place of Communism. He would also ask us, I suspect, whether our reading the century in terms of an East-West struggle was not all too parochial; perhaps, after all, the more important political development on the world scene in the twentieth century was not the rise and fall of the Soviet Union and the Cold War, but rather the throwing off of European colonialism by the nations of Asia and Africa after World War II. And, Barth would doubtless be challenging churches in the wealthy West about their responsibility for global economic justice in the face of the vast disparities in the world. The premise of these challenges is that the church is called to be the church, the free people of God for all humanity, in and beyond every nation — another way of saying "one, holy, catholic, and apostolic"; the premise is not Western or American self-interest in religious garb.

2. *Historical thinking* is essential to good political analysis, and the reason for this is fundamental to Barth's theology. His most condensed term for God is "the Lord who loves in freedom." Barth understood God's "lordship" Christologically, in the subversive way Jesus defined it in Mark 10;[4] this is the way of the servant, not the way of domination and profane power which was all too evident in the Roman Empire — and its successors. Barth spelled out God's being and lordship in terms of God's "perfections," the perfections of divine loving and perfections of divine freedom. But there is a term that binds love and freedom together, a term that is highly pertinent to Barth's politics, and one that needs to be given more prominence: that word is *life*. Speaking of the being of God, Barth writes: "The definition that we must use as a starting-point is that God's being is *life*."[5] The Creator is the living God, Christ the resurrected Christ, the Holy Spirit the "spirit of life."[6]

One of the consequences of this doctrine of God is that Barth is an astutely historical and contextual thinker. In the field of ethics and politics he quickly dismisses ahistorical thinking as "abstract."[7] This is

---

A Defense of Pluralism and Equality (New York: Basic Books, 1983), of the domination of various aspects of life by money.

4. See Mark 10:42-44; cf. Philippians 2.

5. Karl Barth, *Church Dogmatics*, 2/1, ed. G. W. Bromiley and T. F. Torrance (Edinburgh: T. & T. Clark, 1964), p. 263.

6. Rom. 8:2, Rev. 11:11; cf. Rom. 8:10f., 2 Cor. 3:6, Gal. 6:8.

7. See Barth's critique of Emil Brunner on the relation of Nazism and Communism (Green, *Karl Barth*, pp. 297ff.). On a positive note, see his statement with respect

why the category of "event" is so central to Barth's theology.[8] Revelation is event, not deposit or entity. The church-community is event, not an institution. And in ethics God commands freedom, not natural law or principles.

Historical thinking is crucial for the future of American ecclesial theology and its reflection on politics because of the powerful ahistorical tendency in our culture. If Henry Ford is its most colorful representative with his declaration, "history is bunk," George Bush is its most recent exponent with his pronouncement after the Gulf War, "We have kicked the Vietnam syndrome." What did this mean? Unlike Robert McNamara, who at least thought there was something to learn by a self-critical review of the Vietnam War,[9] President Bush told us to put Vietnam behind us. Defeat has been wiped out by a swift and supposedly decisive victory. The Cold War is over, America is the world's sole superpower and is standing tall. On this reading we apparently have nothing to learn from misreading an anti-colonial revolution in terms of the monistic Cold War doctrine; nothing to learn about the limits of military power; nothing to learn from the fact that the Vietnam War compromised the Civil Rights Movement, brought down a president, and caused the greatest division in the country since the Civil War. This was America's "shaking of the foundations," to use Tillich's phrase. And yet the sort of crisis that World War I represented for Europe — and for Barth's early theology — is not to be entertained, according to the presidential pulpit. All the more reason why the Christian church and its theologians have to be more perceptive students of history, and better teachers of the nation.

---

to gender: "Different ages, peoples, and cultures have had very different ideas of what is concretely appropriate, salutary, and necessary in man and woman as such" (*Church Dogmatics* 3/4, p. 154).

8. In George Hunsinger's *How to Read Karl Barth* (New York: Oxford University Press, 1991), this is the motif of "actualism" and the one he calls "the most distinctive" (pp. 4, 30ff.).

9. Robert McNamara, *In Retrospect: The Tragedy and Lessons of Vietnam* (New York: Random House, 1995). Cf. p. xvi: "We of the Kennedy and Johnson administrations who participated in the decisions on Vietnam acted according to what we thought were the principles and traditions of this nation. We made our decisions in light of those values. Yet we were wrong, terribly wrong. We owe it to future generations to explain why."

3. Ecclesial theology has to be a more constructive critic and interpreter of the prevailing doctrine of *freedom* in our culture. Why did Barth think we needed to demythologize the Statue of Liberty? This was a gentle critique of the reigning social philosophy in our version of liberal democracy. According to this essentially individualistic doctrine, freedom is our capacity as individuals to choose and to act (within the outer limits of the law) as we see fit. "Freedom of choice" is for many people an ethical trump card — regardless of what one chooses. It is the central doctrine of moral laissez faire. Indeed, the economic allusion is not accidental: the exercise of choice at the temple of the supermarket is a paradigmatic enactment of this doctrine of freedom. The essence of this doctrine is that freedom is choice, and that freedom itself has no content.

In distinction from this, Barth follows the classical Christian understanding of freedom, which stretches back through Augustine to the New Testament, according to which true freedom is freedom to do good, to do the will of God, to love God and our neighbor. Here freedom has *content*, which is why Barth filled it out with illustrations: it would be freedom *from* inferiority vis-à-vis Europe, freedom *from* superiority vis-à-vis Africa and Asia, and freedom *from* sundry principalities and powers. Positively he called it "freedom *for* . . . humanity," that is, an analogy and imitation of God's freedom in the incarnation — the freedom which, as the gift of Christ, "is the one real human freedom." This is neither an empty freedom nor an individualistic one. It is freedom which is realized in community, the freedom of co-humanity and pro-humanity. Can a pluralistic democracy advance beyond our prevailing individualistic, liberal doctrine of freedom? I believe we did so for a brief time during the Civil Rights Movement. The cry "Freedom Now!" had real human content. It meant equal treatment, decent housing, good schools, and fair employment opportunities for African Americans; it did not mean the empty capacity to choose between these goods and their opposites. An ecclesial theology, then, needs to know the fundamental difference between the Christian doctrine of freedom and the empty, individualistic one — which is why Barth always spoke of freedom and responsibility in tandem.[10]

10. See, for example, "The Christian Community and the Civil Community," §19 on political freedom; *Karl Barth*, p. 285.

4. Barth's theology is ecclesial public theology. This is the presupposition of everything in this chapter. Ecclesial public theology is an alternative, on the one hand, to that privatized Christianity so common in American culture, what Barth in another context called "pietistic sterility."[11] In a nutshell his view is this: "This gospel . . . is political from the very outset. . . ."[12] It is worth pondering what difference it would make if more American Christians were to regard the state not merely as a profane infringement on individual liberty, nor simply as a utilitarian creature of the democratic will, but as an ordinance of God. On the other hand, a truly ecclesial theology will beware of uncritical acculturation to prevailing assumptions, social doctrines, and "realities." It will always be asking about its own distinctive identity, insights, and contributions to political life.

Economic Justice, Peace, and Ecological Ethics

1. Barth's Socialism: Economic Justice as an Imperative of Ecclesial Theology

From his early adult years, Karl Barth was a lifelong socialist. In his 1946 essay, "The Christian Community and the Civil Community," he drew the political conclusion from Christ's coming to seek and save the lost that the church must concentrate first on the lower and lowest levels of human society. The poor, the socially and economically weak and threatened, will always be the object of its primary and particular concern, and it will always insist on the state's special responsibility for these weaker members of society.[13] There is nothing novel about that — from the Bible's advocacy for the poor, the widow, the orphan, and the stranger to the pastoral letter of the U.S. Catholic bishops, *Economic Justice for All*,[14] this is a familiar Christian stance.

11. Cf. "Church and State," in Will Herberg's edition of Barth, *Community, State, and Church* (Garden City, N.Y.: Doubleday, 1960), p. 105; Barth juxtaposed to this the "sterility of the Enlightenment [secularism]."

12. Green, *Karl Barth*, p. 293.

13. "The Christian Community and the Civil Community" in Green, *Karl Barth*, p. 284.

14. National Conference of Catholic Bishops, *Economic Justice for All: Pastoral Let-*

86

What is noteworthy, at least to American Christians, is how Barth continues from this premise:

> The church must stand for social justice in the social sphere. And in choosing between the various socialist possibilities (social-liberalism? cooperativism? syndicalism? interest-free economy [*Freigeldwirtschaft*]? moderate or radical Marxism?) it will always choose the movement from which it can expect the greatest measure of economic justice. . . .[15]

For Barth it was axiomatic that social and economic justice entailed socialism. At the same time he was remarkably unideological about the form of it, as the foregoing list of options indicates; he always placed serving concrete human need above theory and political dogmas.

The very mention of socialism in America usually generates severe allergic reactions. So it needs to be said that Barth was a Democratic Socialist and no Bolshevik.[16] One can find many disavowals of the system of Soviet communism in his writings, and it is not necessary to de-

---

ter on Catholic Social Teaching and the U.S. Economy (Washington, D.C.: United States Catholic Conference, 1986).

15. Green, *Karl Barth,* p. 284, rev.; cf. *Church Dogmatics,* 3/4, p. 545, where Barth writes that the political task of the Christian community is to "espouse various forms of social progress or even of socialism." Barth mentions several quite different approaches to "socialism" in the passage quoted. Social liberalism in Barth's time is about equivalent to "social democratic" in Europe today, namely a moderate socialist position consistent with liberal democracy. A cooperative is a voluntary nonprofit association of consumers or producers for the benefit of its members. Syndicalism is a revolutionary strategy for reorganizing society by overthrowing the state, which it regards as intrinsically oppressive, and substituting the trade union as the key unit of productive labor and government; the motive is socialist in that production is for use, not profit (*Columbia Encyclopedia,* 1963). "Freigeldwirtschaft" is mistranslated as "free trade" or "free market economy." It refers to the economic theories of Silvio Gesell (1862-1930) about an economy in which money would be available without interest (hence "free money"), and would also depreciate like other capital assets. According to Andreas Pangritz (Aachen), to whom I am indebted for the following information, Gesell's theories in 1946 were discussed in Swiss anarchist circles and perhaps among the friends of Leonhard Ragaz. Elsewhere in Barth, "radical socialism" meant Soviet Communism; cf. Green, *Karl Barth,* p. 307.

16. For a summary sketch on Barth's socialism, see Green, *Karl Barth,* pp. 41ff.

tail them here.[17] A letter to his son Christoph in 1950 summed up his view: "Anyone who does not want communism — and none of us do — should take socialism seriously."[18] What did socialism mean for Barth? I think it comes down to two things: first, his inability to make peace with the injustices of a sinful world, what Bruce McCormack calls Barth's "revolutionary unrest: constantly being urged forward by the longing for something better than anything offered by this world."[19] The magnetism of the eschatological kingdom of God was for Barth a powerful stimulus to political and economic change in the world. And this connects to the second thing: in the face of those who said that "realism" demanded accommodation to capitalism and nationalism, Barth said "we should expect more from God."[20]

Why, a decade after the demise of Soviet communism, is Barth's socialism a crucial challenge to the future of ecclesial theology? First, because it makes us ask "What do we expect from God?" Do we expect "revolutionary unrest" or a complacent and comfortable security in the status quo? After answering that — or perhaps before answering it — we should ponder facts like these in a 1998 United Nations report:

> Even in the world's wealthiest countries, the ranks of the poor are growing and many people are being denied the basic rewards of affluence. For example, 16.5 percent of Americans live in poverty, even though the United States leads the world in per-capita con-

17. When Emil Brunner asked Barth why he was not combating Communism as he did National Socialism, he replied that though he did not believe Communism presented the temptation and threat which National Socialism did, he nevertheless did not consider that the Soviet system "conform[ed] to our standards of justice and freedom" and that anyone who wanted from him "a political disclaimer of its system and its methods may have it at once" (Green, *Karl Barth*, p. 299). In "The Church between East and West" Barth wrote that "the profoundly unsatisfactory nature" of Eastern communism is obvious to everybody — though, in contrast to National Socialism, he credited communism with at least having a positive intention of dealing with "the social problem"; cf. Green, *Karl Barth*, pp. 315, 313.

18. Cited in Eberhard Busch, *Karl Barth: His Life from Letters and Autobiographical Texts* (Philadelphia: Fortress, 1976), p. 382.

19. *Karl Barth's Critically Realistic Dialectical Theology* (Oxford: Clarendon Press, 1995), p. 109.

20. *Die Christliche Welt* 28 (15 August 1914): 776, cited in McCormack, *Karl Barth's Theology*, p. 110.

sumption of goods and services. Sweden was ranked the best among developed nations in spreading the wealth, with fewer than 7 percent of its people in poverty. In the industrialized world, at least 37 million people are unemployed, 100 million are homeless, and nearly 200 million have a life expectancy of less than 60 years.[21]

The picture in the United States is also one of increasing disparities. Income disparity is widening at the extremes. In 1979 the top 5 percent of U.S. earners earned ten times the bottom 5 percent. Fourteen years later, in 1993, the top 5 percent earned twenty-five times the bottom 5 percent.[22] According to a 1999 Public Television program entitled "Luxury Fever,"[23] the wealthiest 1 percent own 50 percent of the nation's wealth — though one-third of those earning over $100,000 say they can't make ends meet.[24] Meanwhile the median American income has not increased in the last twenty years, and the earnings of people in the bottom fifth have declined more than 10 percent.[25]

The increasingly interdependent global economy raises more critical issues. Not least among them is the fundamental question: Who controls the global movement of capital? Who benefits and who suffers from this movement? This is not solely a question for investors — it also involves responsible and irresponsible borrowing.[26]

Third World debt is another critical issue in the global economy. Both the World Council of Churches at its Harare assembly in 1999 and the United States Roman Catholic bishops have called for debt relief to

21. *The New York Times*, September 13, 1998, Sec. 3, p. 2. See United Nations Development Program, *Human Development Report 1998: Consumption Patterns and Their Implications for Human Development* (New York: Oxford University Press, 1998).

22. Statistics from Robert H. Frank, Cornell University economist, quoted in interview on PBS News Hour with Jim Lehrer, "Luxury Fever" program, May 20, 1999, and confirmed in Frank's e-mail of June 7, 1999. See Robert H. Frank, *Luxury Fever: Why Money Fails to Satisfy in an Era of Excess* (New York: Free Press, 1999).

23. News Hour with Jim Lehrer, May 20, 1999.

24. Juliet Schor, Harvard economist, quoted in News Hour "Luxury Fever" interview.

25. Robert H. Frank, "Our Climb to Sublime: Hold On, We Don't Need to Go There," *The Washington Post*, January 24, 1999, p. B01.

26. See the four-part *New York Times* series, "Global Contagion: A Narrative," February 15-18, 1999.

poor nations.[27] In comparison to the burden of Third World debt, just one percent of the U.S. national budget is devoted to foreign aid, far less than other developed countries.[28]

On the crises of the global economy, here are some comments from an experienced practitioner, worth quoting at length:

> Market fundamentalism relies on an allegedly scientific economic theory. Basically, I think it was Ronald Reagan and Margaret Thatcher who were the main movers in adopting a vulgarized version of laissez-faire economics, turning it into a kind of fundamentalist position. . . . I also worry about inequity. The markets are good for expressing individual self-interest. But society is not simply an aggregation of individual interests. There are collective interests that don't find expression in market values. Markets cannot be the be-all and end-all. These collective decisions, and even individual decisions, must involve the question of right and wrong. I think markets are amoral. . . . But moral values are necessary to prevent their excesses and inequities. . . . In the case of labor markets, work itself is turned into a commodity. As such, the labor markets often work very efficiently. But you can also sack someone even if he has an ailing mother and may have nowhere to turn. People have to be treated as people. . . . I am worried about . . . the replacement of professional values by market values. Turning law or medicine into businesses. I think it changes the character of those activities. In the case of politics, the huge role of money in elections undermines the political process. [The new global economy resembles the internal crises of capitalism in the past.] After each crisis, we made institutional changes. . . . We have national institutions that keep excesses from going too far. During this period when market fundamentalism has become the dominant dogma, however, markets have become truly global. And we don't have comparable international institutions to prevent the excesses.

27. See Gustav Niebuhr on "A Jubilee Call to Debt Forgiveness" (U.S. Catholic Conference Administrative Board), *The New York Times*, April 25, 1999.
28. This is a widely quoted statistic, for example, in *The New York Times*, July 6, 1999, p. A4, in a story on the departure of J. Brian Atwood, director of the Agency for International Development for the previous six years.

These are not the words of some left-leaning, tweed-jacketed, pipe-smoking, academic theologian in his ivory tower. This is George Soros, the billionaire New York financier, in an interview about his book, *The Crisis of Global Capitalism.*[29]

Christians like Barth who lean to the left will surely acknowledge that the market has won out over state planning as a more efficient way of allocating resources. But those who lean to the right need to recognize that markets have long antedated modern capitalism, and that there are fundamental ethical and policy issues that the market can never address. Those who lean to the left need to recognize that capitalism has proved to be a very successful generator of wealth — which is surely needed to improve living standards among the poor both nationally and internationally. Those who lean to the right need to admit that even moderately controlled capitalism cannot equitably distribute that wealth. The *Church Dogmatics* does not provide a Barthian socialist recipe to magically solve these economic problems. But Barth does call the church to a passionate commitment to social and economic justice. If socialism as Soviet state capitalism and command economy is dead, socialism as the question of economic justice is more urgent than ever.

Finally I submit that it is precisely in economic theory and practices that we find embedded the operative social philosophy of most people today. This is where the agenda of theological anthropology is actually located. It needs to be engaged in a self-critical way in our theological seminaries and our preaching. What philosophy of religion used to be in the seminary curriculum needs to become economic education.

2. *Barth's "Pacifism": The Peace Imperative of Ecclesial Theology*

Barth's ethic of peace is grounded Christologically, for the command of Jesus that we should love our enemies (Matt. 5:44) is rooted in God's being and action in the incarnation, cross, and resurrection. According to Romans 5:6-11, it is God's enemies who are reconciled to God by the cross; the disciples of Jesus, accordingly, are commanded to love their

---

29. (New York: Public Affairs, 1998); see George Soros and Jeff Madrick, "The International Crisis: An Interview," *New York Review* (January 14, 1999): 40.

enemies. For Barth this leads to what he calls his "practical pacifism" — not pacifism as an abstract principle, not an absolute pacifism that ruled out the use of force in certain circumstances — but a definite imperative to peace.[30] From this perspective we can briefly review Barth's course from World War I through the Cold War.

Among the various influences that disillusioned Barth with nineteenth-century Protestant theology, what played a decisive role for him personally, he said, was "the failure of the ethics of modern theology at the outbreak of the First World War which led to our discontent with its exegesis, its conception of history, and its dogmatics."[31] When it came to defeating National Socialism in World War II, however, Barth as vigorously roused Europe to the cause as Reinhold Niebuhr did America. But, typically, as soon as Hitler was defeated Barth became an advocate for the reconstruction of Germany.

One of Barth's major efforts during the Cold War was opposition to nuclear weapons. Working to eliminate these weapons must surely be at the top of the international agenda for the universal church in the present century. Perhaps we have been lulled into complacency in the last decade, but there are still estimated to be over thirty thousand nuclear weapons in the world.

In the 1980s we saw important declarations on peace and atomic weapons by the World Council of Churches' Sixth Assembly (Vancou-

30. In *Church Dogmatics*, 4/2, p. 550, Barth wrote: "According to the sense of the New Testament we cannot be pacifists in principle, only in practice. But we have to consider very closely whether, if we are called to discipleship, we can avoid being practical pacifists, or fail to be so." Cited in Hunsinger, "The Politics of the Nonviolent God: Reflections on René Girard and Karl Barth," in his *Disruptive Grace* (Grand Rapids: Eerdmans, 2000), pp. 21ff.; also in *Scottish Journal of Theology* 51, no. 1 (1998): 61-85, esp. 77ff.

31. In his 1956 essay on "The Humanity of God"; cf. *Karl Barth*, p. 49. Here is the fuller version: "One day in early August 1914 stands out in my personal memory as a black day. Ninety-three German intellectuals impressed public opinion by their proclamation in support of the war policy of Wilhelm II and his counselors. Among these intellectuals I discovered to my horror almost all of my theological teachers whom I had greatly venerated. In despair over what this indicated about the signs of the times I suddenly realised that I could not any longer follow either their ethics and dogmatics or their understanding of the Bible and of history. For me, at least, nineteenth-century theology no longer held any future." From "Protestant Theology in the Nineteenth Century," in Barth, *The Humanity of God* (Atlanta: John Knox Press, 1978), p. 14.

ver, 1983), the U.S. Roman Catholic bishops, the United Methodist Church, and others.[32] These documents were striking in the degree to which they diverged sharply from the official national policy of American governments of both parties. They declared that the use of nuclear weapons was completely outside the bounds of any Christian ethic, and they urged church members not be to involved in the production or use of these weapons. Barth and his colleagues had reached this conclusion almost thirty years earlier.

In March, 1958, people like Martin Niemöller, who had been members of the Confessing Church and were then leading a peace movement in the German churches, presented a petition to the National Synod of the Evangelical Church. The several hundred signatories "challenged the Synod to declare that atomic war was a *status confessionis* issue for the church," that is, a situation requiring a confession of faith by the church because the heart of the gospel and therefore the very existence of the church was at stake. Further, the petition called on the Synod to declare that "the church's position was a categorical No to nuclear war, and that Christians may not participate in any way in preparations for atomic war." A deeply divided Synod passed a resolution against weapons of mass destruction and called for the end of atomic weapons research; but it did not adopt the petition's stance. A rumor circulated that Barth disagreed with the petition. In reply he published a letter in *Junge Kirche* saying: "You may say to all and everyone that I am in agreement with these theses . . . as if I had written them myself. . . ." In fact, Barth himself was the author of the petition![33]

A few months later Barth wrote to the European Congress for Outlawing Atomic Weapons. Everyone, including governments, Barth wrote, knows the "evil and danger of atomic weapons," but they still develop and accept them. Intellectuals, including "a large group of church leaders," Barth said sarcastically, "devote themselves to profound philosophical and theological discussions about such problems as the tragic dimension of human existence in the atomic age, but they stubbornly avoid making any specific decision against atomic weap-

---

32. The Assembly's "Statement on Peace and Justice" calls the production and use of nuclear weapons "a crime against humanity" and calls on Christians to "refuse to participate in any conflict involving weapons of mass destruction."

33. Green, *Karl Barth*, pp. 319ff., citing also Busch, *Karl Barth: His Life*, p. 431.

ons." Atomic weapons are rationalized by the supposedly greater threat posed by the respective adversaries in the Cold War. Therefore every effort must be made to end the Cold War, an effort in which Christian faith can bring some creative insights. In the meantime, opposition to "the blasphemous . . . development of atomic weapons" must continue on all levels. Finally Barth asked the Congress to consider encouraging active resistance, perhaps by inviting people "to refuse to serve in military units employing such weapons."[34]

If we can never regain our innocence by putting the nuclear genie back in the bottle, it is all the more urgent that we build up international institutions such as the United Nations and the International Court of Justice where raw violence can be sublimated as much as possible into law, politics, and economic sanctions. The posture of the protagonists in the Cold War has greatly hindered this development, and outmoded ideas of the nation state continue to do so. The church, itself an international institution, needs to be both more willing and better organized to mobilize its resources for transcending, mediating, and reconciling national and ethnic interests. An international institution like the United Nations will not be able to avoid the use of force from time to time. Particularly in genocidal situations like Rwanda and Kosovo, the need for international police action will continue to arise. But cross-cutting political interests in the United Nations will not make decisions to employ force easy.

In the history of the church the pacifist and just war traditions have jostled each other for centuries. Just war doctrine — more aptly called the "just defense doctrine" — intended its canons to constrain violence and sanctioned it only as a last resort under strictly limited conditions. But the self-interests of rulers and states have usually overridden the church's canons of constraint. So sanctioning the use of violence has been the dominant tradition. We are living after the end of the bloodiest of all centuries. From the machine gun at the beginning of the century to the nuclear bomb in the middle, we have proved that every increase in weapons technology will be used for increased death and destruction. In light of this, is it too much to hope that we can shift the balance, that the ecumenical church will become an active

34. The text, translated by Robert McAfee Brown, is found in Georges Casalis, *Portrait of Karl Barth* (Garden City, N.Y.: Doubleday, 1963), pp. 73f.

peace church, a builder of bridges, an agent of reconciliation, an advocate of economic development? This seems to me the direction of Barth's peace witness.

3. Nature in Creation: Dogmatic Roots of Ecological Ethics

I take it for granted that the issue of ecology is a self-evident political and global issue. The brevity of this section is itself a symptom of the problem it discusses. I want to highlight a critique of Barth's doctrine of creation, as it bears on ecological ethics. Here I am following Paul Santmire and his Harvard dissertation on the status of nature in Barth's doctrine of creation.[35] A concise summary of his analysis is found in his book, *The Travail of Nature*,[36] under the rubric "the triumph of personalism." The problem here concerns the fundamental status of the natural world — as distinct from humanity — as part of creation in Barth's theology.

Santmire characterizes Barth's position as "radical the-anthropocentrism." In the doctrine of revelation the Word is "*God's* address to *humanity* in Jesus Christ"[37] and consequently Christian doctrine, Barth says, "has to be exclusively and conclusively the doctrine of Jesus Christ as the living Word of God spoken to us human beings."[38]

In Barth's doctrine of election this focus on God and humanity discloses its eternal ground. Election is the eternal basis of everything that happens in history,[39] it is the internal basis — the raison d'être — of the creation. Jesus Christ, the eternal Son, is the electing God. Jesus

35. See "Creation and Nature: A Study of the Doctrine of Nature with Special Attention to Karl Barth's Doctrine of Creation," Th.D. dissertation, Harvard University, 1966.

36. H. Paul Santmire, *The Travail of Nature: The Ambiguous Ecological Promise of Christian Theology* (Philadelphia: Fortress Press, 1985), especially pp. 145-56; see also his *Nature Reborn: The Ecological and Cosmic Promise of Christian Theology* (Minneapolis: Fortress Press, 2000).

37. Santmire, *Travail of Nature*, p. 149.

38. Barth, "How My Mind Has Changed," *The Christian Century* 56 (September 1939): 37f., cited in Santmire, *Travail of Nature*, p. 253.

39. It is "the principle and essence of all happening everywhere" (*Church Dogmatics*, 2/2, p. 83n, cited in Santmire, *Travail of Nature*, p. 150).

Christ, as the incarnate Son, is the elect human being. But election also involves, as Santmire puts it, "the ontological prefiguration of a *community of humans* united together in the person of the 'God-Man'."[40] But the nonhuman creation has no eternal ground. It is rather the "external ground of the covenant," the "theater"[41] where the eternal covenant is played out in history. Santmire summarizes:

> We now see formally speaking that nature for the first time has come into view in Barth's schema, as a kind of stage to allow the eternally founded drama between God and humanity to run its course. So, whereas humanity has a dual status — it is elected in eternity and it is also created "as such," in order to fulfill its eternal determination — the whole world of nature, outside of humanity, has a single status only. It has no eternal determination. Its reality is purely instrumental. It is merely the temporal setting for the really real, for the exfoliation and the consummation of the eternal covenant of grace with humanity. . . . Nature has no divinely bestowed meaning of its own.[42]

This does not mean that the cosmos is evil, inhospitable to humanity, or dualistically opposed to God. It is, Barth says with Genesis, "very good." But, Santmire concludes, "it has no evident permanent meaning in the greater scheme of things, as the human community obviously does."[43] The issue raised all too briefly here concerns the deep structure of a dogmatics and its deficiency as regards ecological ethics. Worth further exploration in this context are two places where ecclesial theology cannot avoid dealing with matter: the human body, and the sacraments; this also relates to Barth's understanding of liturgy.

---

40. Santmire, *Travail of Nature*, p. 150, citing *Church Dogmatics*, 2/2, pp. 116f.

41. Cf. *Church Dogmatics*, 3/3, p. 48; cp. 3/3, p. 46 where Barth says its status is "pure service," which means, according to Santmire, p. 152, "purely instrumental."

42. Santmire, *Travail of Nature*, pp. 152f., where supporting citations are given for Barth's argument that humanity is the point of the created world, the meaning and goal of the whole creation.

43. Santmire, *Travail of Nature*, p. 154.

Church Practice as Political Witness

Barth's 1946 essay on "The Christian Community and the Civil Community"[44] describes church and state in terms of two concentric circles of which Christ and the kingdom of God are the center, with the church as the inner circle and the state as the outer. Thus church and state have an analogous relation to covenant and creation, of which Barth said that the covenant of grace is the internal basis of the creation while the creation is the external basis of the covenant. Barth does not advocate a theocratic state. "The tasks of the Christian community in the political realm are secular and profane. . . . Political systems are human inventions, to be tested experimentally to see if, through law and peaceful order, they provide 'an external, relative, and provisional humanization' of existence."[45]

As is well known, Barth regards the state as an "analogue" of the eschatological kingdom of God. Political activity by members of the Christian community should therefore be "parabolic." Christians work to make law, policy, and practice in the public realm point to and reflect in some degree what the church knows of Christ and the reign of God. Hence the incarnation of the eternal God means specific things. It means putting real, living human beings ahead of all causes and ideologies. It means that divine justification points to the constitutional state, and that Christ's coming to save the lost means a preferential option for the most vulnerable members of society. Baptism into one Spirit means the equal freedom and responsibility of all citizens. For restricting "the political freedom and responsibility not only of certain classes and races but, supremely, that of women," Barth said, "is an arbitrary convention" that must be abandoned forthwith.[46] These are some of the dozen examples Barth gives of this parabolic politics whereby civic life can point to God's kingdom for which the church hopes, prays, and works.

Well and good. But now let us ask about turning this procedure back on the life of the church itself, that is, looking to *the actual practices of the church as enacting the doctrines it proclaims*. I am asking about the church which is not only a community of Word, sacrament, and the

44. Green, *Karl Barth*, pp. 265-96.
45. Green, *Karl Barth*, p. 265.
46. Green, *Karl Barth*, p. 285.

Spirit, but also an economic and political community. I am asking how the Christian community, in its own life and practice, can better become *itself* a socio-political parable of the gospel, an enacted parable of God's reign and realm.

I am prompted in this direction by the account of the birth of the church at Pentecost. According to Luke in the Acts of the Apostles, the coming of the Holy Spirit created a new political and economic community in the world. *A new political community:* the Christian community was first constituted by devout Jews "from *every nation* under heaven."[47] Their names are all listed, from Persia in the east to Libya and Rome in the west. The first form of the church was not, pace colleagues in "congregational studies," the local congregation — the dominant form of church life in North America — but a new international community, the first "united nations."

A new economic community: I find it very suggestive that Luke links liturgy, and specifically the Eucharist, to economics. "And they devoted themselves to the apostles' teaching and fellowship, to the breaking of bread and the prayers. . . . And all who believed were together and had all things in common; and they sold their possessions and goods and distributed them to all, as any had need."[48] They distributed bread, the Body of Christ, and they distributed goods and money to those in need — and they did so "with glad and generous hearts." (Those who celebrate the Eucharist only infrequently, or in the modern, individualistic way, should ponder the economic implications of their liturgical practice.)

We should not get sidetracked by arguments about the early church and "primitive communism," but we should equally recognize that Luke is not talking about "primitive capitalism" either. And who will not admit that structuring a just economic order in a global economy is a complex and demanding task? Here I want to focus on the economic life of the church as political witness.

It is worth remembering that there is a long tradition in the church of making direct connections between economic life and the gospel — I am thinking of monastic communities on the one hand, and communities like Mennonites and Hutterites on the other.

We can begin by recalling that churches are already engaged in a

47. Acts 2:5ff.
48. Acts 2:42ff.

great deal of economic activity. Recall church-based insurance companies; recall millions of dollars given annually through churches for humanitarian aid and disaster relief; think of revolving loan funds supporting sweat-equity, low-income housing, and people donating their labor to build houses through Habitat for Humanity; think of trusts and foundations administered by congregations and denominations; and we should certainly highlight the corporate responsibility movement spearheaded by the Interfaith Center for Corporate Responsibility, which assembled sufficient church funds to influence major banks and corporations in their policies on apartheid in South Africa, for example. Subsidizing with church offerings parochial schools, hospitals, and homes for the elderly is also a substantial economic activity.

Yet all this is unsystematic and relatively modest in scale compared to the actual economic resources under the control of church members. What might a more ambitious organization of churches as an economic institution be able to accomplish, and to do so in a way that embodies church priorities and addressed social injustices in some significant measure?

1. A "Workers of Conscience" fund for church members who resigned their jobs making nuclear weapons to assist them while they found new employment.
2. A church-based health insurance scheme for the very poor — church members and non-members — at least some of them.
3. A vigorous affirmative action hiring program by businesses owned by church members.
4. A training and loan program to help minority young adults start businesses in poor city neighborhoods.
5. Establishing a substantial ecumenical foundation to support activities such as the above.
6. A retired executives organization to volunteer expertise in support of the above.
7. Research and education projects on the church as an economic institution — its resources and activities.

What about parables of a new political community, a polis that more nearly reflects Pentecost and a new humanity and less the class and racial and other conflicts of our cities and world?

CLIFFORD GREEN

1. A top priority has to be racial reconciliation, as a parable of the reconciliation of the world with God. We could begin with a major migration of white, suburban church members to black, urban congregations.

2. Institutionalize the sanctuary movement, along the lines of the German church-based organization "Asylum in the church," which provides legal defense to foreign workers the government was illegally trying to deport.[49]

3. Promote systematic church support of the United Nations and the International Court of Justice.

4. Expand dramatically church programs of international exchange and travel seminars, especially to places of ethnic, religious, and political conflict such as the Middle East, Sudan, Korea, Russia, Vietnam, Rwanda, Ireland, and the Balkans.

5. In Christian-Jewish relations, inaugurate a ten-year, church-wide program of theological research, dialogue, and congregational education.

6. Establish Muslim affairs offices in the main denominations to educate church members about the complex realities of Islam and to counteract media stereotypes.

These are just a few suggestions of initiatives that churches can take themselves, independent of and *in addition to* the direct service of Christians in the public world of economics and politics. Let Barth himself have the last word in a concluding passage from "The Christian Community and the Civil Community":

> The real church must be the model and prototype of the state. The church must *set an example* so that by its very existence it may be a source of renewal for the state and the power by which the state is preserved. The church's preaching of the gospel would be in vain if its own existence . . . were not a practical demonstration of the thinking and acting from the gospel which takes place in this inner

---

49. The church-based organization is Asylum in the Church (Asyl in der Kirche), in Berlin-Kreuzberg and connected to the Kirche Zum Heiligen Kreuz. The address is: Asyl in der Kirche, Zossener Strasse 65, 10961 Berlin. The pastor in charge of the project is Pfarrer Jürgen Quandt. I believe the organization is funded by the Ev. Kirche.

circle. How can the world believe the gospel of the King and of his kingdom if by its own actions and attitudes the church shows that it has no intention of basing its own internal policy on the gospel? . . . Of the political implications of theology which we have enumerated there are few which do not merit attention first of all in the life and development of the church itself. So far they have not received anything like enough attention within the church's own borders.[50]

50. Green, *Karl Barth*, p. 294.

Concrete Levels of Being and Their Political Implications

Jean Bethke Elshtain

A perduring theme of John de Gruchy's life and work is the question of who we — Christians as citizens — are in relation to the wider socio-political worlds of which we are a part. His answer, typically, is complex: at times the Christian must stand apart and struggle against a given order of things in the name of neighbor love and service. At other times, a measure of loyalty to the polity is in order, but civic identity and loyalty must not be allowed to trump Christian identity. There is a complex dialectic between the two. Alliances between "throne and altar," as they were once called in the now long-ago past of Christendom, are to be avoided just as assiduously as is a project of secularization that requires not only a properly secular (in the sense of non-denominational and non-confessional) state but a thoroughly secular society shorn of all religious symbols, songs, and words.

The debate about who we are in relation to the *civitas* is an ancient one, ongoingly refracted and contested. The dialectic de Gruchy advocates, one that resists putting flags of a country on the altar of the church but that very much advocates Christian citizens engaging the country, has been made possible by the many potent forces that add up to what we call modernity. Christianity is one of those forces. But to tell this tale takes a bit of effort. I will explore the question from my perch as a social and political theorist. My effort will be one of clarification and interpretation. I will not so much answer a specific question as display the deep backdrop to how such questions are posed in the first place, from both Christian and non-Christian perspectives. I begin with a famous brief by a famous political theorist against the notion of universal human rights, a notion that is now the lingua franca of the world as we know it and that formed the very heart of protest against the old apartheid regime in John de Gruchy's South Africa.

In her masterwork, *The Origins of Totalitarianism*, Hannah Arendt famously argued against universal human rights. Such rights were posed too grandly and abstractly. When the crunch came, they were more or less worthless. Not one to mince words, Arendt claimed that those who were first stripped of citizenship in a *particular* polity, as Jews had been in Nazi Germany, could not make their claims stick anywhere else. You need to have rights guaranteed by a particular polity in order for these rights to be fungible anywhere else. What happened to the Jewish citizens of Germany under National Socialism is that, having been stripped of civic identity, they indeed became what they were accused of being by the National Socialists: the scum of the earth, tossed hither and yon, not particularly welcome anywhere. There is a distinct Burkean flavor to Arendt's criticism with her emphasis on the concreteness of citizenship by contrast to the abstractness of universal rights. For Arendt, universal identity was a chimera and a rather dangerous one at that.

In times of civic peace the proposition of universal identity does not get tested. In times of war it does and there it is found wanting *unless* — and this is a vital caveat — there are international conventions in place that guarantee certain modes of conduct, whether to refugees or prisoners of war. These conventions, like the Geneva Conventions, may be violated in the breach. But it is vital that they be there. One can at least appeal to *something* and hope that that something has some heft in a crisis situation. (It is, by the way, rather remarkable that prisoners of the Wehrmacht were treated quite well on the whole and in line with international conventions: this by contrast to prisoners of the Japanese in World War II.) In sum, Arendt's view is that rights must be lodged concretely within the statutory armamentarium of nation-states — must be attached to a polity — or they are not worth the paper they are written on.[1]

---

1. Arendt makes this argument in a number of places, most notably in *The Origins of Totalitarianism* (New York: Harcourt Brace Jovanovich, Harvest Paperback, 1973), especially chapter 9, "The Decline of the Nation-State and the End of the Rights of Man," pp. 267-304.

A major development of the post–World War II era is, of course, the universalization of human rights discourse and the insistence that these rights attach to being-as-such. There is a "something" about the human person such that that being is not to be violated in certain ways, whatever the exigencies of a political situation. As well, tables of positive rights — lists of the claims such beings can reasonably make upon the polities of which they are a part — attempt to go beyond preventing harm to persons to promoting the good of persons. The idea that identity transcends national boundaries is not a new one. It lies at the heart of ancient Stoicism, or one version of it does. It is the epicenter of Christian belief: that human beings are created in God's image and, as such, possess an inviolable dignity that is God-given, not the revocable privilege of a political body. Christian deterritorialization of identity is powerfully present in one of my favorite moments from St. Augustine's great *Confessions*. Augustine, his Christian brothers, his son, Adeodatus, and his formidable mother, Monica, are making their way down the Italian boot for embarkation to their native Hippo when Monica dies near Ostia. This was a cataclysm in the ancient world — to go into the soil, the foreign territory, of a site that is not one's homeland, not, therefore, the giver of one's identity. (Here it is worth remembering that Socrates calls Athens his "mother.") Augustine, knowing this powerful belief (although his mother is a Christian), begins to fret and Monica tells him not to worry, that surely God will know where to find her. "It does not matter where you bury my body. Do not let that worry you! All I ask of you is that, wherever you may be, you should remember me at the altar of the Lord."[2]

The Christian deterritorialization was correlative with a downgrading of the centrality of membership in a particular *polis* or *civitas*. The prototypical Christian identity is not that of citizen but of pilgrim. The peregrinus or peregrina wanders across and through territories but he or she is not essentially *of* them. This does not mean Christians are to ignore civic matters utterly: here Augustine's discussion of the vocation of the judge and why a Christian should undertake such an inherently tragic vocation is instructive. Yes, one does have responsibilities to one's time and place through the forms of its concrete expres-

<hr>

2. St. Augustine, *The Confessions* (New York: Penguin Books, 1961), Book IX, p. 199.

sion in households and polities: in both *domus* and *civitas*. Most importantly, however, the concrete expression of one's identity is revealed within the body of another institution: the *ecclesia*. The body of Christ on earth benefits from conditions of civic peace but is not a creature of the city or empire. It possesses real autonomy. If a member of *ecclesia* is called upon by the city or empire to violate his or her faith, loyalty to faith trumps other loyalties, even to the point of martyrdom. There could, in other words, be a real clash between layers or levels of identity and in such a case, although, for the most part, one is enjoined to be a loyal subject, one's faith takes precedence. One is reminded of the famous last words of St. Thomas More: "I die the king's good subject, but God's first."

Augustinian universalism is far more concretized than is Stoic universalism, in part because of Augustine's complex, dynamic layering of institutions. The household is a component part that contributes to the completeness of the wholeness. Our work in small ways and about small things contributes to the overall harshness or decency of any social order. On earth there must be compromises between human wills if there is to be anything resembling civic peace; indeed, the heavenly city on pilgrimage helps to forge peace by calling out "citizens from all nations and so collects a society of aliens, speaking all languages." She — the *civitas dei* — does not annul or abolish earthly differences but even "maintains them and follows them," so long as God can be worshiped; in this way, she makes "use of earthly peace" and it is in her interest, as we might now say, to help contribute to earthly peace.[3]

Temporal peace is a good, whether it is the peace of the body (health and soundness), or fellowship with one's own kind, or "light, speech, air to breathe, water to drink, and whatever is suitable for the feeding and clothing of the body, for the care of the body and the adornment of the person." Amidst the shadows that hover over, above, among, there are nonetheless two rules we can follow: "first, to do no harm to anyone, and, secondly, to help everyone whenever possible."[4] This is the ethic of the pilgrim-citizen — of the one who is tethered to

---

3. The commentary here embodies the general thrust of Augustine's famous Book XIX of *The City of God* (Baltimore: Penguin Books, 1985), especially chapter 18, p. 878.
4. Augustine, *City of God*, Book XI, chapter 8, p. 437 and chapter 26, p. 459.

this earth and its arrangements through bonds of affection and neces-sity but who recognizes at the same time that these arrangements are not absolute and not final.

We have two briefly sketched alternatives on the table at this point. Arendt insisted on the centrality of particular citizenship of par-ticular polities. She was adamant that no one can be a citizen of the world as he or she is a citizen of a bounded nation-state. By contrast, St. Augustine de-emphasizes citizenship of a particular polity by stress-ing two alternative forms of membership: the first in a concrete and particular body — the *ecclesia* — and the second in a universal body, a universal *oikumene* — that calls out people from all nations and binds them to one another through Christian love and belief. If one were do-ing this spatially, one might say that Augustinian identity is both "be-low" and "above" that of particular states or empires — not, remember, to the utter exclusion of responsibility to and for one's polity given his emphasis on the good of temporal peace and the importance of neigh-bor love, wherever one may find oneself.

Augustine did not talk about rights, of course, but he certainly put in play a universal identity based on God-given dignity. And his definition of to whom that dignity attaches is extraordinarily expan-sive. Augustine tells us that there are many accounts — his chief au-thority is Pliny's *Natural History* — of strange creatures whose existence raises questions about human derivation and human definition. There are:

> the so-called Sciopods ("shadow-feet") because in hot weather they lie on their backs on the ground and take shelter in the shade of their feet. . . . What am I to say of the Cynocephali, whose dog's head and actual barking prove them to be animals rather than men? Now we are not bound to believe in the existence of all the types of men that are described. But no faithful Christian should doubt that anyone who is born anywhere as a man — that is, a ra-tional and mortal being — derives from that one first-created hu-man being. And this is true, however extraordinary such a creature may appear to our senses in bodily shape, in colour, or motion, or utterance, or in any natural endowment, or part, or quality. . . . If these races are included in the definition of the "human," that is, if they are rational and mortal animals, it must be admitted that they

trace their lineage from that same one man, the first father of all mankind.[5]

There is a double trajectory to Augustine's universalism, then: of identity and of definition. So long as a creature can talk some sort of language, that creature is human and belongs within the broad domain of the unique and infinitely precious. These identities are revealed only through concrete, local, and contingent associations. His two cardinal rules — do no harm and help whenever you can — conform to the two tables (so to speak) of the Universal Declaration of Human Rights: the negative (you cannot treat human persons in the following way) and the positive (you must treat human persons in the following way, if at all possible).

Leapfrogging ahead many centuries, let's take stock of the fate of this double trajectory. We see straight away that human identity was reterritorialized in a major way and that human definition was circumscribed. Let's take the latter point first as I shall spend less time on it. With the triumph of Cartesian rationalism, indeed with the entire Enlightenment project, the boundaries of humankind narrowed. No longer was "talk" privileged but, rather, the capacity for certain sorts of abstract, rational operations. This narrowing rationalism had profound effects, most obviously for persons with mental disabilities, but women as a category were also implicated given their alleged lesser rationality. Of course, this is an old story in many ways: Aristotle saw women as rational beings but less fully so than men. Christianity, by contrast, did not privilege rationality, emphasizing instead human capacities for love, loyalty, belief, and perseverance, and defining the human as the capacity for communication. Pushing this definitional boundary, we confront the spectacle in our own time of a tug of war between those who want to dethrone a too narrow understanding of reason as definitional of the human (without dethroning reason altogether) and those who seek to privilege a particular version of rationality or consciousness as defining the human and, in so doing, even offer up the possibility of elimination of those categories of persons who are not capable of self-consciousness, whether because of a mental disability or because they are newborns: there are no barriers to

---

5. Augustine, *City of God*, Book XVI, chapter 8, pp. 662-63.

their elimination.[6] (I am thinking here of the resurgence of eugenics with its correlative notion that imperfect human beings can be destroyed *in situ* on this basis without restraint and, some going further, even after birth if the parents so choose.)

It is the reterritorialization of identity (that Arendt so powerfully represents in her caustic remarks about the uselessness of abstract, generic human rights as such) that is my real concern. The solidification of this effort is certainly the Treaty of Westphalia, but the truly fatal move is the Peace of Augsburg, 1555, with its *cuius regio eius religio* principle, for this deranged the universalism of the Christian dispensation and sought to confine it within the boundaries of particular political configurations. The church, in effect, became subordinate to the state and existed at the sufferance of the prince. This is one of the reasons I speak of "the Protestant nation-state" in my book *Women and War*.[7] Let me remind you of a portion of that argument. Luther prepares the way for the political theology that underlies the emergence of the nation-state. In the future, the triumphant state becomes more difficult to resist, churches having been disarmed in their relation to the state, that is, hedged in by a *cordon sanitaire* that muted their potential political force or, more decisively, constituted churches as arms of the state (in England and Prussia, for example). The implications of Augsburg were profound. All one need do is to observe the way the Prussian State Lutheran Church lined up with the National Socialist regime — with Dietrich Bonhoeffer and a small number (the numbers are actually more substantial than we once realized) — resisting and often paying with their lives — to lament this territorialization of religious identity.

If to Augsburg and Westphalia, one adds the growing love for the *patria* that became the basis of modern nationalism, you have a potent force for internationalism defined as the alliance or the clash of particularisms. There were profound consequences for political good, too, including over time agitation for constitutional and democratic forms of governance. Much of this agitation arose from patriotic love

---

6. For a more complete discussion of these and related themes see Jean Bethke Elshtain, *Who Are We? Critical Reflections, Hopeful Possibilities* (Grand Rapids: Eerdmans, 2000).

7. New York: Basic Books, 1987; second edition published by the University of Chicago Press in 1994.

for one's nation and a commitment to her and to what sort of place she was.

Jean-Jacques Rousseau went overboard on this score, but his insistence that one must gaze upon the fatherland every waking moment and that one's every thought should be of her is an extreme statement of a potent and very real sentiment.[8] Within the strongest versions of the nationalist configuration, no institution within the *patria* can be said to have autonomy, beginning with the family. The family becomes a subset of the nation-state's definitional imperialism, so to speak. The household exists for the good of the polity rather than being, as it was in Augustine's view, good for its own sake as a way human sociality reveals itself in social configurations that involve love, duty, necessity, loyalty, fidelity, and powerful emotion.[9]

Alternative three, then, is the Augsburg-Westphalian model of identity as congealed around the nodal point of national identity and citizenship. I take this to be a stringent form of the privileging of national citizenship of the sort that Arendt emphasizes. Arendt clearly believed that it was possible for potent friendships to transcend the circumscription of national identity, but even here she notes that one is never at home in a language not one's own, at least not fully, so friendship is most powerfully realized with those who speak the same tongue. The Rousseauian model presupposes a nigh exclusivity of relationality confined to the national, if I read him correctly. (Although there are so many Rousseaus one could probably find some counter-evidence to this claim without too much difficulty.) Arendt's life experience also puts another identity fragment on the table — it is not an identity people seek willingly to realize — and that is refugee under duress. This by contrast to the adventurer or, indeed, the pilgrim. The refugee is not an identity that gains institutional expression, either, save for those temporary institutions that spring up to serve those in such an unfortunate position. (To the extent that this

8. The two key Rousseau texts on this score are the famous *Social Contract* (New York: St. Martin's Press, 1978) and the less well-known *Government of Poland* (Indianapolis: Bobbs-Merrill, 1972).

9. Perhaps the clearest statement of this is in Hegel's *Philosophy of Right*. I would simply refer the reader to my discussion in *Public Man, Private Woman: Women in Social and Political Thought* (Princeton: Princeton University Press, 1981; 2nd ed., 1992), pp. 170-83.

status becomes permanent or quasi-permanent, it probably needs to be called something else.)

Let's take stock: in the Arendtian model, little attention is paid to concrete, local arrangements beneath the level of the state save for friendship (which also transcends the local) and education, which helps to project one beyond the local. In the Augsburg-Westphalian model, all institutions within the boundaries of the nation-state are finally indebted to it for their very existence: they persist at its sufferance and a premium is put on the ways all institutions reinforce national loyalty. The most perverse form of this is the twentieth-century totalitarian *Gleichshaltung*, or coordination, of all institutions and functions at the behest of the state. In the Augustinian model, there is a flow between the concrete, beginning with the *domus* or household, and that of a vast arena, the entire *mundus* or world. Each layer of institutionalized identity contributes to the *ordo* or ordering of the whole, or its disordering as the case may be. And disordering does not mean tension, conflict, alienation, unintelligibility: Augustine assumes that these are constant features of the human condition. Rather, disordering means the wrongful subordination of one layer of identity or institution to another that possesses more power in the sense of earthly rule *(potestas)*.

John Milbank, in his provocative work *Theology and Social Theory*, argues that Augustine offers up the possibility for a complex "metanarrative realism." The implications for how we understand concrete levels of being and their political implications are clear. Here is a very difficult passage from Milbank that makes the point, although it does so in a way that will require some unpacking:

> . . . from a postmodern perspective, Augustine's philosophy of history appears more viable than that of either Hegel or Marx. These two provide "gnostic" versions of Augustine's critical Christianity by giving us a story in which antagonism is inevitably brought to an end by a necessary dialectical passage through conflict. Augustine, on the other hand, puts peaceful reconciliation in no dialectical relationship with conflict . . . but rather does something prodigiously more historicist, in that he isolates the codes that support the universal sway of antagonism, and contrasts this with the code of a peaceful mode of existence, which has historically arisen as

"something else," an *altera civitas,* having no logical or causal connection with the city of violence.[10]

For Milbank, what Augustine achieves is nothing less than an immanent critique or "deconstruction of antique political society." Augustine agrees that the earthly city is "marked" or "stained" by sin. But this sin of violence is not given ontological priority, as it is in the work of Thomas Hobbes and much of modern political theory. Rather than ushering into a demand for a totalized particular, if I may deploy such an awkward construction, Augustinian realism ushers into a rueful recognition of limits rather than a will to dominion that requires others for one to conquer or to absorb or to banish. If one makes the project of peace, and its good, a project for all levels of identity and being, then it is possible for the good work of a more capacious, less violent way of being to start small and to grow larger, so to speak.

But, in the Augustinian model, the way this happens is rather mysterious — it isn't pellucid at all — because there is much that goes on that alters the direction of human willing that is not visible to the naked eye. I mention this because Augustine would not want the small, generous things we do, the necessary, neighborly work, to be downgraded in the overall scheme of things. Augustine's *tranquillitas ordinis* is a right ordering of human relationships that, ideally, requires as little coercion as possible. The level of coercion will rise as one moves through the various levels, but even here Augustine analogically links those who would be masters and have others at their "beck and call" whether in households or empires.

Loyalty to one's polity is definitely a good in this scheme of things but it isn't the only good: it is not a superordinate good. If any institution is privileged, it is the *ecclesia* as the site of deepest human loves, beliefs, and commitment as this institution works to achieve intimations of the peaceable kingdom during its earthly sojourn. That sort of kingdom can also be presaged in political life, but this is far less likely given the abiding temptations of that life and how easily it is given over to the *libido dominandi.*

Working analogically, through layers and levels of being, one can

10. John Milbank, *Theology and Social Theory* (London: Basil Blackwell, 1990), p. 389.

see how disorder in one sphere can create tension and conflict in the other — if one is working from the top down, so to speak. Civic chaos wrenches families and friendships and churches, too, apart. It is more difficult to see how it works the other way around, although here we now have mountains of empirical evidence on the overall social or public costs of widespread disorder or breakdown in the family: another story for another time.

Let me refract the issue one final way. Many early twentieth-century reformers in women's peace efforts hoped that the virtues, values, and goods of households — of women's work — could ramify out to change cities (they called it civic or municipal housekeeping) and, eventually, the international realm in which states relate. A chief spokesman for this view was the American social theorist and reformer, Jane Addams. She observed that within the turn-of-the-century immigrant city — hers was Chicago, which was composed of over 80 percent foreign-born immigrants in 1900 — those who would be part of warring and hostile factions and enmities in the Old World found ways to work together and get along under the very different conditions of the New World. She observed their ordinary kindnesses and sharing with one another and took note of the fact that friendships and even marriages took place across what would be hardened lines of identity in Europe.

Analogizing from the pluralistic-relationality of the immigrant city, she argues that well-ordered nation-states can and should function much the same way. And, while we are at it, could not the international sphere benefit from this lesson as well? Is it not possible for different nations to be placed in a role analogous to the different "foreign" configurations of the immigrant city and to learn to harmonize their differences rather than warring over them? By "harmonize" she did not mean moving toward a vast homogeneous world-state project but, rather, a pluralistic relationality of an internationalist sort.

But here this project surely breaks down, and this breakdown is very instructive. The city acted as a boundary within which immigrant peoples related to one another. (Some twenty-two nationalities found themselves within the nineteenth ward of Chicago, the ward in which Jane Addams's pioneering settlement-house, Hull House, was situated.) The fact that the turn-of-the-century immigrant was no casual boundary-crosser but, rather, one who had made a permanent change from which there was no looking back, surely aided and abetted this change. One didn't look to one's compatriots in the homeland any longer but to one's neighbors, for better or for worse, in the new land. To argue that different cultures as they culminate in nation-states are analogous (or can be) to groupings of immigrants in the city presupposes that one can adumbrate an entity that will play a role analogous to the city. But where is the international arena's "Chicago," so to speak?[11] There is no overall ordering principle, no glue to hold the different identity configurations together, even in a loose way. Especially so in our day and age when temporariness comes more and more to define human living. Our abodes are less permanent, from household to nation. This creates incentives to "hang loose" rather than to commit on all levels. It detracts from the citizenship held so dear in the Arendtian and the Augsburg-Westphalian models. But it also detracts from the commitments, loves, and loyalties central to the Augustinian model.

Any viable model has to account for layers of identity and their relationship. It has to make room for the privileging of one aspect of identity should it come into conflict with others. It must acknowledge both our propensity for conflict and violence as well as our ability to seek out and attempt to live out alternatives. It must make provision for our desires for rootedness as well as our yearning to roam. Human beings move through, across, and over landscapes. Any important feature of identity, to be important, must be concrete. Concrete means it must be more than a sentiment or conviction: it must be embodied in some institutional or relational form that has some sturdiness and capacity for perdurance. I see something along the lines of a fusion of the citizen with the pilgrim or peregrinus, and this I believe to be the gravamen of John de Gruchy's work. To be a pilgrim is very different from merely drifting, crossing boundaries, or proclaiming one's cosmopolitanism. There is moral purpose in pilgrim identity. There is the realization of identity in and through pilgrimage that is very different from the fleeing of identity (or being forced to flee) of the refugee or the mere wanderer.

Working all of this out is much beyond the scope of this paper —

11. For a full critical airing of Jane Addams's view and that of social feminism more generally, see Jean Bethke Elshtain, *Jane Addams and the Dream of American Democracy* (New York: Basic Books, 2002).

and perhaps beyond the scope of my abilities — but it would be an interesting challenge to try. Perhaps Vaclav Havel is gesturing in a similar direction in his very interesting discussion of "Home," although, as with much of Havel's thought, to which I have been drawn for many years now, a kind of vagueness pertains when it comes to concrete institutionalization, for at least some of the levels and layers of identity he articulates. But it is a capacious vision and a good place from which to end — one might say to really begin.

My home is the house I live in, the village or town where I was born or where I spend most of my time. My home is my family, the world of my friends, the social and intellectual milieu in which I live, my profession, my company, my work place. My home, obviously, is also the country I live in, the language I speak, and the intellectual and spiritual climate of my country expressed in the language spoken there. The Czech language, the Czech way of perceiving the world, Czech historical experience, the Czech modes of courage and cowardice, Czech humor — all of these are inseparable from that circle of my home. My home is therefore my Czechness, my nationality, and I see no reason at all why I shouldn't embrace it, since it is as essential a part of me as, for instance, my masculinity, another aspect of my home. My home, of course, is not only my Czechness, it is also my Czechoslovakness, which means my citizenship. Ultimately, my home is Europe and my Europeanness — and finally — it is this planet and its present civilization and, understandably, the whole world. . . . I think that every circle, every aspect of the human home, has to be given its due. . . . I am in favor of a political system based on the citizen, and recognising all his fundamental civil and human rights in their universal validity, and equally applied: that is, no member of a single race, a single nation, a single sex, or a single religion may be endowed with basic rights that are any different from anyone else's. In other words, I am in favor of what is called a civil society. . . . To establish a state on any other principle than the civic principle . . . means making one aspect of our home superior to all the others, and thus reduces us as people. . . . The sovereignty of the community, the region, the nation, the state — any higher sovereignty, in fact — makes sense only if it is derived from the one genuine sovereignty, that is, from the human sovereignty, which finds its political expression in civic sovereignty.[12]

Augustine would argue, of course, that if you give up God's sovereignty all these other forms of human sovereignty will be driven to become superordinate and you will be back in the usual fix. (Unless the point of superordination is not, as it was not for Augustine, political in the usual sense of that word.) Let the discussion continue, with appreciation for the openings to robust conversation John de Gruchy has offered us over the years.

12. Vaclav Havel, *Summer Meditations* (New York: Knopf, 1992), pp. 30-31.

On Religion and Theology in a Civil Society

James R. Cochrane

As I write, the world confronts what the President of the United States has baldly called a "war against terrorism." Some describe it as the possible beginning of a third world war of a kind, and yet others regard it as a war of terrorism in itself. The leaders of the notorious Al-Qaeda network implicated in the horrific attacks in New York and Washington on September 11, 2001, have another way of describing it, echoing the thesis of Samuel Huntington — as a clash of civilizations, Islam against Christianity (Judaism as well).

It is far too early to understand just what these times mean. It is to be hoped that the attempts of many people of faith to undercut any definition of this present conflict in terms of a war between faiths will succeed over the long haul. Yet it is difficult to avoid hearing echoes of the Enlightenment, specifically the deep suspicion about the capacity of religious people and communities to provide any secure future for humankind. This suspicion is occasioned by the way in which wars and horrible deeds are enacted and legitimated on all sides in the name of the sacred, though they are as much about perfectly material interests.

At the beginning of the twenty-first century we may once again ask: Does religion have a positive role to play in public life? Or is it intrinsically negative, despite the good contributions ordinary religious people make to their local communities, by virtue of what Jacques Derrida has called the "threat" of community — its inherent drawing of boundaries against the other through what one may describe as "auto-immunity"?[1]

If religion in this sense has a suspect future, it is only one step further to ask if theology has a future. Is its memory of the poor sort that only works backwards, the last refuge of provincial minds? Or is McGaughey right when he says that "The profound paradox of our circumstance is that as individuals and communities, we are a spiritual project in a material world. We are a spiritual odyssey of faith seeking understanding in order that we may act in ways that are enhancing, liberating, and healing"?[2]

Theology remains an ongoing reality inside a particular faith community; it will not disappear as long as faith communities exist. But, as the reflective practice of believers or believing community, it is often blinded by its internal logic to the realities of the world within which it is situated, to the presence of the other who does not belong. Think of how theology entered into black South African reality in the missionary era: As Jean and John Comaroff show in their study on the encounter of the Tshidi tribe of Botswana with the early missionaries, their relationship produced a profound conflict of interpretations over the meaning, status, and direction of Christian claims, all in the context of an avowedly political and material struggle.[3]

The conflicts of our world, even if articulated in the medium of religious language, have as much if not more to do with resource questions, with material deprivation, with economic inequality and political injustice, as anything else. Yet religious convictions and ways of seeing reality have their own independent impact as well, in the case of the World Trade Center towers a very visible, clearly material, and highly symbolic impact all at once. To think again of theology, and religion, in the public place, I would like to focus on the lens offered by the idea of civil society. Admittedly a narrow lens, it still enables us to highlight some important challenges to theology in our time.

1. Jacques Derrida, in Derrida and Gianni Vattimo, eds., *Religion: Cultural Memory in the Present* (Stanford: Stanford University Press, 1998), pp. 42-44, 53.

2. Douglas R. McGaughey, *Christianity for the Third Millennium: Faith in an Age of Fundamentalism and Skepticism* (San Francisco: International Scholars Publications, 1998), p. 10.

3. Jean and John Comaroff, *Of Revelation and Revolution*, 2 vols. (Chicago: University of Chicago Press, 1991, 1997).

JAMES R. COCHRANE

On Religion and Civil Society

At a lecture in 1997 at Oxford, Nelson Mandela noted that Portuguese explorer Vasco da Gama had five hundred years before set out around Africa "in search of Christians and spices."[4] His journey, to South Africa among other places, was not the first imprint of Christianity on Africa — the earliest churches were established in North Africa long before much of western Europe could be regarded, in its later language, as "civilized."[5] Da Gama's voyage did signal, however, the arrival on the African continent of the forces of modernity through the processes of conquest and colonization. The impact upon African peoples of this development is well documented and needs no comment here. Mandela interrogates that history by provocatively asking ". . . whether our generation has the capacity to close the circle on these five centuries."

Mandela sees religion as a necessary part of the transformation required. Noting that strong "inter-religious solidarity in action against apartheid, rather than mere harmony or co-existence, was crucial in bringing that evil system to an end," he suggests that interaction and cooperation between "the three great religions of Africa [Islam, Christianity, African Traditional Religions] . . . could have a profound bearing on the social space we create for the rebirth of our continent," perhaps even assisting in the establishment of a world order "based on mutual respect, partnership and equity."

The possibility of these three religions (or any other) contributing to the social space necessary for renewal in Africa raises the question about the relationship between religion and society, or more narrowly, civil society; hence between Christian churches and civil society.[6]

---

4. Nelson Mandela, "Renewal and Renaissance — Towards a New World Order," lecture given at the Oxford Centre for Islamic Studies, U.K., 11 July 1997.

5. The Coptic Church in Egypt, for example, was in existence by the second century of the Christian era.

6. For an argument on why civil society is an important construct despite its history, see Cochrane, "Religion and Civil Society: Readings from the South African Case," in James R. Cochrane and Bastienne Klein, eds., *Sameness and Difference: Problems and Potentials in South African Civil Society* (Washington, D.C.: Center for Philosophy and Values, 2000), pp. 15-53.

Civilizing Africa: A Colonial Curse
or a Double Emancipation?

A hermeneutic of suspicion is inevitable when an African is confronted by the demand to pay attention to "civil" society. Africa has in the past been viewed by mainstream Northern cultures as "uncivil," more recently as "undeveloped." "Civil" society, with its roots in European cultural constructs and ideologies, was a concept that accompanied the "civilizing" mission of European colonial representatives. This left a negative heritage whose effects are still apparent.[7] Thus a call to civil society evokes deep suspicion in Africa, especially as a rallying cry against "tribalism," "nepotism," "reactionary traditionalism," or other similar epithets favored by critics of Africa.

The suspicion must remain given the genealogy of the concept.[8] But suspicion alone will not resolve the question of how we might define practical relationships of political and economic life in the context of the plural lifeworlds, powers, and practices. Differentiation in African states is an important issue, and much of postcolonial history may be read as one or other kind of attempt to come to terms with this in the kind of large-scale societies that the nation-state represents. This presses us to clarify the idea of civil society.

The colonial "scramble for Africa" coincides with the formal separation, most notably in France and the United States of America, of bourgeois society into three domains of authority: political, economic, and civic — a tripartite conception of society. Yet colonial constructs in Africa distort this construction of social authority and power. As Mahmood Mamdani shows,[9] late colonial practices of direct and indirect rule left a legacy of bifurcated societies, with massive historical consequences. Urban areas, conceived as directly under the control of metropoles or their agents, were regulated through modern notions of civil society and citizenship (differentially accorded to colonizers and indigenous people). Rural areas generally were governed through sec-

7. See the analysis of this heritage, including its impact on comparative religious studies, by David Chidester, *Savage Systems: Colonialism and Comparative Religion in Southern Africa* (Charlottesville: University Press of Virginia, 1996).

8. See Adam Seligman, *The Idea of Civil Society* (New York: Alfred A. Knopf, 1991).

9. Mahmood Mamdani, *Citizen and Subject: Contemporary Africa and the Legacy of Late Colonialism* (Kampala: Fountain Publishers/Cape Town: David Philip, 1996).

JAMES R. COCHRANE

ondary agents, particularly local tribal authorities, who acted on behalf of the colonial power.

These tribal authorities were always constructs in part. In ruling indirectly, colonial authorities drew selectively on traditional foundations of political life, while simultaneously altering their meaning. Tribal authorities became agents of colonial authority under a different structure of law and practice ("customary law"). Here local people were governed as subjects without the rights of the citizens of urban areas. Urban areas became racialized, and in rural areas native authorities were tribalized.[10] This history affects transformation strategies now and shapes a bitter dispute between "modernists" and "Africanists." Modernists, Mamdani argues, seek a political solution to Africa's problems through the development of a vigorous civil society in which individual rights are protected; Africanists place communitarian politics at the center where culture is defended. Mamdani believes that both civil society and communitarian life must be sublimated under a critique of each; thus democratization, still a vital and burning project, will entail "the deracialisation of civil power and the detribalisation of customary power. . . ."[11]

The task of disentangling authoritarian and emancipatory possibilities must be done, I suspect, in light of the warnings from Gadamer against the destruction of tradition and its positive valuing of authority. This leads us directly to consider the matter of religion.

Civil Society and Religion in Africa

The relationship between religion and society in Africa is as complex as anywhere. In South Africa it takes the form of a rich mix of religious traditions (African, Christian, Muslim, Hindu, and Jewish in particular) alongside strong secular or nonreligious traditions (notably liberal humanism and revisionist Marxism). Inevitably these traditions sit within the contradictions of economy and politics common in Africa, particularly in the articulation of different modes of production and social organization.

10. Mamdani, *Citizen and Subject,* pp. 18-19.
11. Mamdani, *Citizen and Subject,* p. 25.

120

This dichotomy between two paradigms enters into the way in which religion is analyzed as well. Thus the dominant dialectic in contemporary discourse on Christianity in Africa lies between those who champion inculturation versus those who promote liberation as the hermeneutic keys to the theological task. Despite attempts to unify these poles — some more successful than others[12] — the dichotomy remains significant. It reveals different visions about what the problem is and how to address it.

In approaches of liberation theologians, the modernist foundations of concepts of autonomy, rights, will, power, and history (usually theorized in terms of some grand narrative) tend to make it difficult to appreciate local, particularized patterns of culture that are not overtly or consciously political. In South Africa, this lacuna is seen most obviously in a widespread inability to find an adequate relationship to the most populous and most popular forms of religion: the Zionist and Zionist-Pentecostal churches. If, however, these are the churches of the poor, the communal centers of participation that give meaning and organizational substance to struggles for survival or for carving out a protected site of existence, then the contradiction becomes almost fatal to liberation theology movements.

In contrast, inculturation approaches, as I read them, emphasize concepts of community, duty, authority, obligation, and spirituality. This tends to accent the local, particularized patterns of culture and tradition in ways that make it difficult to theorize or contest the structural, systemic, and developmental dynamics of a political economy. This makes it difficult to deal with popular, African initiated forms of religion (including the African Initiated Christian Churches), partly because of minimal relationship on the part of AIC's to the concerns of the public sphere (other, perhaps, than those that have do with cultural polity or morality).

These and other contradictions within Christianity — denominationalism and historic alienations, for example — suggest that the prospects of a significant contribution on the part of Christian churches, taken as a whole, to the reconstruction of civil society in Africa are not good. They inhibit the chances of a strong engagement and contribu-

---

12. See, for example, Kwame Bediako, *Christianity in Africa: The Renewal of a Non-Western Religion* (Edinburgh: Edinburgh University Press, 1995).

tion in the public sphere, and thus their role in the development of a civil society.

There are church leaders in many parts of Africa taking a direct interest in the public sphere, particularly in regard to the protection of important elements of civil society. Such advocacy at the level of public leadership has always been vital, even if not always present, as we have seen in South Africa. But it is locally rooted movements that hold a vital space open for the development of a civil society. Such movements are capable of affecting the "steering media of money and power," and of addressing the issues of public life and practices of ordinary people.[13]

One example of such a movement, born of an ecological crisis, is found in southern Zimbabwe, among the followers of Mbuya Juliana.[14] She claims to be a rainmaker, sent to lead her people back to traditional values. These values are, in fact, a mix of African traditional and Christian ideas. The occasion of her prophecy lay in a severe drought, which she blamed in part on modernization processes in the region (e.g., the "cementing of holy places" to make dams). Her mission is the restoration of the land. Juliana's movement challenged the powers of the state, business, church, and indeed traditional authorities, and her success was key in helping restructure social relations on the land and land-use practice.[15] Here is a prime example of a religious movement acting in civil society, drawing on traditional resources, and affecting both political and economic orders.

Constructing Civil Society, Tentatively

This example enables us to pay attention to two claims simultaneously. First, the construction of a strong and healthy civil society must in-

13. The phrase "steering media of money and power" comes from the social theory of Jürgen Habermas.
14. See Hezekial Mafu, "The 1991-92 Zimbabwean Drought and Some Religious Reactions," *Journal of Religion in Africa* 25, no. 3: 288-308; see also Terence Ranger, "Religious Pluralism in Zimbabwe: A Report on the Britain-Zimbabwe Society Research Day, Oxford 1994," *Journal of Religion in Africa* 25, no. 3: 226-51.
15. Ranger, "Religious Pluralism in Zimbabwe," 239. One example of the restructuring of social relations is the imposition by Mbuya Juliana of price constraints on local stores.

clude the institution of processes and mechanisms that allow popular, particular marginalized voices their proper place and dignity. Second, the injection of virtues and values by which a social consensus on the common good becomes possible must draw on the traditions with which people identify and which shape them. Let us consider these claims in relation to the role of Christian churches.

The contemporary idea of civil society points to the ineluctable shift in power under conditions of modernity from small centralized political authorities to large, mostly independent economic agencies with whom nation-states and international political bodies must come to terms.[16] In this shift, the realm of citizen activity increases in complexity, and under democratic conditions, enters directly as a "third" partner into public life alongside economy and polity.

In modern states, religious bodies usually (not always) find themselves out of the centers of power, having neither economic clout nor political muscle.[17] Civil society becomes the prime sphere within which to consider the role and significance of religion. This does not imply a privatization of religion, though that may and does happen under certain conditions, leaving the spheres of political and economic activity outside the realm of church or religious life. A privatized religion, then, is not a result of the development of civil society under modern conditions, but an abdication of a role (by religion or theology) in civil society. It leaves concerns for the material and relational well-being of citizens to other interests and forces than those motivated by the transcendentals of truth, goodness, and beauty, or holiness, justice, and love.[18] In Christian terms, this would be an abdication of the gospel itself.

Interestingly, politicians sensitive to the issues are not unaware of this "spiritual" dimension to political and economic life.[19] They know

16. Jean L. Cohen and Andrew Arato, *Civil Society and Political Theory* (Cambridge, Mass.: MIT Press, 1992).

17. The examples of Poland, of Israel, and of Egypt, to name three disparate locations, suggest that religious bodies continue to have some substantial direct influence on politics, though perhaps less so on economics.

18. For a recent analysis of theological aesthetics along these lines, drawing on the South African context among others, see John W. de Gruchy, *Christianity, Art and Transformation: Theological Aesthetics in the Struggle for Justice* (Cambridge: Cambridge University Press, 2001).

19. See, for example, Thabo Mbeki, "From Liberation to Transformation," Ad-

that social and economic transformation cannot succeed without spiritual foundations, and often a prophetic religious voice. Crime, corruption, graft, a culture of egoism and individual entitlement, violence against women and children, and the like are fundamental threats to the construction of a just and whole society; and they cannot be countered by political or economic policies alone.

If religious institutions and personalities have a critical role to play in civil society, how are they to fulfill it? The question must be posed in the knowledge that religious institutions may well enter into public life by obstructing the development of civil society rather than encouraging it. The very contradictions contained in their own specific heritage, we have noted, often function to inhibit a constructive role in the public sphere.

Let us then conceive of religion in civil society such that religious discourse and practice become integral to public life. Jean Cohen and Andrew Arato help us here, even though they pay no direct attention whatsoever to religion in civil society. They conceive of civil society as a realm of communicative action based on mutually achieved agreements about norms and goals, sufficient — even if minimal — for some action to become possible. Such agreements may be limited, based on a single issue around which a particular coalition or cooperative action becomes possible, or deeper and more durable.

The link between lifeworlds and civil society, and the emphasis on the institutionalization of lifeworld claims in civil society, points to the place religion may occupy — indeed, does occupy in many societies. A religious worldview and tradition often enters directly into the practical negotiation of relationships in civil society, and in economic and political life, and it may engender values and virtues that are essential to civic life. Religious or faith communities thus remain potentially vital in offering resources for the patterns of normative integration and open-ended communication that Cohen and Arato see as necessary foundations of civil society. Equally, they may well damage the emergence of a strong, healthy civil society by insisting on exclusive control over particular norms, by refusing to take into account the other

---

dress to the World Conference on Religion and Peace Consultation, in *Spiritual Power for Nation-Building*, Report on Seminar, Goethe Institute, Johannesburg, 14-16 June 1997, pp. 11-16.

norms, or by aggressively attacking or denying norms. There is clearly a residual ambiguity here that we must also take into account.

The introduction of norms derived from religious traditions into the public sphere must be solidly rooted in particular traditions if they are to have a chance of being materially grounded among citizens who identify with them, in the process of constructing more general civic virtues and values. So we might say then that religious communities best serve a strong and healthy civil society, in its necessary differentiation, if they enter into it with a "strong sense" of their own tradition and its claims as they see it. This is the significance of public theology.

From the point of view of Christian theology — particularly those forms that take seriously the preferential option for the poor — another dimension enters the picture: The needs and contributions of those marginalized by political and economic society or by dominant cultures or structures of knowledge must be foregrounded at least as much as any other. For here we find a store of local, appropriate practical experience and wisdom necessary to a well-rooted civil society. Further, they have important inputs to make into political and economic policy, not in terms of generalized theory or analysis but in terms of the actual constraints and possibilities that confront policy makers on the ground.[20]

A "thick description" of moral life in the public sphere depends not on a kind of rationality abstracted from the particular, but on bonds of affection, on the imitation of significant others who embody or express "how it is to live," on stories that narrate the point of a moral life together — "narratives of possibility" rather than of closure, which help us to see the vitality and importance of everyday life and "the connection of small events to wider streams of life and thought."[21]

---

20. Mbuya Juliana's movement is a test case of this claim. But the claim can be more generally substantiated, and in one form or another it lies behind current "fourth-generation" development theories. See David C. Korten, *Getting to the 21st Century: Voluntary Action and the Global Agenda* (West Hartford, Conn.: Kumarian Press, 1990), and alternative economic theories. For an important theologically linked approach, see Klaus Nürnberger, *Prosperity, Poverty and Pollution: Managing the Approaching Crisis* (Pietermaritzburg: Cluster Publications/London: Zed Books, 1999).

21. Jean Elshtain, "Political Theory and Moral Responsibility," in Joan W. Scott and Debra Keates, eds., *Schools of Thought: Twenty-Five Years of Interpretive Social Science* (Princeton: Princeton University Press, 2001), p. 54.

For Jean Elshtain, such a theory is the necessary foundation of political life. In my view, this allows us to reconceive the importance of the everyday life of ordinary religious communities for the polis, captured in the narratives of ordinary people. This remains true even if we concede that narratives may be hidden, secluded, or silenced by others. Even when such narratives enter into the public transcript,[22] they often do so in coded ways, as may be seen among African initiated churches, the "churches of the people," whose narratives have often been formally absent from the public sphere but present in other ways in civil society.[23]

How then does space become available for excluded, suppressed, hidden, or diminished narratives to enter into the construction of a fully differentiated, healthy civil society? John Coleman notes that religious communities empower civil society by "training ordinary, even poor people in transferable leadership skills . . . : skills of speaking, convoking a meeting, gathering a people together, pursuing public discussions about issues of concern and moment in their society," as well as "by outreach through popular organisations" that enables people to learn how they might "have a voice in the decisions about their life in their neighbourhoods and places of work."[24]

The same phenomenon is visible in the extraordinarily significant presence of clerics or lay church people with a strong Christian activist record in all sectors and levels of the new South African government.[25] Such people, in turn, are important fulcrums of activity within political and economic society around which organizations of civil society may generate knowledge, experience, and influence. They are what Cohen and Arato call "sensors" who organically connect civil soci-

---

22. James Scott, *Domination and the Arts of Resistance: Hidden Transcripts* (New Haven: Yale University Press, 1990).

23. The most visible public movement in the first two decades of the twentieth century was the Ethiopian Movement, influenced by the AME (cf. Joseph T. Campbell, *Songs of Zion: The African Methodist Episcopal Church in the United States and South Africa* [New York: Oxford University Press, 1995]).

24. John A. Coleman, "Civil Society, Citizenship and Religion," draft chapter 3, p. 6, forthcoming.

25. The list includes members of cabinet, senior party leadership who function as national or regional MPs, provincial premiers, top administrators in government institutions, key members of new constitutional bodies such as the Truth and Reconciliation Commission or the Human Rights Commission, and the like.

ety in "ordinary, everyday life" to the institutions of political and economic life and open them to the processes of civil society.[26] They are also often the much needed people who may act as allies or in sympathy with church leaders and assemblies when they address government and business, thus strengthening civil society indirectly in its interaction with matters of polity and economy.

Despite all these possibilities, the insertion of religion into civil society remains unstable. First, many religious institutions are unclear about their role in the public sphere, or abrogate any such role. Second, they are often marginalized within their own public contexts, both ecclesially in the ecumène and socially in the polis. Third, civil society — because it requires normative integration and open-ended communication and because it tends to ground this in nonreligious or nontraditional language — tends systematically to undercut precisely the particular religious and philosophical visions upon which it depends.[27] Fourth, civil society contains its own negativities and deformations; it can degenerate into a mess of private interests and factions, "[evacuating] the larger social world of any sense of truly public or common goods."[28] Fifth, civil society itself is threatened by the imperatives of politics (power) and economy (money), or (as in parts of Africa) by the assertion of traditional patterns of authority and identity against the plurality it defines.

We are faced, therefore, with a situation where civil society remains fragile, in which religious communities may well fail to play the role for which they are, in some respects, well-equipped. Yet that does not diminish the importance either of civil society or the potential of religious communities as part of civil society. In Africa it is a truism to say that people are strongly religious, and the demographic reach of religious communities exceeds that of any other institutional form of life barring perhaps the state. Couple this with a view on civil society that

26. Sensors are elite allies in state and economic systems who are supportive of programs of democratization or cultural revision initiated by social movements or institutions within civil society. Cf. Cohen and Arato, *Civil Society*, pp. 471-72 *inter alia*.

27. This point is strongly made by Seligman, *The Idea of Civil Society*; Seligman's point is developed in relation to faith communities by Lewis S. Mudge, "Traditioned Communities and the Good Society: The Search for a Public Philosophy," Address to the Center for Hermeneutical Studies, U.S.A., April 1993.

28. Coleman, "Civil Society, Citizenship and Religion," p. 21.

emphasizes a multiplicity of voices as essential to the health of the body politic, add to it a religious/theological conviction of the importance of making space for the voices of those who are silenced or marginalized, mix it with the view that civil society is the bedrock upon which a social morality must be constructed under modern conditions, and the task becomes immediately obvious.

The engagement of religious communities in the construction of the values, virtues, and practices of civil society is a moral task as much as it is a public one. As Cohen and Arato put it: "It is on this terrain that we learn how to compromise, take reflective distance from our own perspective so as to entertain others, learn to value difference, recognize or create anew what we have in common and come to see which dimensions of our tradition are worth preserving and which ought to be abandoned or changed."[29] In this sense, the engagement of religious communities in public life, as a project of ethical formation, begins and ends in an act of faith.

Theology Once More

Let us turn again to the question of religion with which we began. Among those who have recently considered this question is Jacques Derrida.[30] He gives me my lead. Religion is a word, *religio*, of Graeco-Latin origin; from a particular culture, history, worldview; not a universal thing; carrying connections, assumptions, a way of seeing and of judging — and of not seeing and of *pre*judging. A word that transports a culture, a history that dominates others — or hides its domination, or refuses to look it in the face. A word that totalitizes, absolutizes, or as Derrida puts it in linguistic irony, "Globalatinizes." Could we not say much the same sort of thing about *theologia*/theology?

We have *this* word "theology," thus *this* complex of ideas, histories, logics, and illogics — in Africa. Penetrated by Greece and Rome in the north, probed and dissected by the heirs of Graeco-Roman culture in later colonial ventures, Africa is also deeply touched by Islam and the Semitic world — hybrid, mixed, heterogeneous; changed and changing

29. Cohen and Arato, *Civil Society*, p. 23.
30. Derrida and Vattimo, *Religion*.

over the *longue durée*. Yet still Africa, not Greece, Rome, Arabia, Europe, or North America.

What does it mean to do this Greek thing, to engage in the *logos* of the *theos* in Africa? Does it mean *one* thing? *Can* it mean one thing? Does it mean *anything*? It clearly does mean something, at least for some people, sometimes, in some places. But perhaps it changes even for them at other times, in other places.

What do we mean when we speak of "African theology"? African *Christian* theology, or not? Or should we think of theologies in the plural; or simply, of ways of reflecting on faith, or is it culture, or both faith and culture, or neither? Are these questions not potent enough to drive us away from thinking, believing, having faith in . . . the idea, the claim, the presumption, that *one* kind of *theologia* is sufficient, or likely, or even possible? Is pluralism our necessary theological condition, a condition of the health of theology?

What about orthodoxy — another Greek word, imposing sameness on us, setting us against difference, thrusting "right teaching" upon us, without which we would be "wrong," in need of detection, correction, and perhaps expulsion? Orthodoxies do not stand up well under the set of questions I have elaborated. They often suppose one theology, one belief, one truth, one path, one way through; hence unable to deal with the idea that there might be "no way through" — an *aporia*, an impassable path, an unknowable knowledge, a bridge that cannot be crossed — at the heart of theology itself.

If orthodoxies, of whatever kind, cannot deal with the *idea* of the *aporia*, or the many *aporiai*,[31] at the heart of theology (one would have to be able to show that), then they cope even less well with the *practices* of those who have other ways of believing and thinking, or no particular way at all. Such people from the point of view of orthodoxy must be stopped, converted, or thrust away. Such people are treated as *fundamentally* misguided. The word "fundamental" is intentional. Fundamentalisms are not merely the territory of conservative evangelical literalists. The geography of all expressions of faith that claim the one

---

31. For a profound discussion of six *aporiai* central to the Christian tradition, all of them compromised as often or not in Western theology at least over the last many centuries, see Douglas R. McGaughey, *Strangers and Pilgrims: On the Role of Aporiai in Theology* (New York and Berlin: De Gruyter, 1997).

thing as the only thing, the only right thing, maps fundamentalisms into the roots of doctrine, dogma, and decree. They work against "what is to come," in order to protect "what is." Why? Because *what is still to come* is unknown, uncontrollable. It escapes all authority except the authority of faith, to which none but the faithful themselves can testify.

If what is to come is decisive and cannot be controlled — and I believe it is so — then theology, in as much as it looks to what is to come, is a risky business. It has no business in determining, possessing, the truth, for it cannot and does not possess the truth. Here Karl Barth was right at least in his *Römerbrief,* that theology is a parable of the truth, if there is a truth.[32] A parable is slippery, a narrative that leaves much open, concealing as much as it reveals. It prevents us from both closing truth down and naming the truth as ours, so that we may possess it — and thus lay claim to the status of God. Then theology is a demon to be exorcised. Not to possess the truth is to be forced to search for it, unceasingly. It is being forced to think, and to act differently, taking responsibility for ourselves and each other. And if Ricoeur is right, then acting is always accompanied by suffering.[33]

Why? Because acting, as human, is the power to actualize ourselves and this always means embodying the other in ourselves, recognizing ourselves as another, in the other. But our power to actualize ourselves is always curtailed in myriad ways, some more devastating than others. This diminishes us, and the other. Being prevented from actualizing ourselves, concretely, in our material and spiritual being in the world, is suffering. Ask a poor person, an unemployed person.

To take responsibility, then, is to take responsibility for acting and for suffering. It is the root of relationality, of life together, and thus of justice. This somewhat lengthy train of thought has a surprising conclusion. *Not to possess* the truth, as I have exegeted it, but to keep the

---

32. McGaughey, in his *Strangers and Pilgrims,* speaks in what I take to be a similar fashion about the crucial role of "possibility" as the driving force of theology, in relation to "actuality." Possibility always breaks open actuality, revealing what is new, at the same time concealing something else. This dialectic of revealing and concealing, at the heart of theology, also prevents any certainties about our claims and forces upon us the need for a critical appraisal of both actuality and possibility, both in theory and in practice.

33. For Ricoeur's central statements about the basis of his philosophical ethics, see *Oneself as Another* (Chicago: University of Chicago Press, 1991).

truth open, is *also* to act justly. It is not that the one thing follows from the other; they are the same thing.

The opposite statement poses the challenge for theology in South Africa today. To possess the truth, to close it down, is to act unjustly. It is a tyranny. It diminishes the actualization of human being, causing or excusing suffering. It works against the truly other and tries to force them to be the same. To confront that statement would indeed be a challenge for theology!

This is not a naïve challenge, a mere intellectual game, a play on words. On the contrary, it may be applied directly to the key practical challenges that face us in the society we are trying to construct. This is a society in which exclusivity is *not* the mark of our life together, where separation from the other is *not* the defining character of our citizenship, where difference is *not* an excuse for domination, and where sameness is *not* achieved at the cost of the subjugation of the other.

I sum up with a brief autobiographical comment. At an early stage, I was faced by the deep negative impact of our social system on people in South Africa. Directly and indirectly, explicitly or implicitly, my subject was apartheid and all its synonyms — a racially defined political economy of oppression and subjugation, with a correlative set of religious and other legitimizing ideologies.

In my consciousness, it began with what was a still naïve and early question on my part: If the summary of the laws, the commandments, and the prophets is contained in the aphorism, love God and your neighbor as yourself (Matt. 22:36-40), what did this mean for those around me who were not white,[34] whom I saw as if in a distant mist, and who clearly did not share my privileges or have my opportunities? How far does love extend, and who is my neighbor? Among the conservative evangelical Christian circles that contained me, the answer was poor: "Don't get involved in politics." Why this unexplained limitation of the scope of love, this artificial restriction of the meaning of "personal" to exclude the interpersonal? Why this deficient, even false, view of spiritual life in relation to the world we inhabit?

It has led me to conclude, above all, that anything that restricts, in the name of a humanly imposed authority, the question of oneself, of one's claims, of one's particularity, of one's actions and patterns of

34. Later this became also "those who are not male" in a patriarchal society.

behavior, of one's interpretation of the world, is bad theology. While such restrictions might serve some interests, especially those of the imposed authority, and while they might well have some value, such as the preservation of the wisdom of an enduring tradition, they must in principle be open. Authority and tradition must in practice be questionable and questioned, even at the most fundamental levels, else it degenerates all too easily into unfaith.

The aim of such questioning would not in the first place be a destruction of faith or a denial of the worth of reflections on faith by others through history. Rather, it would serve the *deconstruction* — not destruction — of claims and counterclaims, in order to *reconstruct* them again in a new time and place, for changed circumstances and demands. In that sense, one might say that the very method of theological reflection is eschatological in character — anticipating a complete vision of a whole and healed future while acknowledging a flawed and fragmented present.

Thus responsible theological reflection seeks to break open new possibilities amidst the limits of present actualities. It partakes of what is to come, refuses to possess the truth, supports the struggle of human beings to actualize themselves, takes its stand against suffering, and incorporates the other in just institutions and ways of living well together. It is not difficult to test our thought and our action against these criteria. And they should help us grasp what the task is of religion, or practical faith, in civil society.

Like Moses, We Always Perish Outside the Promised Land: Reinhold Niebuhr and the Contribution of Theology to Development

Steve de Gruchy

A considerable amount has been written about the involvement of the church and Christians in social development, both globally and in South Africa.[1] As John de Gruchy, among others, has reminded us through almost forty years of theological writing, there are many connections between the Christian faith with its concerns for love and justice, and the struggles to make life better for those who are poor and marginalized. While we take this seriously as the background to all that is said here, this is not the direct focus of this essay. Here, instead, we focus specifically on the contribution to development by *theology* — as a theoretical and reflective undertaking. Through theological insights from Reinhold Niebuhr we argue that this contribution lies in two important areas, namely, (1) the deconstruction of the false creed of redemption through development; and (2) reconstructing development as the practice of democracy.

The "Right to Development"

One hundred and forty-nine leaders, and thirty-eight representatives from 187 member states adopted the United Nations Millennium Dec-

---

1. For some of the more recent essays, see the special issue on Theology and Development, *Journal of Theology for Southern Africa (JTSA)* 110 (July 2001).

laration, a range of statements and recommendations on the challenges facing the world, its nations, and the UN itself at the start of the Millennium Assembly in September 2000.[2] Included is a reference to the "right to development":

> 11. We will spare no effort to free our fellow men, women and children from the abject and dehumanizing conditions of extreme poverty, to which more than a billion of them are currently subjected. We are committed to making the right to development a reality for everyone and to freeing the entire human race from want.

Yet, for all the good intentions of the UN, of many nations of the North, and of many international institutions, the fact of the matter is that "development" has not happened. There is a growing body of literature that suggests just the opposite is in fact the case. Arturo Escobar comments:

> Development was — and continues to be for the most part — a top-down, ethnocentric and technocratic approach, which treats people and cultures as abstract concepts, statistical figures to be moved up and down in the charts of "progress." Development was conceived not as a cultural process (culture was a residual variable, to disappear with the advance of modernisation) but instead as a system of more or less universally applicable technical interventions intended to deliver some "badly needed" goods to a "target" population. It comes as no surprise that development became a force so destructive to Third World cultures, ironically in the name of people's interests.[3]

Some simple figures illustrate the depth of the problem. While the world's income multiplied by 2.5 between 1950 and 1987, the gap between the richest 20 percent and the poorest 20 percent grew from 30:1 to 60:1.[4]

2. See www.un.org/millennium/assembly.htm. See also Steve de Gruchy, "Introducing the United Nations Millennium Declaration," *JTSA* 110 (July 2001).

3. Extract reprinted as Arturo Escobar, "The Making and Unmaking of the Third World Through Development," in Majid Rahnema and Victoria Bawtree, eds., *The Post-Development Reader* (Cape Town: David Philip, 1997), p. 81.

4. Serge Latouche, "Paradoxical Growth," in Rahnema and Bawtree, eds., *The Post-Development Reader*, p. 142.

Likewise, between 1982 and 1990, poor countries paid $418 billion more in loan repayments to rich nations than what they received, and yet in 1990 were "61 per cent more in debt that they were in 1982"![5] Also, within poor countries, the burden of "development" falls upon those with little access to power, and predominantly therefore upon women. Systems of male domination, and the exploitation of women through a lack of access to economic and political power, means that "when development programmes have negative effects, these are felt more acutely by women."[6] During the period of the United Nations Decade for the Advancement of Women (1975-1985), Sen and Grown note that the socio-economic status of the great majority of women in the Third World "worsened considerably."[7] Furthermore, development has had a devastating impact on the environment. Eduardo Galeano comments:

> During the last twenty years, while the human race increased three-fold, erosion has destroyed the equivalent of the whole cultivable area of the United States. The world, which has become a market for merchandise, loses a million hectares of forest a year, of which 6 million become desert. Humiliated nature has been made over to the service of capital accumulation. . . . Acid rain from industrial fumes is killing the woods and lakes of the world, while toxic wastes are poisoning the rivers and seas. In the South, imported agro-business prospers, uprooting trees and human beings. . . .[8]

These stark figures and descriptions suggest that the "right to development," as promoted in the Millennium Declaration, is thus a very suspect notion. For all the decades of development, the net impact has been a worsening of the situation of poor nations and people, and a continuing increase in prosperity and consumption among the rich nations and the rich elite in the Third World. To understand how this has happened, we must turn our attention to the philosophical roots of development as found in the idea of progress.

5. Susan George, "How the Poor Develop the Rich," in Rahnema and Bawtree, eds., *The Post-Development Reader*, pp. 209f.

6. Gita Sen and Caren Grown, *Development, Crises and Alternative Visions: Third World Women's Perspectives* (London: Earthscan Publications, 1988), p. 26.

7. Sen and Grown, *Development, Crises and Alternative Visions*, p. 16.

8. Eduardo Galeano, "To Be Like Them," in Rahnema and Bawtree, eds., *The Post-Development Reader*, pp. 14f.

The Failure of Development

Gilbert Rist in his book, *The History of Development*, argues that the introduction of the developed-underdeveloped dialectic into international relations after the Second World War struck a powerful chord in Western society because it drew upon deep philosophical and cultural roots that were laid in the Enlightenment around issues such as growth, progress, and optimism.[9] Rather than looking backwards for truth and wisdom, people assumed a forward-looking orientation, as science and technology began to create all kinds of unheard of opportunities. The discovery of human agency in the making of "history," alongside this future orientation, contributed to a growing sense that life can and does get better. This worldview provided the ideological partner to the accumulation of capital, the reinvestment of profit, industrialization, and the search for new raw materials and markets. Colonialism was given ethical status in terms of a growing social evolutionism. Rist quotes Albert Sarraut:

> It should not be forgotten that we are centuries ahead of them, long centuries during which — slowly and painfully, through a lengthy effort of research, invention, meditation and intellectual progress aided by the very influence of our temperate climate — a magnificent heritage of science, experience and moral superiority has taken shape, which makes us eminently entitled to protect and lead the races lagging behind us.[10]

The First World War put an end to naked colonialism, but the League of Nations that followed it replaced it with the notion of mandates. More powerful nations were given authority "to look after" less powerful nations. Then after the Second World War the binary relationship of "colonizer" and "colonized" was completely replaced with that of "developed" and "underdeveloped." Developed nations were called upon to assist underdeveloped nations to develop to become "like them." This was now the meaning of progress, and whole institu-

9. See Gilbert Rist, *The History of Development: From Western Origins to Global Faith* (London: Zed Books, 1997).
10. Rist, *The History of Development*, p. 58.

tions were created in the United Nations to achieve this, while development aid was offered as a solution to underdevelopment.

For anyone to make sense of development and its failures, it is crucial to understand these philosophical roots. Teodor Shanin has captured this with his reflections on the relationship between development and the idea of progress:

> The idea of progress, with its many derivations, has also become an important ideology — a blinker on collective cognition. Up to a point, it became the "normal science" as defined by Kuhn where, once established, a field of knowledge designs its own questions, brushing aside as illegitimate other questions, and evidence, which do not fit its assumptions. That was not all, for service to progress became an important justification employed by both development experts and hardened politicians, enabling them to override whatever did not fit their visions — views and people alike — and to award themselves massive privileges of power, status and well-being, while most people were turned into objects of manipulation (for their own good, of course).[11]

In his book, Rist does give attention to alternative voices in the history of development, but he demonstrates that while most of them promoted themselves as different, the key equation of development with growth and progress was never questioned. This is true of the Bandung Conference of Asian and African leaders in 1947;[12] the work of those who advanced the "dependency theory";[13] and the Brundtland Commission.[14] He sees the same tendency involved in new ideas of development such as the "basic needs" approach, structural adjustment, sustainable development, and even globalization. Rist would find agreement with David Korten's comment:

> We have become prisoners of an obsolete vision of our global reality and the nature of human progress. This vision equates human

---

11. Teodor Shanin, "The Idea of Progress," in Rahnema and Bawtree, eds., *The Post-Development Reader,* p. 69.

12. Rist, *The History of Development,* p. 81.

13. Rist, *The History of Development,* pp. 118ff.

14. Rist, *The History of Development,* p. 183. The quotations are from the report, pp. 6 and xii respectively.

progress with growth in the market value of economic output and subordinates both human and environmental considerations to that goal. The result has been the extravagant consumption of the world's resources by a favoured few with little recognition of the social and environment costs borne by the many. These costs have now accumulated to the point of endangering the continued well-being of everyone on planet earth.[15]

Development as Religious Myth

The question now arises, If development is failing, why not abandon it? For Rist the answer to this question is that development is a myth — something that everyone believes in, and provides legitimation for all kinds of practices, but does not actually exist.[16] The fundamental argument of his book is that "development" is "an element in the religion of modernity,"[17] allied to ideas of progress, growth, and linear notions of history:

> At the origin of the broad "development" movement, we find a belief whose roots lie deep inside the Western imagination; political leaders, economic agents, public and private international organisations as well as sections of the population in both North and South, were willy-nilly converted to it. According to this belief, the "good life" can be assured for all through technological progress and ever-rising production of goods and services — from which everyone will eventually benefit. . . . The belief does not, however, correspond to any historical reality: the world never has been and never will be true to this high-minded dream, although it does shape some of the relevant practices. If modern societies all proclaim the necessity of "development," this is because they have made it into a holy truth symbolising their practices as a whole and conferring on them an obligatory force. If people are made to believe, it is so that they can be made to do something.[18]

15. David Korten, *Getting to the 21st Century: Voluntary Action and the Global Agenda* (West Hartford, Conn.: Kumarian Press, 1990), p. 3.

16. Rist, *The History of Development*, p. 24.

17. Rist, *The History of Development*, p. 21.

18. Rist, *The History of Development*, p. 214.

We are now at a point when we can begin to engage theologically with development theory, making use of key themes in the thought of Reinhold Niebuhr. Niebuhr is an extremely helpful theologian to work with in this context because he advanced a similar critique of the Western or "modern" worldview — what he calls secular liberalism — and its belief in progress. This theme is at the heart of his two-volume magnum opus, *The Nature and Destiny of Man*.

> The idea of progress is the underlying presupposition of what may be broadly defined as "liberal" culture. If that assumption is challenged the whole broad structure of meaning in the liberal world is imperiled.[19]

Niebuhr argues that through the advances of reason and science in Europe, people came to have a very optimistic view of what they could achieve in history. In fact, the very discovery of *history* itself — human agency and the ability to change things for the better — all characterize this emerging worldview. In *Faith and History*, Niebuhr argues that what unites and characterizes the different strands of thought that emerge from the Renaissance, and that separates them from earlier, Classical thought, is a fundamentally different conception of time, and therefore of history. Time "became the principle of interpretation by which the mystery of life was comprehended."[20] The passing of time, allied to a belief in pedagogical technique and technical mastery over nature and society, came to be seen as intrinsically good so that history itself held the key to human redemption. In one of his sermons, Niebuhr puts it like this:

> Modern culture . . . believes that the historical process is such that it guarantees the ultimate fulfillment of all legitimate human desires. It believes that history, as such, is redemptive. Men may be frustrated to-day, may live in poverty and in conflict, and may feel that they "bring their years to an end like a tale that is told." But the modern man is certain that there will be a tomorrow in which pov-

19. *The Nature and Destiny of Man*, vol. 2 (New York: Charles Scribner's Sons, 1943), p. 240.

20. *Faith and History: A Comparison of Christian and Modern Views of History* (New York: Charles Scribner's Sons, 1949), p. 2.

erty and war and all injustice will be abolished. Utopia is the simple answer which modern culture offers in various guises to the problem of man's ultimate frustration. History is, according to the most characteristic thought of modern life, a process which gradually closes the hiatus between what man is and what he would be.[21]

Because he understands these commitments to progress and the redemptive character of history to be *a priori* to any scientific or historical truth, Niebuhr — like Rist — considers modern secular liberalism to be as much a faith as any other religion. It is a faith in human reason, a faith in the human ability to redeem the world, a faith in the redemptive character of history itself, and in the end a faith in history:

> Believing itself to be irreligious but wise, it would regard the judgment with shocked incredulity. Yet the truth is that its confusions arise not from its irreligious knowledge but from its heedless and unwise religion.[22]

Taking Sin Seriously

The degree of similarity between Rist and Niebuhr on this matter is quite remarkable, given the differences of approach. They both note the intrinsically religious character of the worldview that underpins the Western, modern, or liberal belief in progress — and has such a powerful impact on the notion of development. The difference lies in the proposed solution to the problem. Rist offers a *sociological* critique, in which he desires to "shatter the religious structure which protects 'development.'"[23] This "belief-dissolving" work is the task of historians and anthropologists (i.e., people like himself) who must extricate "thought from the circle of belief."[24] Here is his conundrum. He is an active participant in the very worldview that he is trying to critique, for

21. "Mystery and Meaning," in *Discerning the Signs of the Times: Sermons for Today and Tomorrow* (New York: Charles Scribner's Sons, 1946), pp. 144f.

22. *Beyond Tragedy: Essays on the Christian Interpretation of History* (New York: Charles Scribner's Sons, 1937), p. 229.

23. Rist, *The History of Development,* p. 245.

24. Rist, *The History of Development,* pp. 247f.

in the act of critiquing the modern idea of progress he has drawn on its deepest desire — the idea that through reason the vestiges of religion will be overcome. Anthropologists and historians will replace priests and prophets, and (so the argument goes) we will all be better for it. Progress!

Niebuhr, on the other hand, offers a *soteriological* critique in which he takes religion for granted, but asks whether the promises of salvation being offered by that religion are adequate in the light of human experience.[25] He too would be concerned to shatter the religious structure that protects "development," not in order to dissolve belief, but to promote true belief. For Niebuhr the problem is not religion but *sin*. Religion — any worldview for that matter — is false insofar as it either does not take sin seriously or it promotes a false salvation from sin. The question that Niebuhr poses as much for Rist as for believers in development is whether they have adequately accounted for sin.

For the strongest criticism of the liberal creed of redemption through progress lies in the "facts of history." This is a constant and familiar theme in Niebuhr's writing, as he is convinced that all the facts cry out that history itself is not redemptive: "Since 1914 one tragic experience has followed another, as if history had been designed to refute the vain delusions of modern man."[26] Every new step in the direction of progress brings with it new possibilities for both good and evil. "We have learned that history is not its own redeemer. The 'long run' of it is no more redemptive in the ultimate sense than the 'short run.'"[27] There is no linear progress towards "goodness." "No simple victory of good over evil in history is possible."[28] Thus Niebuhr writes of Western secular culture:

> Its profoundest belief is that the historical process is itself redemptive and guarantees both the meaning of life and its fulfillment. There is indeed progress in history in the sense that it presents us with continually larger responsibilities and tasks. But modern his-

---

25. See my essay, "Not Liberation but Justice: The Task of South African Theology in Shaping Public Discourse," *Missionalia* 21, no. 1 (April 1993): 57-73.

26. *Faith and History*, pp. 6f.

27. *The Nature and Destiny of Man*, vol. 2, p. 206.

28. *Beyond Tragedy*, p. 145.

tory is an almost perfect refutation of modern faith in a redemptive history. History is creative but not redemptive.[29]

The reference to the "creativity of history" is a pointer to the way that Niebuhr understands human nature, freedom, sin, creativity, and destruction. He wrote a tremendous amount on these themes, and here we can but summarize them. For Niebuhr, human life is the complex interaction between, on the one hand, the limitations of our physical realities — the specificities of who we are, the things that we cannot transcend like our bodies, our nationalities, our cultures, our language, our identity — and, on the other hand, the transcendence of our spirits or minds — the creative ability to imagine ourselves to be something else, to picture a different reality. Living at this intersection, the self is anxious. This anxiety is the basis of creativity, for the advances in human history occur through human anxiety in the present and the determination to transcend it in the future. But the anxiety caused by this tension is also the grounds of temptation, and therefore of sin.

Sin is the collapse of that anxious tension in the inevitable, though not necessary, claim of universal and transcendent meaning for a contingent, limited, and historically relative action: "Human life points beyond itself. But it must not make itself into that beyond. That were to commit the basic sin of man."[30] Because of the freedom that is the basis of history, and due to the presence of sin, human beings are free to be both creative and destructive. In other words, the same freedom that is creative can also, through sin, be destructive. To eliminate the freedoms that are destructive can only mean the elimination of all freedoms, and thus the historical self is the sinful self, as human beings cannot transcend sin in history without putting an end to history. Writing to a pacifist about the Second World War, Niebuhr says: "Your difficulty is that you want to try and live in history without sinning. There is no such possibility in history."[31]

This, then, is Niebuhr's fundamental criticism of the idea of

29. *The Children of Light and the Children of Darkness* (New York: Charles Scribner & Sons, 1944), pp. 131f.

30. *The Nature and Destiny of Man*, vol. 1 (New York: Charles Scribner's Sons, 1941), p. 158.

31. "An Open Letter to Richard Roberts," in D. B. Robertson, ed., *Love and Justice* (Philadelphia: Westminster Press, 1957), p. 270.

progress. He argued again and again that the modern Western world-view has too optimistic an account of life and history, and too great a confidence in its own ability to change things for the good. It sees sin in terms of limitations that could be overcome by education, piety, hard work, or political struggle. Thus it sees the historical process as one that will enable human beings to ultimately transcend the ambiguities of history itself.[32] It has failed to perceive that because of the existence of sin in human nature, the present holds as much potential for good and evil as the future, and that humans cannot escape from history and its constant tension between necessity and freedom.

> Man, as the creature of both necessity and freedom, must, like Moses, always perish outside the promised land. He can see what he cannot reach.[33]

The Two Contributions of Theology to Development

Drawing on Niebuhr's understanding of sin and history, we would argue that theology — as a critical reflective discipline — has two crucial contributions to development. The first is to deconstruct the false creed of redemption through development, and the second is to reconstruct development as the practice of democracy. We turn to the first task.

A. To Deconstruct the False Creed of Redemption Through Development

Niebuhr does not see the liberal belief in progress to be just a false interpretation of reality, but a false scheme of redemption. In other words it is itself symptomatic of the problem of sinfulness in history. Niebuhr is cutting in his rejection of the false "schemes of world redemption,"[34] which fail to understand the facts of history, and whose

32. *Faith and History*, pp. 70f.

33. This is the quotation from which the title of this essay is taken. From *An Interpretation of Christian Ethics* (New York: Harper Brothers, 1935; New Edition, New York: Seabury Press, 1979), p. 90.

34. See "The Christian Witness in the Social and National Order," in *Christian Realism and Political Problems* (New York: Charles Scribner's Sons, 1953), pp. 106f.

very desire to offer hopes of redemption in willful denial of these facts is illustrative of the whole problem of sin and redemption:

> There is a profound pathos in these failures. They prove that . . . the ultimate form of sin is a corruption of man's quest for redemption.[35]

There is no doubt that Niebuhr would say the same of Rist and his solution. To seek the answer to history in anthropology and sociology, in the rejection of all faith and the exalting of human reason is itself a redemptive solution, and a false one at that. The liberal, modern, secular, Western vision of utopia is, "the Kingdom of God minus the resurrection, that is, minus the divine transformation of human existence."[36]

This alerts us to Niebuhr's solution to the ambiguity of history. The resolution to the struggle created between freedom and necessity, creativity and destruction is found only in God and God's mercy. Sin cannot be overcome in history save by the forgiveness of sins. For Niebuhr this makes the doctrine of the Atonement the key to interpreting history, "a revelation of what life actually is."[37] It is

> the beginning of wisdom in the sense that it contains symbolically all that the Christian faith maintains about what man ought to do and what he cannot do, about his obligations and final incapacity to fulfill them, about the importance of decisions and achievements in history and about their final insignificance.[38]

The wisdom that is gained through the Atonement is the recognition of our limits in history, and the resolution of these limits only in God's mercy. This resolution does not happen in history, but only at the end of history. While we can experience this mercy now, the full experience of God's grace remains unfulfilled in the interim between the death of Christ and the Second Coming. The full meaning of the Atonement is therefore only understood from the perspective of the

35. *Faith and History*, p. 205.
36. *Beyond Tragedy*, p. 299.
37. *Beyond Tragedy*, pp. 19f.
38. *The Nature and Destiny of Man*, vol. 2, p. 212.

kingdom of God to be established at the end of history. Niebuhr sees this confirmed in the Christian understanding of the Parousia. The idea of a last judgment even at the end of history is a reminder that all historical actions, even those of the redeemed, stand under the judgment of God.[39]

Furthermore the New Testament speaks of the appearance of the Antichrist at the end of history. At the time of the coming of the kingdom there will be "wars and rumors of wars," and the ultimate struggle between good and evil, between God and Satan, will therefore take place at the end of history.[40] In other words, even in the light of the Cross of Christ history is not moving progressively towards higher and higher possibilities of love, truth, and justice, but rather continues to exhibit the same potential of creativity and destruction. The Christian faith "believes that the Kingdom of God will finally resolve the contradictions of history; but for it the Kingdom of God is no simple historical possibility."[41] History and all human endeavor must be understood from within the "interim" between this fulfillment and promise, and it remains under the judgment of God. The full experience of redemption awaits the second coming of Christ, the end to history, and the establishment of the kingdom. With this as part of the gospel, Christian theology has no option but to deconstruct the false creed of redemption through development.

B. To Reconstruct Development as the Practice of Democracy

Niebuhr is absolutely convinced that an awareness of God's mercy should not lead to complacency in the life of the believer. Rather, it ushers in an attitude of thankfulness and humility that should characterize our dealings with history. The desire to claim too much for ourselves is gone, and with it a new realism about what we can and cannot

---

39. *The Nature and Destiny of Man,* vol. 2, p. 293.

40. *The Nature and Destiny of Man,* vol. 2, p. 138: "The Antichrist stands at the end of history to indicate that history culminates, rather than solves, the essential problems of human existence."

41. *Christianity and Power Politics* (New York: Charles Scribner's Sons, 1940), pp. 20f.

achieve. This is the "nonchalance of faith"[42] that enables us to be free agents of history, delivered from the false creed of redemption through development, unencumbered by hopes of redemption in history, and thereby more able to contribute towards justice. In *Discerning the Signs of the Times* Niebuhr puts it like this:

> We cannot live by historic achievement alone, though we cannot live meaningfully without historic achievement.[43]

We are now at a point where we can consider the second contribution of theology to development, namely, to reconstruct development as the practice of democracy. If history is not redemptive, and if the claims for progress, development, and social redemption are thus rejected, then what is a legitimate historical task? For Niebuhr it is the practice of justice and the promotion of democracy. To understand this, we must understand Niebuhr's reflections on power.

Niebuhr sees power as a necessary force in society, crucial to the defense of good against evil. Power, however, like freedom is neutral. It can be used both creatively and destructively, for both good and evil. Because of the presence of sin in the world, the just exercise of power is needed to ensure that evil does not triumph over good. Yet, because of sin, the same power that is used for good can be used for evil. Just as an individual needs freedom in order to be creative, and yet discovers that that same freedom is the source of destruction; so society needs power to sustain itself against evil, and yet that very power can itself be turned to evil. Society is never able to transcend this ambiguity of power:

> History is, for this reason, not a realm of indeterminate growth and development. It is a realm of conflict. In this conflict new forces and forms of life challenge the established powers and orders. They are a reminder to the established forms and powers of the contingent character of all historic configurations and a judgment upon the pretension which denies this contingency.[44]

---

42. See Gordon Harland's discussion on Niebuhr's use of the term "nonchalance of faith" in *The Thought of Reinhold Niebuhr* (New York: Oxford University Press, 1960), pp. 147ff.

43. "The Age between the Ages," in *Discerning the Signs of the Times*, p. 52.

44. *Faith and History*, p. 224.

Holding society together in the midst of this conflict is a difficult challenge. This awareness led Niebuhr to one of his great intellectual tasks, namely, to rescue the notion of democracy from its liberal roots and establish it upon a more realistic basis. This found clearest expression in *The Children of Light and the Children of Darkness,* published in 1944 just as World War II was coming to an end. The book grew out of his conviction that "democracy has a more compelling justification and requires a more realistic vindication than is given it by the liberal culture with which it has been associated in modern history."[45]

Niebuhr was concerned to rebuild the democratic tradition in light of the experience of Nazism and Fascism, the rise of Stalinist Russia, and the obvious weaknesses of liberal democracy. He felt that democracy needed to take sin into account, thus both the possibilities of human creativity and human destruction, and the use of power for both good and evil. This ability to balance power and to ensure that it was open and transparent is what makes democracy viable: "Man's capacity for justice makes democracy possible; but man's inclination to injustice makes democracy necessary."[46]

Democracy, then, is the way in which power can best be used for justice. It provides the balance necessary to hold the creative and destructive uses of power in check and to ensure human agency and control of these in an open, accountable, and transparent manner. Rather than some unattainable utopian vision of a kingdom of God on earth, democracy is the best that society can achieve in history. It is the space in which human beings can exercise their freedom for creativity, and be restricted from using their freedom for destructive means. It is the way in which power can be used for justice and restricted from its use for injustice. The struggle for democracy, then, rather than a faith in growth or progress, should guide our social vision and engagement. Interestingly, this has some creative connections with current development discussions around sustainable livelihoods and sustainable community as a legitimate social vision.[47]

45. *The Children of Light and the Children of Darkness,* p. xii.
46. *The Children of Light and the Children of Darkness,* p. xiii.
47. See *Sustainable Rural Livelihoods: Practical Concepts for the 21st Century,* Robert Chambers and Gordon L. Conway, Institute for Development Studies Discussion Paper 296, 1992.

We have relied on Niebuhr in this essay because we believe that he is right in his theological critique of the liberal notion of progress, which provides the foundations for development practice that has gone wrong. His ability to think through issues of faith, power, history, and social engagement from a theological perspective makes him a creative dialogue partner. But it is important to note as we draw this essay to a close that while Niebuhr helps us see the importance of building democracy, his own understanding of democracy and justice had some important limitations that contemporary development practice would have to transcend. Two of the most obvious are his lack of awareness of gender bias in struggles of democracy and justice, and of the way in which the environment is also a victim of progress. Clearly there is still much work to be done in taking Niebuhr's vision forward.

That would not surprise Niebuhr himself. All our deeds in history — our theology and our praxis — are tainted with sin, and are limited and relative. We struggle through the desert towards the Jordan, but progress is not guaranteed, and it finally eludes us. As creatures of both necessity and freedom, we like Moses perish outside the promised land. We can see what we cannot reach.[48]

---

48. Paraphrase of the quotation from which the title of this essay is taken. From *An Interpretation of Christian Ethics*, p. 90.

THEOLOGICAL PERSPECTIVES ON SOCIO-CULTURAL AND POLITICAL REALITY

Does Africa Need Theology
in the Twenty-First Century?

Chirevo V. Kwenda

In 1995, when I was fairly new in the Department of Religious Studies at the University of Cape Town with John de Gruchy as one of my esteemed colleagues, the department experienced an internal crisis. There was a proposal to rename the Department the "Department of Theology and Religious Studies." Various positions were taken and arguments adduced to support them. This situation serves to introduce and highlight a theoretical problem in which theology as a discipline has long been trapped and in which it may continue to be locked in the twenty-first century, despite noble intentions on the part of theologians to free it.

Tinyiko Maluleke discusses some aspects of this problem, charging that Christian theology is in crisis in South Africa.[1] For one thing, it does not engage meaningfully, if at all, with the African Traditional Religions (ATRs), with the result that the study of religion in Africa is drastically compromised. For him the culprit is not theology per se; it is rather "Western Christian Theology." And to the extent that African theology is implicated in the style and habits of Western theology, it too will be tarnished. Maluleke sees no point in seeking a remedy in re-

---

1. Tinyiko Maluleke, "Theology in (South) Africa: How the Future Has Changed," in Speckman, T. McGlory, and Larry Kaufmann, eds., *Towards an Agenda for Contextual Theology: Essays in Honour of Albert Nolan* (Pietermaritzburg: Cluster Publications, 2001), pp. 384-85.

ligious studies, for it too, as a Western discipline, is implicated in disre-
gard for the ATRs. This whole area, he points out, is waiting to be studied properly and seriously. To indicate a way forward Maluleke suggests
the litmus test of "African presence" in the departments of religious
studies. By this he means that proper study of religion in Africa must
be predicated on a serious commitment to promoting "African interests"; the mere presence of "people of African descent" will not be
enough. Thus, whether one is doing theology or religious studies, the
chosen discipline must be practiced in service of African interests, however these might be defined.

I would like to carry this debate forward in three ways. In agreement with Maluleke I shall first critique the role of religious studies in
the study of African religions. Second, I shall take Maluleke's critique
of Western Christian theology to the next logical stage, namely, a critique of theology as a genre for the study of religion generally, and African religions in particular. Third, I shall briefly suggest a possible way
forward by proposing the adoption of discourse X as an approach to
studying religion in Africa. By calling the new suggested method "X"
we are declaring that we do not yet know what it is or what shape it will
take when it has set. As yet it is in the process of being formed, along
the lines of Mudimbe's notion of an African gnosis or knowledge in
movement.[2]

We shall return to this later. For now we take a critical look at a
crucially important component of religious studies, viz., the science of
religion. Let me make it clear from the start that by science of religion
we shall understand what has come to be known as the history of religions in North America, but is practiced all over the world wherever religion is studied through rigorous analysis utilizing a suite of disciplin-
ary tools and culminating in an attempt at understanding the meaning
of specific religious phenomena through interpretation of texts, rituals, symbols, and the like. The title of this chapter asks about the need
for theology in twenty-first-century Africa. No similar question is addressed to the need for religious studies, despite Maluleke's argument
that religious studies is no alternative to theology as it too is impli-

2. Valentin Y. Mudimbe, "African Gnosis. Philosophy and the Order of Knowledge: An Introduction," *African Studies Review* 28, nos. 2 and 3 (June/September 1985):
149-233.

cated in the bad habits of the West. The reason this question is not addressed to religious studies is clear, presented in two parts. On the one hand, to the extent that religious studies is a child of theology we could apply the rule that what's good for the goose is good for the gander, meaning that what is said for theology applies to religious studies. But this would not be quite accurate, as some significant differences exist. For instance, the possibility, or perhaps simply an aspiration, that religious studies may be free of (overt) theological norms places it close to the new proposed discourse X. Thus the case of religious studies is answered by its affinity with theology on the one hand, and its kinship with discourse X on the other.

Religious Studies: The Case of the History of Religions

The simple thesis of this part of the paper is that the history of religions, in common with other human sciences, is of, by, for, and about the West.

Some people have written epic histories about The Rise of the West.[3] Others have predicted, rued, or celebrated its decline and decay.[4] Still others have, with what approximates prophetic fervor, pronounced its triumph and renewal in the form of modernity.[5] Wishing for the demise of the West, as many non-Westerners obviously do, may well be tantamount to a contemplation of suicide, given Ashis Nandy's caution that the West is in all of us[6] and Appiah's pessimism about the possibility of disentangling a "unitary Africa" from a "monolithic West."[7] The clock of history cannot be turned back. The most we can do is negotiate the best deal from within the belly of the dragon that is the West, that is

3. Francis S. Philbrick, *The Rise of the West, 1754-1830* (New York: Harper & Row, 1966), and William H. McNeill, *The Rise of the West: A History of the Human Community* with a retrospective essay by William McNeill; drawings by Bela Petheo (Chicago: University of Chicago Press, 1991).

4. Oswald Spengler, *The Decline of the West* (London: Allen & Unwin, 1954).

5. Anthony Giddens, *The Consequences of Modernity* (Polity Press, 1990).

6. Ashis Nandy, *The Intimate Enemy: Loss and Recovery of Self Under Colonialism* (Delhi: Oxford University Press, 1983).

7. Kwame Anthony Appiah, *In My Father's House: Africa in the Philosophy of Culture* (New York: Oxford University Press, 1992), p. 155.

partly us. Yet while this may be descriptively accurate, it is not helpful politically, flying as it does in the face of the self-arrogated normativity of a self-conscious West. It is in recognition of this latter fact that we will speak below as if this epistemological divide, this signifying game, were also a descriptor of a concrete reality.

The History of Religions Is of the West

The history of religions was born under a bad star, shrouded in an ominous cloud. It was begotten in the swell of the European Enlightenment, in that euphoric moment when Europe's cultural pendulum swung to the rationalist extreme, the continent having drunk to the dregs its cup of witch-huntings and burnings at the stake. Now, there is nothing wrong with being born in such a watershed moment. In fact, such a birth may actually be cause for jubilation. The trouble lies in some of the details. The birth of the history of religions reminds me of Zimbabwean singer-composer Paul Matavire, who likens an independent-minded young woman to a child born when the attending midwives had retired to drink beer. Sexism apart, the idea of a child coming into this world unattended is a powerful analogy for the birth of the history of religions. What could one do with the truant midwives? In this litigious world we could sue for culpable negligence, especially if the absence of midwives adversely affected the baby. Or, perversely, we might blame the infant for bad timing (sorry, child, you chose a bad time to be born!).

However, in the case of our subject we are faced with criminal negligence; the midwives (the parents, actually) — science and theology — were present but busy fighting. We cannot chide the child for bad timing, even if this were permissible. The right time was right for it to be born, a kind of kairos for a world come of age. However, the child entered the world without the proper fortifying and humanizing rituals. Perhaps it is as a result of this that it never quite achieves majority status, its induction into the hall of science being stiffly opposed by the deposed queen of sciences — theology.

This was no "I want a place in the sun, too" kind of brawl; it was a total war of supremacy to decide who possessed the truth, the whole truth, and nothing but the truth. Of course, the question about why anybody would want to shoulder such a heavy responsibility presents insatiability as a fundamental characteristic of the West and Western culture. Now, this is only partially a problem of modernity; it is the spirit of Westernism. What we call Westernism is born at the point at which modernity graduates from manipulation of nature to domination of other peoples and cultures. And this transmutation is not secular; it is religious, a fact that is effectively concealed by the West's close alliance with Christianity, and the latter's quasi-esoteric definition of religion. Perhaps it is not surprising that theology, which for a long time viewed other cultures only as fields ripe for the harvest, should lead the opposition of any possibility of a different way of looking at the religious world. We must not forget that it had balked at the pretensions of modern science to custodianship of a new, autonomous method of acquiring and certifying truth.

Apparently Wach's truce allocating the field of Christianity to theology and the territory of foreign religions to Religionswissenschaft[8] was not accepted by theology, which insisted on recruiting the history of religions as an ancillary (a nanny) of theology. To this day, theology has not quite managed to kick this backward habit of looking at other cultures merely as darkness in which the light of the gospel comes to shine. This could be summed up as the Christian West's habit of wanting to dominate everything, from the world's gold to the world's gods. What is hard for a non-Westerner to figure out is why theology and the history of religions (and the other human and social sciences, for that matter) think the misfortune to referee this tragedy is something to fight for.

The History of Religions Is by the West

We have seen above that where modernity sought to dominate nature, the West desires to dominate other peoples and cultures, not only as a strategic and pragmatic maneuver, but as the inevitable outworking of its very nature and essence. We are here faced with a problem in the stra-

---

8. Joachim Wach, "Introduction: The Meaning and Task of the History of Religions (Religionswissenschaft)," in Joseph M. Kitagawa, ed., *The History of Religions: Essays on the Problem of Understanding* (Chicago: University of Chicago Press, 1974), p. 2.

tegic division of intellectual labor. The history of religions had to originate in the West, but something certainly is seriously wrong if one hundred years later it is still a Western enterprise, as the paucity of non-
Western historians of religions would seem to indicate. It probably is
not by chance that most of the practitioners of the history of religions,
especially in Africa, are theologians or have that background. Notwithstanding the sterling efforts to Africanize Christianity in the past generation, the internal logic of the Christian message militates against the
integrity and continuity of non-Christian cultures. Such cultures are
destined for demise, whether the euphemism used is transformation or
fulfillment. The goal is always the same — the old culture must go. Any
study of it, therefore, can only be in service of this missiological goal.

In this, theology is in tune with modernity insofar as the ideology
of change is concerned.[9] Thus, we see here the secularizing forces of
modernity making common cause with the de-sacralizing impulses
and designs of theology in the dethronement and demise of pagan cultures. But as recent studies in the social sciences and humanities have
shown, classic secularization theory is hard put to explain the new religious vigor in Africa and the world generally. It would seem then that
the traditional religions of Africa are dealing with modernity in their
own terms, thereby holding out hope of a viable field of study for the
history of religions. However, as Maluleke reminds us, as long as the
West is the dominant factor in the study of religion in Africa, it does
not matter whether the method used is religious studies or theology.
What matters is that the Western dominance on the theoretical and
conceptual levels must be broken.

The irrational division of intellectual labor, it seems, is closely
linked to the next issue for our consideration.

The History of Religions Is about the West

Here we go beyond the division of labor itself to the more immediate issue of the distribution of attention. The thematic of the West as the

9. Pierre L. van den Bershe, "Major Themes in Social Change," in John N.
Paden and Edward W. Soja, eds., *The African Experience*, vol. 1 (London: Heinemann,
1973), pp. 252-75.

center or metropol and the rest of the world as its periphery has become a cliché. But it should serve to illuminate our thinking on this issue of who gets attention in the world. All roads lead to the West, literally and symbolically. Among goods ferried in all this trafficking are cultural forms, all the way from artifacts to ideas. Now, there is nothing intrinsically wrong with cultural borrowing; that is how the world enriches itself. But the kinds of borrowing we find here are well known for creating imbalances and distortions in intellectual exchange as they are often driven by a cultural ideology of superiority. The fathers[10] of the history of religions make it quite clear that their subject aims at the study of otherness. Thus Wach:

> Quantitatively and qualitatively Religionswissenschaft thus has a field of study distinct from that of theology: not our own religion but the foreign religions in all their manifoldness are its subject matter.[11]

Wach goes on to identify these foreign religions as the "religions of exotic or primitive peoples." One may reasonably ask: Where is the subject matter of the history of religions scholar who cannot identify with the "we" of Wach and Eliade and the rest of them? Where do the African historians of religions look for their subject matter? According to Wach what justifies this project is "desire for truth." Now, in my case, can I at once be grist for the truth machine and the researcher operating that machine? Can I as a member of an "exotic culture" legitimately be a historian of religions in the Wachian sense? Or a theologian in the traditional Western sense? Or shall I be constrained to force a revolt in the disciplines and bring about another unassisted birth? If I read him well, this is close to what Maluleke is calling for when he insists on championing of African interests as opposed to mere presence of people of African ancestry in departments of religious studies or theology.

It is clear then that the reason the history of religions is by and about the West resides in the definition of the subject matter and de-

---

10. Editors' Note: Our aim in this volume is to encourage the use of inclusive language as far as possible. There are times, however — as in this case — when it is appropriate to use masculine terminology.

11. Wach, "Introduction: The Meaning and Task," p. 2.

lineation of the field of study. To a large extent this question, especially as regards theology, has been answered in the rise to maturity of African theology in its manifold approaches,[12] but let us come back to this later. For now, we shall look at another aspect of the problem, namely, for whom the history of religions is practiced.

The History of Religions Is for the West

The history of religions is not only a Western project practiced by Westerners; its stated goal is the self-understanding and reconstruction of the West. Thus, the history of religions is for the West. Charles Long makes this clear:

> Every adequate hermeneutic is at heart an essay in self-understanding. It is the effort to understand the self through the mediation of the other. By self-understanding I do not mean the reduction of the other to the dogmatic categories of contemporaneity. Self-understanding through the mediation of the other involves the principle of reciprocal criticism. It is this *reciprocal criticism of self and other* which permits the interpolation of the phenomenon into our lives.[13]

There is tremendous potential in this proposal for shock to the other and scandal on the part of the perpetrator in the use of the other to mediate self-understanding to the Westerner. But, as Long points out, these potential outcomes can be averted or cushioned, if not transformed for constructive creativity, through the principle of reciprocal criticism. Long is taking the bull by the horns here, for lack of reciprocity is one of the gravest crimes against humanity perpetrated over the years by the human and social sciences. And before we are elated at the possibility of doing the right thing by the other at last, we must be sobered by the realization that in practice there continues to be no reciprocity. Yes, there is criticism both of self and other, but the subjectivity of this act remains in the West. And this is a problem, although

12. Malukeke, "Theology in (South) Africa," p. 366.
13. Charles H. Long, *Significations: Signs, Symbols, and Images in the Interpretations of Religion* (Philadelphia: Fortress Press, 1986), p. 46 (emphasis added).

seeds of its redress are clearly identifiable in recent developments in intellectual history.

Long[14] goes on to cite positive developments in hermeneutical sensitivity, coming out of the philosophical work of Ricoeur. But even here symbols from other cultures are used in the renewal of Western philosophy, and thus the revitalization of Western culture, and not in a global project of general intellectual liberation. Even in the case of Eliade, whom Long praises for going further to challenge the still very Western orientation and character of these new philosophical directions, the goal is still that of rejuvenation of Western culture. And how am I as an African supposed to respond to this? With jubilation? Of course not: a rejuvenated West is bad news for "foreign and exotic cultures," just as a strong U.S. dollar wreaks havoc on developing economies and their currencies. And all this is not unrelated to the epistemological fact that the West possesses the truth, the whole truth, and nothing but the truth. We must note, of course, that postcolonial and postmodern critiques have begun to challenge this whole paradigm.

What, then, do we propose should be done?

As far as the history of religions is concerned, steps must be taken to transform the discipline from being of, by, about, and for the West alone. This will allow other peoples to participate in the discipline authentically and meaningfully, and with intellectual honesty and integrity. It will also mean that instead of serving the narrow interests of Western intellectual and cultural narcissism, the discipline will broaden its interests to focus on the self-understanding of the entire human race. Where, up until now, the discipline has striven to discover avenues of renewing Western culture, from now on it would seek transformation and affirmation of the cultures of the world in their diversity, plurality, and integrity. Instead of continuing to participate in a culture of unilateral and arbitrary taking, of insatiable expropriation of the rest of the world's resources, the history of religions must now accept a culture of giving back and receiving (as opposed to taking), and of sharing in a spirit of true critical and creative reciprocity.

This would go a long way in eliminating the violence that is endemic to the Western intellectual enterprise. It might also answer some of the concerns raised by Maluleke about the inadequacies of both reli-

14. Long, *Significations,* p. 50.

gious studies and theology. At this point, the history of religions might learn a few useful, though ambiguous lessons from its parent and age-old rival, theology, where indigenous peoples have wrested some space for themselves and are now empowering themselves to transform the discipline into an instrument of African and broader human liberation.

However, it must guard against what I consider a serious error that continues to haunt theology. This is the problem that Maluleke identifies as the unsatisfactory, even injurious, relationship between Christianity (Christian theology) and African Traditional Religions.

Christianity, the African's Burden

When I spoke on the theme of religion and diversity at the University of the Western Cape in 1995 it created a palpable dissonance. As justification for its take and tone one could have appealed for precedent to Mark Anthony's plea that he had come to bury Caesar, and not to praise him. Except that I had come neither to praise anybody nor bury anything. In fact, I had come to exhume some things, some skeletons from the cupboard of respectable religion. If the present discussion has a jarring effect in a collection of harmonious essays, it may very well have achieved its purpose, thereby finding a humble place in the old prophetic league whose specialty was hailing discomfort at both Samaria and Jerusalem.

It is not that hard to see that theology as a genre may, consciously or otherwise, do more concealing than revealing. For instance, where indigenous African religions are concerned, the zealous glossing of their distinctive details in a rush to Christianize them and to christen them as *praeparatio evangelica* has left those religions distorted and the product of inculturation, anemic to the point of monstrosity. Take the case of the Holy Spirit, for example. The scramble to demonize local understandings of spirit, in a bid to establish dominance and normativity for the biblical Holy Spirit, served to hide, diminish, and discredit indigenous African understandings of spirit and spirituality.

One of the saddest aspects of Christianity is its unfortunate intolerance of other traditions, its claim to not only possess, but be the truth, the whole truth, and nothing but the truth (so help me God, I need it!). In the pluralist world of today this primitive outlook becomes a sin against the diversity that is the imprint of everything the Creator thought worth making. In South Africa, the new socio-economic dispensation makes it not only possible but imperative to ask the question about diversity of any kind, and religious diversity specifically. An assumption that is generally held in the country is that diversity is an asset and not a liability. But in order to put some substance into this hope we must examine the contribution each of the religious traditions of the country has to offer in the building of a new society.

Here we address this question in respect of indigenous African religions. This tradition that has nurtured generations of Africans since the time of the beginning brings rather unique problems to the debate. It is true that it shares with other non-Christian traditions the vagaries of demonization and being besieged as targets for conversion. What is unique in its experience is its relationship of captivity to another religion, namely, Christianity. It is one thing to be targeted for proselytization (which is the inescapable fate of all non-Christian religions); it is quite another to be targeted for total annihilation, as envisaged by the culture policies of mainline missionary societies,[15] and some early as well as later African converts.[16]

I am aware that this assertion puts some people on the defensive such that they find themselves arguing that one tradition cannot captivate another tradition. So, let me put the matter rather differently. Christian theologians, especially African ones, in response to the theological and pastoral issues raised by the existence and power of the indigenous religions, actively toil for the demise of the indigenous religions of Africa. Of course, being the sophisticated operators they have become, they will not use the crude approach of a head-on collision or overt cultural genocide (although this has not been ruled out completely). By and large they espouse the more refined and enlightened strategy of inculturation. The result is the same, though: the targeted religion is written off. The only difference is that in the one case the aim is to crush, while in the other the intention is to swallow up. Our

---

15. Kwame Bediako, "The Roots of African Theology," in *International Bulletin of Missionary Research* (August 1989): 58.

16. David Chidester et al., *Christianity in South Africa: An Annotated Bibliography* (Westport, Conn.: Greenwood Press, 1997).

concern here is to concentrate on the indigenous African religions as the religion of many Africans by birth and their relationship to Christianity as the religion of choice for millions of Africans.

It is useful to spell out as clearly as possible what we mean by the indigenous African religions. These are the religions that have been designated by the academic appellation African Traditional Religions. Here I find Oduyoye's definition quite helpful:

> There are those who are to a lesser degree Islamised or Christianised. There is also a group that we may refer to as "traditionalists." Some of these are simply theorists, but there are masses of people in Africa who hold to the traditional religious beliefs and practices of their forebears to the exclusion of the *missionary religions*. Their religious customs blend with their social life and are at the base of all their institutions and festive celebration.[17]

Now underlining the autonomy of what Oduyoye here calls "traditionalists" is not to deny "African-ness" to those who have embraced missionary religions. In fact, one does not need to claim a primordial African identity for Christianity, as does Kwame Bediako,[18] in order to observe that Christianity has become one of the ways of being African. The move is merely a convenient way of distinguishing "traditionalists" from Africans of other faiths. Traditionalist, in its complexity, means much more than embracing or espousing specific beliefs and practices. It refers to a stance, an overall orientation, one that is marked by either indifference to or defiance of certain essential elements of Western culture and religion. This distinction is of the utmost importance especially in South Africa, a country that prided itself on being a Christian country and continues to think so of itself, in spite of all the current talk about diversity. Despite the fact that this purported Christian identity of South Africa was a child of apartheid hegemonic politics, some Africans embraced it and wave it threateningly at anyone who seems to be forgetful or ignorant of the statistics. It is not my intention

17. Mercy Amba Oduyoye, "The Value of African Religious Beliefs and Practices for Christian Theology," in Kofi Appiah-Kofi and Sergio Torres, eds., *African Theology en Route,* 2nd ed. (Maryknoll, N.Y.: Orbis Books, 1979), p. 109 (emphasis added).

18. Kwame Bediako, *Christianity in Africa: The Renewal of a Non-Western Religion* (Edinburgh and Maryknoll: University Press and Orbis, 1995), p. 93.

to enter the debate about religion statistics here. Some good studies already exist on the issue.[19] All that should be said, though, is that even if South Africa were to be declared 90 percent Christian that would not, in a democratic secular state, deny the indigenous African religions an independent identity and a space to be.

It is common knowledge that there was a time in the past when the driving force behind world affairs was the white person's burden to civilize and Christianize. Now that the mission fields of yesteryear can boast of being Christian countries in their own right, as we have just seen in the case of South Africa, we can safely assume that this burden has largely been discharged. Unfortunately, in the process a new phenomenon was born: the African's burden. But unlike the white person's burden which, as a burden of the powerful, of empire-building conquerors, may be construed as a burden of choice that could be discarded at will, the African's burden is the burden of the weak, the powerless, the vanquished, the dispossessed. It cannot be laid down at will. It refuses to be discharged. It threatens to self-perpetuate indefinitely.

To those who have converted to Christianity it is alleged to be the burden of a split consciousness[20] or the related but different doubleness spoken of by du Bois with reference to Black America.[21] For those who have not converted it is the burden of being under constant siege, of being denied being, identity, and space. As Chidester observes, "the Hottentots were credited with a religion that discredited them. Even when granted a religion, therefore, the Hottentots were denied."[22] This is especially pernicious when the power and influence of academic institutions and discourses participate in this cultural atrocity. There are reputable liberal scholars (black as well as white), for instance, who hold that there are no independent indigenous religions to study; that all there is to consider is the encounter with Christianity. If this is true,

---

19. David Chidester, "Worldview Analysis of African Indigenous Churches," in *Journal for the Study of Religion* 2, no. 1 (March 1989): 15-29 and John W. de Gruchy, *The Church Struggle in South Africa,* 2nd ed. (Cape Town and Grand Rapids: David Philip and Eerdmans, 1986).

20. Desmond Tutu, "Whither African Theology?," in E. W. Fashole-Luke et al., eds., *Christianity in Independent Africa* (London: Rex Collings, 1978).

21. W. E. B. du Bois, *The Souls of Black Folk* (New York: NAL Penguin, 1969), p. 45.

22. David Chidester, *Savage Systems: Colonialism and Comparative Religion in Southern Africa* (Charlottesville: University Press of Virginia, 1996), p. 70.

then there is no need to consider the possible contribution of the indigenous religions to the development of a new South Africa. Since this is crucial to this debate we must look at it in greater detail.

Battle for Ownership of Symbols

Even at this late hour some people hold the view that indigenous religions must be treated as quarries from which different religious traditions may excavate what they want and take it away. Indeed, this is largely the use to which many African theologians have put indigenous religions; they use these religions as raw materials for the theological enterprise. Now, there is nothing wrong with this. Traditions thrive by borrowing from one another. In the case of African Christians there is the added need to Africanize their faith. However, if this becomes the basis of denying indigenous religions an independent identity, then we have a problem. What this shows quite clearly, however, is that indigenous religions are not there simply to be interpreted as meaning systems; rather their symbols are carriers of power the ownership of which is contested by various parties in pursuit of their respective goals.[23]

So far Christianity, as the religion of conquerors par excellence, has had an unfair advantage in the battle for the souls of African folk. In many cases it succeeded in silencing the traditionalists' voice, or in driving it underground, only to see it re-emerge in the scarcely disguised form of new religious movements. As the religion of victors, and itself by its very nature a conquering religion, Christianity has dictated how the indigenous religions were to be used. To date most African intellectuals who have concerned themselves with indigenous religions have been Christian theologians who were interested in inculturation, that is, making the gospel at home in African culture and African culture comfortable with the gospel. However, as David Bosch pointed out, "Inculturation suggests a *double movement*: there is at once inculturation of Christianity and Christianization of culture."[24]

Many inculturation theologians would concur over the insepara-

23. Chidester, "Worldview Analysis," pp. 15-29.
24. David Bosch, *Transforming Mission: Paradigm Shifts in Theology of Mission* (Maryknoll, N.Y.: Orbis, 1991), p. 454 (emphasis added).

bility of the two currents. This, of course, is in keeping with the ethical and missiological model of Christ as the transformer of culture.[25] But in the case of the indigenous religions and the unhappy history of their encounter with Christianity, this model poses the danger of denying indigenous religions an authentic identity by reducing them to this invention, this product of the Christian project of inculturation, and debasement to the status of "a basic raw material for Christian theology."[26] A good example of this is the Christianization of the role of the ancestors as intermediaries between God and the living. This reductive transformation may be good for Christians insofar as it helps them in dealing with the problem of the split, the doubleness that runs through their consciousness. But it would be absurd to insist, as many Christian theologians do, that this is what all Africans do believe and should believe. In fact, even within the framework of African theology, this proposal seems to lack persuasive power, and is fraught with insurmountable logical hurdles.

Once again we see that what we are faced with is a contestation of the ownership of religious symbols. If history is anything to go by we could create a scenario that is disquieting to Christianity of the triumphalist type. History shows that in spite of concerted attempts to destroy them, there is a marked "resurgence" of the traditional or primal religions all around the world. In South Africa vicious persecution and marginalization of indigenous religions both by church and state during colonialism and apartheid failed to destroy indigenous religions. Now with the dawning of a new democratic dispensation expressions of indigenous religions that earlier may have gone underground may now be expected to rear their primal heads both in urban and rural areas. Christianity will have to be a good neighbor and learn to live with this. This is by no means to suggest that the church must now stop preaching and propagating its message. But it is to say that in the spirit of the new missiological model of dialogue the church will have to exercise a charitable attitude that will allow indigenous religions space in which to be themselves. And it will have to redefine the mean-

---

25. H. Richard Niebuhr, *Christ and Culture* (New York: Harper & Row, 1951), pp. 190f.

26. E. Bolaji Idowu, *Towards an Indigenous Church* (London: Oxford University Press, 1965), p. 25.

ing of the lordship of Christ, which John de Gruchy insists is at the center of the church's task,[27] and spell out its implications for a world that has come of age again. To put it in the poignant words of M. M. Thomas, Christians must be prepared to "risk Christ for Christ's sake."[28]

The university, for its part, can play a key role in the concretization of the notion of diversity. Instead of conceptualizing, teaching, and researching indigenous religions as if they were pastoral problems of Christianity, the university must create enough space for indigenous religions to be and become themselves, complete with the theoretical and methodological implications of doing so.

However, to claim space and an identity for indigenous religions is not to suggest that these religions were or will remain static, oblivious to both the reality of and need for change. It is rather to affirm their subjectivity and agency as active players in the tug-of-war for ownership of symbolic resources and strategies. It is to acknowledge their character and identity as dynamic power relations.[29] The words of Emilio Castro in relation to dialogue as a strategy for mission powerfully capture this idea:

> Dialogue insists that the other is a subject, a protagonist, and not simply an object of missionary endeavour. The dialogical attitude is one of respect for the others *in their self-definition.*[30]

Today self-definitional stirrings abound among traditionalists in South Africa. If Christians are serious about recognizing diversity, the least they can do to atone for the sins of the past is let go and let indigenous religions be.

This, however, is easier said than done. Indigenous religions are variously seen as the umbilical cord that attaches contemporary African Christians to their past, thereby anchoring their identity in their heritage. The nature of the burden in this respect has been construed

---

27. De Gruchy, *Church Struggle*, pp. 243-44.

28. Emilio Castro, "Mission in a Pluralistic Age," *International Review of Mission* 75, no. 299 (July 1986): 209.

29. David Chidester et al., *African Traditional Religion: An Annotated Bibliography* (Westport, Conn.: Greenwood Press, 1997), p. 12.

30. Castro, "Mission," p. 204 (emphasis added).

on the level of consciousness as that of psychological schizophrenia.[31] Whether there is a connection here with the theological split vision of a depressed Africa on the one hand and a thriving Christian Africa on the other may be an interesting question in its own right. But for now, I will attempt to comment briefly on the issue of psychological split personality.

African theologians have considered it a major responsibility of theirs to overcome this schizophrenia, employing all sorts of theological gymnastics to this end. But is this really an issue, a problem for the ordinary man or woman in the street, in the field, Christian or non-Christian? At least two statements can be made in response to this question. First, it would appear that ordinary folk do not suffer from the alienating effects of this perceived split in consciousness, for the simple reason that on the level of practice they do not perceive any contradictions between the two hemispheres that make up their world. To a large extent, the problem of a divided consciousness is an ailment of the elite African professional theologian. Second, one feels constrained to ask if it is indeed necessary to bridge the split. I am thinking here of the view of "person" that would make it possible to raise the question, let alone necessitate such a drastic measure as seeking to eliminate the split. Is not this a symptom of the Western view that sees ideal personhood as characterized by a centered, autonomous subject that as free agent must confront the integrity of the world that informs its actions? Speaking of theology, it is not difficult to trace this view back to its Augustinian roots[32] (where the contextual nature of Augustine's response in both personal and historical terms is clear).

Developments and ramifications into phobias of otherness were only one short step away from this patristic anxiety over a life and consciousness that were feared to be scattered about and to which the necessary response consisted in "returning" and "gathering" the self into an integrity, in a religious context fraught with contestations between purported orthodoxies and perceived heresies. Granted, this is an im-

---

31. Tutu, "Whither African Theology?," p. 366, and Maluleke, "In Search of 'The True Character of Christian Identity': A Review of the Theology of Kwame Bediako," *Missionalia* 25, no. 2 (August 1997): 217.

32. Margaret R. Miles, "Roman North African Spiritualities," in Jacob K. Olupona, ed., *African Spirituality: Forms, Meanings and Expressions* (New York: Herder and Herder, 2002), p. 367.

portant way of understanding what it means to be human. But it certainly is not the only way. It may not even be the best way. Doubleness of consciousness may be offensive to Western sensibilities, but to ex-slaves (victims of slavery and colonialism) this may very well be a permanent condition.

It may not be that difficult to understand why Westerners hate this prospect. First, as we have seen, it cuts counter to their notion of a centered self. Second, it reminds them of the failure of their project of cultural imperialism. Hence resolution of the split is always prescribed as imperative and must always assume the form of a Western Christian synthesis, never an indigenous African integrity. Unfortunately, Westernized Africans (especially Christian theologians) have begun to believe that this is their problem too. They seem easily to forget the composite nature of African conceptions of personhood.[33] No wonder they become all worked up at even the mention of spirit possession, the epitome of psychical decentering and fragmentation of the personality. It may very well be that it is alright to have a double consciousness. That is our colonial heritage.

It is also the way of postmodern postcolonialism. Those purporting to have only one consciousness, in spite of their creolizing experience within colonial practice, may be excused if they are caught envying those who boast a double consciousness. They suffer from the psychological anxiety induced by awareness of a lack. The historic denial and rejection of indigenous African religions may be a flight from double consciousness. It is a form of erasure of history, and entry into self-induced amnesia. Africans cannot reject this double consciousness without rejecting themselves. For it is the indigenous religions, the older leg of the bifurcation, that retain the memory of the encounter, the contact. The contact and its aftermath — the newer arm of the fork — cannot hold a memory of itself, as affirmed by the Shona saying that an ax cuts and forgets, but the tree that was cut forever remembers the pain.

---

33. Dominique Zahan, *The Religion, Spirituality, and Thought of Traditional Africa* (Chicago: University of Chicago Press, 1979), p. 9.

Way Forward

What then should be the way forward for us? At this point I find Maluleke's insights helpful, though somewhat self-consciously hesitant. In an insightful 1997 article he proposes a programmatic route predicated on transcendence of the status quo, imploring that theological endeavor go "beyond the two Africas approach." Here, as opposed to the case of psychological schizophrenia, it is not only legitimate but imperative to smash the split.[34] He then proposes that the African theological agenda go "beyond Christianity as a foreign and convenient entity." Rejecting as irrelevant to Africa's contemporary problems Bediako's assertion that Christianity is not a foreign religion in Africa,[35] Maluleke boldly underlines the foreignness of the religion but goes on to propose that, because of its long presence in the continent, and its impact on African life, Christianity must now be made to lose its foreignness through a process of domestication. Third, there is a need to go "beyond obsession with missionaries and colonialists." Fourth, theologizing in Africa must go "beyond the universal gospel." Of special significance in this respect is relativization of the authority of the Bible, the radical distinction between the gospel and Christianity, and the oft-posited distinction between Christianity and the other religions. In this I think Maluleke is on the right path. It is very easy for theological production to degenerate into a fruitless exercise in marking time, with no real ground being gained. Hence the call to going "beyond." However, he stops short of this inevitable conclusion: the need to go beyond theology itself.

Beyond Theology

Maluleke goes further in developing an earlier critique of theologians who, as Bediako, espouse an easy and comfortable relationship between Africans and Christianity. He cogently speaks of "troubled relations between Africans and Christianity."[36] Using biographies of early

34. Tinyiko Maluleke, "Christianity in a Distressed Africa: A Time to Own and Own Up," *Missionalia* 26, no. 3 (November 1998): 336.
35. Bediako, *Christianity in Africa*, passim.
36. Maluleke, "Christianity in a Distressed Africa," p. 378.

converts to Christianity in South Africa he paints a painful picture of the Africans' experience with their new faith. One convert, Ntsikana, speaks of his conversion in terms of an invasion by a "thing" that came into him, an experience correctly interpreted as "violent" by Maluleke. But the violence did not end there; living the Christian life was in itself a trauma that wove a tapestry of racism, rejection both by blood family and the new family of faith, and no doubt, disillusionment and despair. He asks harrowing questions:

> Why has Christian adherence not been enough glue to create a new society of Black and White, male and female? Why is it that even the deepest symbols of Christian reconciliation have not managed to do this?[37]

These are very disturbing questions indeed for those who are Christian theologians in Africa. I shall return to them later with a proposal as to what to do about them. For now let us listen further to Maluleke's painful analysis. Examples are adduced from the relationship of Christianity with African Traditional Religions and the theoretical and methodological problems encountered in studying them.[38] What he has to say about what he calls "Reconciliation Discourse" begs to be quoted.

> In South Africa, reconciliation is largely a discourse of a few Black elite and White males. There is an amazing and very loud silence of lower ranked and working class Blacks on the subject. An even more resounding silence is that of Black women. This silence may be deliberate, but it is also *an indicator of the extent to which the power-less remain powerless* even in post-independent South Africa. My proposal here is simple: African Theology must enter the fray of the reconciliation discourse; it is a discourse which cannot be left merely to the powerful in society.[39]

These questions and observations are not only theological; they are also epistemological, having to do with types of knowledge, ways of

37. Maluleke, "Theology in (South) Africa," p. 378.
38. Maluleke, "Theology in (South) Africa," p. 384.
39. Maluleke, "Theology in (South) Africa," pp. 386-87 (emphasis added) and "'Dealing Lightly with the Wound of My People': The TRC Process in Theological Perspective," *Missionalia* 25, no. 3 (November 1997): 335-36.

knowing and voicing, and means of leveraging the public platform. No doubt Maluleke would only be too aware of this. For in his critique of Bediako he charges that Bediako had unfairly criticized Edward Blyden and Kwabena Damuah "in terms of categories and criteria that are too 'Christian' — criteria which fall outside of their own schemes."[40] If I read him correctly, Maluleke is saying that Blyden's and Damuah's works must not be read as if they were theology; they ought to be read as something else. This issue of genre specificity is crucially important. But it does not relate to reading only. It also applies with regard to writing or speaking. Theology is a highly specialized way of writing, speaking, arguing, persuading, and so on. There was a time when it was thought to be a specifically Christian enterprise, although today other traditions are said to do theology in their own right.

Whatever else it does or may be, theology may be defined as a way of stating as a rational proposition what is cast in mythological terms. It is this detail that links theology to speculative philosophy. Through theological discourse theologians have endeavored intelligibly and rationally to communicate mystical things (about messiahs, virgin births, resurrections, life after death, sin, ethics) to a rational audience. Conversely, theologians have tended to reduce ordinary reality to mythologies of sorts before they could theologize about them. This is what critics mean when they charge that theologians' reflections are not based on empirical reality. Maluleke touches on this when he rejects the "Two Africas Approach" which arbitrarily separates analytically the real Africa of grinding poverty, corruption, crime, disease, and squalor from a posited mythical Christian Africa of hope and integrity.

This reduction of the raw material of theology to mythology prior to (as an unstated procedural condition for) the moment of theologizing has the net effect of concealing rather than revealing, obscuring rather than unveiling. This comes out clearly in Maluleke's analysis of and prescription for the love-hate relationship of theology to African Traditional Religions. The prescription is that African theology must cut itself loose from "the violence of Western Christian theology and then from there work out its relationship to religious studies,

40. Tinyiko Maluleke, "In Search of 'The True Character of Christian Identity,'" p. 215.

if there is any."[41] Moreover, it is not as if the discipline of religious studies is any better than the discipline of theology. Both are implicated in the problematic of epistemological violence and cannot transform from within. The litmus test will be the authenticity of African presence that is in service of African interests in these disciplines. But is it only Western Christian theology that is caught up in the violence of knowing? Or may it be the case that the problem lies not so much in a specific type of theology as the theological genre itself?

Maluleke's demands are tough. Can they be met? Perhaps only time will tell. Maluleke himself does not quite say where transformation will come from. Or what will be the nature of the new discipline. I propose that the solution lies not so much in tinkering with theology as in transcending it. As for religious studies, a child of theology, it partially shares in the fate of its parent. However, to the extent that it possesses some of the traits of the new proposed discourse X, it may be spared the severity of the former's plight.

One may be tempted sometimes to think that the world might actually be better off without theology. Africa would especially benefit from such an eventuality. There is no doubt that theology is an elitist genre. It is a complicated way of saying simple things. That is the reason the powerless remain disempowered to the point of not participating in theological discourse. For people who want to say simple things, or complex things, for that matter, simply, theology seems uninviting. Theology mystifies, conceals, and disempowers.

What notoriously religious Africa needs now is a discourse about religion that calls a spade a spade. It can be called anything; discourse X will do for a start. Its brief will be to investigate, analyze, and report on the state of religion in the continent and seek to interpret its powerful symbols in relation to the power relations that arise from and define society, economy, politics, and culture.

However, it seems neither necessary nor possible to simply go beyond theology or all the "beyond theologies" that Maluleke alludes to.[42] What is needed is to put theology in proper perspective within the ordinary order of things. This means, among other things, that we do not have to be doing theology every time we open our mouths or turn

41. Maluleke, "Theology in (South) Africa," p. 385.
42. Maluleke, "Theology in (South) Africa," p. 372.

on the computer. We can talk about theology, religion, faith communities, and the world in a non-theological discursive manner. A civic manner that does not reduce reality to mythology first, and one that is accessible to ordinary folk.

Strictly speaking this is already happening, and has been for a long time. For instance, the descriptive treatments of African Initiated Christian Churches that Maluleke complains about as lacking theoretical and hermeneutical radar to guide them[43] are, in fact, of this nature. Except that they have pretensions to being theology. I would venture to suggest that, in some of his recent writings, John de Gruchy himself comes close to realizing this possibility although, for obvious reasons, he cannot think of it as anything but theology. We need to accept these departures from the theological norm as the budding of a legitimate genre for talking about religion, and be deliberate, purposive, and explicit about the practice of this genre. And we must be prepared to develop this genre to the highest point of discursive refinement.

The theologians can use this intermediate discourse as raw material for their specialized expositions if they so choose. They and others must, however, first learn how to talk about life and the world in ways that are not constrained by theological norms and intentions. However, this middle talk is not supposed to replace theology, I must reiterate, because faith communities need the latter. As dealers in mythologies at the point at which these touch reality and are configured into rational propositions, faith communities and their theologians need theology in mediating the enterprise.

As long as theologians want to talk simultaneously as ordinary folk and theologians, obfuscation takes place. To pretend that theologians can disengage and talk theologically as if they were ordinary people, engaging in ordinary talk, is shamefully disingenuous. Even narrative theologies such as Musa Dube's, to the extent that they are governed by biblical or Christian norms, cannot be ordinary talk. Thus, going beyond does not mean doing away with theology. Instead it entails acknowledgment of the existence, legitimacy, and need further to develop a middle discourse between religious phenomena and theological production.

It could be argued that this is already being done by the social sciences and the humanities. There indeed is some truth in this view.

43. Maluleke, "Theology in (South) Africa," p. 375.

These disciplines discuss reality in a manner that is different from theology, and do produce a discourse that could function to mediate between the mythologies of theology and the realities of the world. However, it must be noted that they too are problematic. For the norms that guide them, though different from those of theology in some essential respects, are no less elitist and epistemologically exclusionary of ordinary people. To some extent, this might go also for religious studies. Thus, the need for a discursive X, a middle discourse about religion, remains an urgent item on the African intellectual and academic agenda. The needs of the twenty-first century, the African century, not only invite us to this task. They demand that we tackle it and see it through to a satisfactory conclusion.

Secularism, Pluralism, and the Afrikaner Churches in the Twenty-First Century

Jaap Durand

A Society in Transition

South African society is a society in transition. As is commonly known, the major changes that took place from the early nineties through to the first democratic elections in 1994, and thereafter, were of a political nature and only the beginning of a process of transformation.

In many instances these changes are very slow in getting off the ground, especially in the economic and social spheres. Huge challenges lie ahead, and there is a widespread awareness among responsible and thinking citizens that, if these challenges are not adequately met, South Africa faces a bleak future. The lack of urgency on the part of the "established" (Reformed) Afrikaner churches to transform and adapt themselves to this new situation is therefore, on the face of it, remarkable if we consider the influential, even pivotal, role these churches played in the shaping of the old South African society.

To many, though, this reluctance to change may not seem remarkable after all. It can be argued that the Afrikaner people, realizing that their political power has been irrevocably lost and feeling that their cultural heritage, the Afrikaans language above all, is under real threat, still find in their churches the last vestiges of a still longed-for past and one of the few remaining safe havens of Afrikanerdom. However, I believe that this is only partly true. The reluctance to change has also to do with a profound crisis of identity that goes far beyond the mere loss of political power. It has to do with forces, other than political (although in many instances precipitated by political changes), that were unleashed during the last few decades of the twentieth century. These forces can be rubricated under the headings of secularism and pluralism, both phenomena concomitant with the dynamic process of democratization and the new sense of freedom in South Africa. These two factors, secularism and pluralism, although not altogether unknown in the past, have taken on such proportions during and since the political break with the past that the leadership in the established Afrikaner churches is left baffled, uncertain how to cope with these forces and, paradoxically, with the new forms of spirituality these forces engender. It is this bewilderment that paralyzes them, rendering them incapable of dealing with those issues of transformation that the uncomprehending "outsiders" expect of them.

The obvious question to ask in this regard is why the onslaught of secularism and pluralism is only manifesting itself forcefully now in the wake of the dramatic political changes and, consequently, at such a late stage in the history of Afrikanerdom. The answer to this question is not self-evident, because it has to do with the complexities of South African society at large.

Secularism, Pluralism, and the Afrikaner[1]

Broadly speaking, South Africa encompasses two vastly different worlds of African and Western orientation with various ethnic and cultural inflections. It speaks for itself that there is no watertight division between the different groups. Cross-cultural influences are very much in evidence. One outstanding example is that the Western lifestyle is not limited to the white section of the population. Many Africans, especially in the urban areas, have adopted it fully or in part. For the purposes of this article, however, a distinction must be made between the two groups that traditionally represent the way of life of the modern West: the English- and Afrikaans-speaking sections of the populace

---

1. Although people of various population groups in South Africa regard Afrikaans as their home language, the term "Afrikaner" has historically referred exclusively to white Afrikaans-speaking people.

and more specifically the Afrikaners among the latter group. Only then will we be able to get a clear focus on the specific Afrikaner reaction to and ways of dealing with the forces of secularism as part and parcel of Western modernism.

What do we mean by Western modernity or modernism with respect to the South African situation?

"Modern" and "modernism" usually refer to a worldview and a lifestyle that developed under the impact of science, technology, rational thought, and a strong sense of the worth of the individual that culminated in the typical culture of the West. The origin of this development can be traced back to the breakdown of medieval scholasticism which, encouraged by the Oxford tradition to demand certitude of material evidence, contributed to the liberation of scientific thought. A century later a new sense of spiritual freedom developed during the time of the Renaissance and the Reformation, leading to a form of individualism that henceforth would characterize the thinking of the West. The real cradle of the modern West, however, is the Enlightenment of the seventeenth and eighteenth centuries in Europe. Enlightenment thinkers opposed the pervasive influence of religion and dogma, and wished to replace them with a more reasoned approach to everyday practical life. It was never the idea to eliminate religion completely, but to restrict it to the sphere of the transcendent. But even here reason was elevated to be the measure of what could possibly be true.

It is not difficult to see how such a worldview could eventually lead to the elimination of the idea of the transcendent and thus to a secular society in the full sense of the word: a society that has no other horizon than the *saeculum* (world) itself. Max Weber did not use the term "secularization," but spoke of the "disenchantment of the world": human beings were passing from the enchanted garden of primeval religiosity into the cold comfort of modern reality. This, however, does not mean that secularization is inextricably linked with modernity. Peter Berger argues persuasively that on the one hand secularity occurred long before the advent of modernity, and on the other hand, many societies, even countries, are as religious as ever, despite being in every sense of the word modern. No one, he says, will propose that the United States is not a modern society; indeed in some respects it may be more modern than any other. Yet by all conventional criteria it continues to be an intensely religious country. There is, according to Berger, one geographical region and one cross-national group of people among whom secularization took firm hold. The region is Europe, and the group refers to people with Western-type higher education everywhere. In the case of Northern Europe the process of secularization can be correlated fairly accurately with the advance of modernity.[2] These remarks of Berger are all very pertinent to the South African situation to which we shall return in due course.

We often hear talk of postmodernism, and the impression one gains is that South Africa, together with the rest of the world (we live after all in a period of globalization), is caught up in a new dispensation in which modernism and its concomitant secular life-orientation are left behind. Nothing is further from the truth. It is not true with regard to the Western world as a whole, which still is very much a modern world with a modern outlook and, in many a region, a rampant secularism despite so-called postmodern signs. It is a moot point whether many indicators that are now associated with postmodernism are not in fact phenomena that could be properly placed within the "old" modern outlook.

As far as South Africa is concerned it is even less true. South Africa is years, even decades, behind most of the Western world. The process of secularization as described above has only now begun to make significant inroads into the lifestyle and outlook of South African society at large. South Africa is only now really being challenged by modernism in the secular sense of the word. This is not only due to the fact that South African society exhibits a diversity of conservative ethnic cultures and traditions, but is also due to the success of the otherwise West-oriented section of society, and more specifically the Afrikaans-speaking section, in keeping intact its traditionally non-secular way of life to quite a remarkable degree. It is only now, since the disintegration of Afrikaner hegemony, that it seems as if the forces hitherto kept at bay are unleashed to the complete bewilderment of those caught up in these processes and, above all, the churches that serve them.

The reasons for the successes of Afrikanerdom in its resistance to secularism are varied and complex. Reference could be made to South

2. Peter L. Berger, *A Far Glory: The Quest for Faith in an Age of Credulity* (New York: The Free Press, 1992), pp. 25-46.

Africa's geographical isolation which, however, would not explain why the Afrikaner section resisted the secularization process more effectively than their English counterparts. It has more to do with Afrikaner history, which drove Afrikaners into a mindset and lifestyle of isolation by choice and into a form of civil religion that has demonstrated a remarkable resilience. Their chosen isolation produced a way of dealing very effectively with the phenomenon of pluralism. In the second half of the twentieth century this became one of the most important factors in the Afrikaners' resistance to secularism. Before pursuing this thesis further, it is necessary to say something about the link between secularism and pluralism.

Pluralism denotes a physical as well as a mental state. Physically pluralism is the coexistence of groups of people of different cultures in a society, living together in a more or less peaceful manner despite these differences. Pluralism is self-evidently not a new phenomenon. It has always existed to a greater or lesser degree depending on various demographic situations. A process of urbanization intensifies the impact of pluralism and this is one of the main reasons that modern pluralism is different from the past. Cities have become gigantic and increasingly heterogeneous. More and more people of many cultures, languages, religions, and persuasions live together in large, sprawling metropolitan areas, drawn together by economic necessity. Despite the natural inclination of the like-minded to flock together, the nature of urban life and the inescapable needs of the workplace prevent any possibility of isolation. Physical nearness leads to the breaching of fences. The physical side of pluralism is therefore but a step towards the mental side. This whole process is intensified and deepened by modern technology's ability to influence the masses. Through mass communication people encounter different cultures and worldviews. This, of course, is not limited to urban settings. Through modern technology (television, the Internet, the quicker dissemination of newspapers and literature etc.) even people living in remote places are exposed to pluralism.

Apart from its many other consequences pluralism has a secularizing effect. Peter Berger is of the opinion that being exposed to different cultures and worldviews leads to a pervasive relativism. We start to think that our own traditional way of looking at things may not be the only plausible one. The worldview that was taken for granted suddenly becomes less certain. There are few certainties; convictions become mere opinions. Berger then concludes by stating that Christianity is particularly vulnerable to these secularizing consequences of pluralism.[3]

As we have said, the Afrikaners' resistance to secularism has among other things to do with their history, the development of a civil religion, and the way in which they tried to contain the effects of pluralism. It is now time to take a closer look, albeit very briefly.

Civil Religion and Afrikaner Hegemony

The indissoluble link between Afrikaner history and Calvinist religion has been acknowledged by most historians, although not always with the necessary nuances. What many historians fail to explain or appreciate is the sheer conservatism of the brand of Calvinist religion of the small group of West European people who colonized the Cape in the middle of the seventeenth century, a conservatism that had its roots in English Puritanism. The novelist-historian W. A. de Klerk has explored this relationship,[4] but to my knowledge very few scholars have taken his thesis seriously. There are, however, in my opinion cogent reasons for looking again at this relationship.

Pietistic Puritanism was introduced at the Cape very soon after the arrival of the Dutch settlers. The spirituality of the Calvinist religion and ethic that the Dutch settlers brought was characterized by its origin in the Reformed Pietism that swept across the European continent, especially the Low Countries in the seventeenth century. This Reformed Pietism, which developed as a protest against the spiritual and ethical sterility in the Reformed churches of the day, found its stimulus in the Pietism of Puritan England. There is overwhelming evidence of a very close contact, personal as well as through correspondence, between the English Puritans and the leaders of the Pietists in the Reformed Netherlands. Teelinck, who must be regarded as the father of Reformed Pietism, was in England several times where he came under the influence of John Dod and others, while Amesius, who may be regarded as the early theologian of the Pietistic movement, was a student

---

3. Berger, *A Far Glory,* p. 41.

4. W. A. de Klerk, *The Puritans in Africa: A Story of Afrikanerdom* (London: Rex Collings, 1975).

at Cambridge and a disciple of William Perkins.[5] Note also that many English Puritans moved to the Netherlands to escape persecution. The Pilgrim Father William Bradford — first governor of Plymouth Colony in New England — had lived with others in Leiden for nearly twelve years before going to America.

The English Puritans were representatives of an aggressive Protestantism that increasingly exerted pressure toward a pattern of Calvinist piety with a fundamental characteristic of rigid adherence to the text of the Bible, a persistent emphasis on the need for a profound experience of salvation, and an ethical code that hovered in the vicinity of perfectionism. The two pillars of Puritan thought were the sovereignty of God in his divine activity of election and the human response to God's election and covenant by a life of devotion and practical piety in which the law of God was applied to every conceivable condition of human life. Latent in this spirituality was a militant radicalism, which among other things manifested itself in the Cromwellian revolution and the urge to reshape society in its most "Christian" form, setting things right for both God and his people.

Due to their geographical isolation at the southern tip of Africa the Afrikaners escaped the secularizing influence of the Enlightenment that swept across Europe in the eighteenth and nineteenth centuries. The nineteenth century was also the period during which the inherent conservatism of the Puritan heritage was strengthened by the Afrikaner resistance to British authority (the Great Trek) and British imperialism which culminated in the Anglo-Boer War (1899-1902).

During this period a new injection of Calvinism, this time of purely Dutch origin, began to play a significant role in bringing about an even more conservative Calvinist orientation in the Boer Republics than was prevalent in the Cape Colony where the Afrikaners and the British coexisted more or less peacefully side by side. But even in the Cape liberal theology never really succeeded in finding a foothold, not least because of the influence of Scottish ministers who came to serve in the Dutch Reformed Church. They brought with them an orthodox evangelical piety that did not differ substantially from the Reformed Pietism that was part and parcel of Afrikaner spirituality in the Cape.

---

5. F. Ernst Stoeffler, *The Rise of Evangelical Pietism* (Leiden: E. J. Brill, 1965), pp. 117-21.

The twentieth century saw the beginning of an important new development. Because of the awakening of Afrikaner nationalism during the latter half of the previous century, strengthened by the suffering of the Boer War, the idea of a *volkskerk* (a church of the people) took firm root among the Afrikaners and became part of their spiritual make-up. The idea of a *volkskerk* was much more than a merely theoretical identification of church and people. It took concrete shape in the church's concern for the plight of the impoverished Afrikaners who trekked in large numbers to the cities after the Boer War. The nationalist aspirations also made themselves felt in the educational field, where the battle for what was called Christian-national education was directed against British cultural imperialism. Eventually an attempt was made to restructure not only Afrikaner, but South African society as a whole — radically and fundamentally according to Afrikaner ideals and aspirations. This was supported by the sometimes outspoken, but mostly unspoken, desire to reshape the South African world once and for all in terms of a newly defined Afrikaner ideology.

It is remarkable that they came very close to succeeding, to a great extent due to the fact that they gave this worldview a religious basis, distinctively Christian and Calvinist in the way it was presented. A firm injection of Kuyperian neo-Calvinism played a not insignificant role in this development. The end result was a kind of "civil religion" that not only had an exceptional resilience but also an extraordinary power of persuasion among the Afrikaners, with dissident voices few and far between.

The whole concept of an Afrikaner "civil religion" which, in the course of the twentieth century, eventually developed into the ideology of apartheid is controversial and the theme of many a historical debate, especially as far as its origins are concerned.[6] I do not intend to enter this debate. I am only interested in it insofar as, in the first place, it provided the theoretical and ideological basis for a political strategy to deal with the problem of pluralism and, in the second place, it devel-

6. T. D. Moody, *The Rise of Afrikanerdom: Power, Apartheid and the Afrikaner Civil Religion* (Berkeley: University of California Press, 1975); John W. de Gruchy, "English-Speaking South Africans and Civil Religion," *Journal of Theology for Southern Africa* 19 (June 1977); I. Hexham, *The Irony of Apartheid: The Struggle for National Independence of Afrikaner Calvinism Against British Imperialism* (New York: The Edwin Mellen Press, 1981); A. J. Botha, *Die Evolusie van 'n Volksteologie* (Bellville: UWC, 1986).

oped into a very powerful social substratum which underpinned the notion that South Africa was a Christian country and which kept the South African "public square" from being secular and empty.

Although not justifiable, the lure of the Afrikaner ideology of apartheid becomes almost understandable when viewed against the complexities of the context within which it developed. It provided the rationale for dealing by social engineering with the perceived threat of an overwhelming pluralistic society within which Afrikaners saw themselves as an endangered minority group. This not only applied (and still applies) to their coexistence with the great majority of black Africans of various ethnic groupings, but also to their daily exposure to the pervasive influence of English cultural and economic power. Although apartheid as such was never directed against the white English-speaking section of South Africa, the mindset of an apartheid worldview inclined towards a disposition of self-consciousness and self-interest and even a tendency towards isolation from "alien" influences. The fact that the majority of English-speaking South Africans fell in with apartheid as a political device made no difference to this basic Afrikaner attitude. The Afrikaner's history made inconceivable the idea of cultural assimilation with the English.

The existence of Afrikaans churches, schools, universities, cultural organizations, et cetera gave the feeling of security against outside influences, a feeling strengthened by the knowledge that these institutions were protected, directly or indirectly, by legislation and an Afrikaner-friendly government. Above all there was the conviction, mostly unspoken, that Afrikaner (predominantly Calvinist) religion formed the basis of the Afrikaner ideals and aspirations embraced by these institutions. Even the Afrikaner political parties were considered by many to be imbued with religion at their very roots, and to some were a seamless extension of the church.

In this way the Afrikaner civil religion not only tried to deal with the threats inherent in pluralism, but also enabled Afrikanerdom to make its influence felt in the public sphere out of all proportion to its numbers. Hence the myth of South Africa as a Christian country, not in the sense that the vast majority of South Africans were nominal Christians, but that the South African civil society as such was penetrated with Christian values.

The notion of a Christian civil society was upheld by the very obvious influence of the Afrikaner churches in the formulation of public policies. Apart from the fact that cabinet ministers, National Party members of parliament, and senior officials of the civil service were generally members of the Afrikaans churches, these churches tried to influence public policy directly by resolutions taken at official meetings. Although the overt and official theological justification of apartheid only took on its final form two decades after the National Party had come to power, some of the early building bricks of the apartheid edifice, the Mixed Marriages Act and Section 16 of the Immorality Act, had been promulgated under the direct and public instigation of the Afrikaans churches, thereby strengthening the perception that the social structures engineered by the government were indeed Christian.

Apart from the theological justification of the policy of apartheid and the moral and theological support the Afrikaans churches lent to the war strategies of the security forces against the "total onslaught" of Communism during the seventies and eighties,[7] these churches saw it as their responsibility to influence public policy with special regard to education, welfare, and public morality.

A typical example of the churches' stance on matters that affected public life, reminiscent of their Puritan roots, was their insistence on legislation to enforce a formal public observance of the Sunday as a Sabbath. Even as late as the early nineties the Dutch Reformed Church waged a fierce battle to prevent the repeal of the legal prohibition of gambling and commerce on Sunday, declaring that "in a Christian country" no economic or other principles but those of Holy Scripture may determine legislation on commerce on Sunday.

The maintenance of the Christian character of public education was also high on the agenda. When the exclusion of Christian religious instruction and Biblical Studies from the school curriculum was propagated in the early nineties the Afrikaans churches vigorously campaigned for their continuation.

When one looks at the dominant role the Afrikaans churches had played in South African public life, it seems self-evident that the impact on these churches of the political abdication of the Afrikaner in 1994 had to be quite severe. To this we must now turn, although we

---

7. Jaap Durand and Dirkie Smit, *Kerk en Geweld: Teks en Konteks* (Bellville: UWC, 1994).

have to accept that a lack of historical distance makes it difficult to assess fully what is taking place.

Crisis of Identity and Spiritual Fragmentation

The first observation that I would like to make with regard to the reaction of the Afrikaans churches to the loss of Afrikaner political control is their rather muted response, not only after the elections of 1994 but even during the period in which the Afrikaner politicians were negotiating a new dispensation with the ANC. The Afrikaner political leaders were outpacing the religious leaders who, for their part, took on a wait-and-see attitude. This is quite remarkable when one takes into consideration that during the late eighties and the early nineties the Dutch Reformed Church (DRC), the biggest of the Afrikaner Reformed churches, had a particular hand in paving the way for the politicians to come to a negotiated settlement. The qualified criticism of apartheid by the document "Church and Society" adopted by the General Synod of the DRC in 1986 and the even more critical version in 1990 provided a moral foundation for those in the government who wished to dismantle apartheid.[8]

The first period of euphoria and the celebration of the South African "miracle" passed and with it the wait-and-see attitude. By 1998 the General Synod of the DRC received a report called *The DRC and the Transition to a New South Africa*. This report reveals that many members of the DRC have strong negative feelings about the so-called new South Africa because of the cumulative loss of political and cultural power, the negative impact on whites of affirmative action (retrenchments, loss of promotion and job opportunities of members), the diminished status of Afrikaans in public life, and the increase of crime, especially violent crime.

However, what is not clear from the report is the impact that the transition to democracy has had on the attitude of many members *to the DRC itself and the church's own self-perception.*

First and foremost I think it is fair comment to state that the

---

8. Etienne de Villiers, "The Influence of the DRC on Public Policy During the Late 80s and 90s" (unpublished paper, 2001).

DRC as the dominant Reformed Afrikaans church is experiencing a profound crisis of identity. Previously the DRC's self-consciousness as a church was not only determined by its Reformed faith and traditional forms of worship, but also by the experience of its nearness to its people *(volk)* as their spiritual bulwark against the forces that could so easily overwhelm them. The endorsement and justification of apartheid was part of this heritage. The dismantling of apartheid was therefore seen, by arguably the majority of members, not as the exchange of one political policy for another, but as a catastrophe that threatened a crucial part of their belief system and endangered their very existence. It was felt as a betrayal that the church, through its official organs, in the last decade before the political shift, started to criticize apartheid, albeit with qualifications, and eventually even went so far as to accept that apartheid had been a mistake. What the church for a long time had called the will of God suddenly became a mistake, even a sin.

The church is not only no longer the guarantor of the people's ideals and aspirations, but it has also lost its extensive influence over the public sector. There is little doubt in the minds of adherents of the Reformed Afrikaans churches that their churches have little or no influence at all on what is taking place in the public domain. For the first time in their existence the Afrikaans churches are faced with a secular state, a state that is indeed determined to make the public square secular and empty. The faith tradition of the Afrikaans Reformed churches, which confess a theocratic ideal for politics, has been replaced by a political dispensation based on a Bill of Rights. The name of God disappeared from the constitution, and all religions are now regarded as equal with one of the consequences being that Christian religious instruction in the public schools could eventually be phased out or relegated to a neutral comparative study of religions. The values that are to be promoted in the public sphere are not Christian values, but common human values as expressed in the Bill of Rights. Visible signs of these shifts can be seen in the rapid change of the face of South Africa on Sundays and in the moral tone set by public broadcasters and other media.

The crisis of identity that is caused by these developments has led to a pronounced uncertainty about the way forward within the ranks of these churches. Only an in-depth survey and analysis of what is happening will be able to determine possible future patterns of behavior. At the moment only a few trends can be discerned.

First, there seem to be enough indicators that, generally speaking, there is very little difficulty in adapting to a more secular public (and even private) lifestyle, for the simple reason that the old patterns of public behavior started to be eroded long before the previous political dispensation finally closed down. The efforts to contain pluralism had been only partially, and for a time, successful. Eventually the dam broke under a lot of pressure when the secularizing effects of pluralism were allowed fully to come into play.

Second, in this process a new sense of freedom began to prevail. There is a general feeling that the old authoritarian ways of enforcing moral and other forms of behavior have lost their validity and that the individual, including the individual believer and church member, is his or her own arbiter in matters of faith, religious practice, and ethics. This sense of being free from restrictive authority also creeps in when standpoints akin to modernist theology are being espoused in publications by theologians of the church with the view to placating those who are dissatisfied with what they perceive as a pre-modernist attitude in the church.

Third, while on the one hand there is the inclination to adapt to a more general secular lifestyle, there is on the other hand a very clear tendency to withdraw from any real involvement in public life. Concomitantly a new inward spirituality is beginning to manifest itself. This withdrawal into an inward spirituality in turn leads to a spiritual fragmentation that becomes visible in different forms of worship, not only in different congregations, but even within the same congregation where the older, more traditional members find their traditional way of worshiping challenged by the new, more informal and charismatic style of the youth. Some congregations now have separate services for these groups.

However, the spiritual fragmentation in the DRC is more than the result of a generation gap. It is the outward manifestation of the inner turmoil this church is going through. When it is said, justifiably, that the new inward form of worship in the DRC predominantly takes place among the youth, it must be kept in mind that this church had been able in the past to keep strict control over its youth and only allowed innovations within certain limits. Today the crisis of identity and the uncertainties caused by the completely new situation in which the church finds itself preclude it from giving clear and concise guidelines to the youth, and to those older members who feel themselves driven into the inner world of the spirit.

A Belated Enlightenment

As pointed out, we can trace the roots of the secularization process in the West to the breakdown of the medieval structures, although it only came to fruition in the Enlightenment which followed on the Renaissance and the Reformation. The Reformation itself was instrumental in changing the face of Europe. To a large extent the Reformation was made possible by the communication revolution brought about by the development of the printing press. Around 1500 printing conquered Europe and would reign supreme over the continent for the centuries to come. When in 1517 Martin Luther posted his propositions against indulgences on the doors of the church in Wittenberg, almost immediately the first modern press campaigns were unleashed throughout Europe in a flood of competing posters, pamphlets, and caricatures. The presses functioned at top capacity to distribute far and wide the works of the Reformer and his followers. Little control of any kind by the German rulers existed, even less by the Roman Catholic Church.

The written word is an instrument of power because it generates the force of public opinion. The Roman Catholic Church completely underestimated this power of public opinion and consequently lost control of the public square it had dominated. This led to a growing sense of freedom and an individualistic piety that gradually became indifferent to the many religious observances and rituals of official church practices. This in turn led to a religious fragmentation of society, giving room, inter alia, for the radical reformation of Anabaptist groups. Sociologically the Protestant orthodoxy of the seventeenth century, including English Puritanism, could be seen as so many unsuccessful efforts to bring back some doctrinal order in the religious fragmentation that had taken place. At the same time they tried to form a bulwark against a rampant humanism that originated in the Renaissance, espousing the supreme authority of scientific knowledge and rationality that came to fruition in the Enlightenment of the eighteenth and nineteenth centuries and started the secularization of Europe.

South Africa escaped this development. Because of the remoteness of Europe, the orthodox Pietism of the Europeans who settled in the Cape was never seriously threatened by humanism. The subsequent history, especially of the Afrikaners, tells us the reason why the secular forces that engulfed Europe were kept at bay in South Africa. But this could not continue forever. South Africa's turn has come.

The similarities between what happened in Europe and the present situation in South Africa are quite amazing: the powerful role of the media and the secularizing effect of a pluralism that has, now, taken on global proportions, the loss of religious control over the public square, the start of a religious fragmentation, these and other sociological phenomena that seem to be ingredients of times of transition. But it is perhaps after all not so amazing. The same forces are at work.

Whether the outcome will be the same is of course another matter. In South Africa the process of secularization takes place against the backdrop of a black African population that is deeply religious and with a tradition and a human value system that differ fundamentally from those of their white compatriots. They are, of course, also exposed to the secularizing effect of a global pluralism. The outcome, however, is not predictable, because history is not predictable.

Christianity and Globalism

Graham Ward

Let me begin by stating that this is a theological study. By that I mean that this essay is not a survey of Christian responses to the cultural phenomenon labeled "globalism." While recognizing that the practices of faith communities, Christian or otherwise, constitute sociological subsystems that play out various anti- and pro-systemic functions with respect to globalism, this essay is not a survey of such responses from a sociological perspective. Beyer[1] and Castells[2] have examined the effects of globalism in terms of the New Christian Right in America, suggesting Christian fundamentalism as one key response to global economics and polity. Beyer also gives an account of liberation theology's response to global culture and explores other "fundamentalist" (Jewish and Islamic) critiques of Westernization and liberal democracy. Mayer,[3] Shahla,[4] and Tehranian[5] provide more in-depth studies of what is taken as the most radical fundamentalist response to globalization in

1. Peter Beyer, *Religion and Globalization* (London: Sage, 1994).
2. Manuel Castells, *The Rise of the Network Society* (Oxford: Blackwell, 1996).
3. Elizabeth Ann Mayer, "Fundamentalist Impact on Law, Politics, and Constitutions in Iran, Pakistan, and the Sudan," in Martin E. Marty and R. Scott Appleby, eds., *Fundamentalisms and the State* (Chicago: University of Chicago Press, 1993).
4. Shahla Haeri, "Obedience versus Autonomy: Women and Fundamentalism in Iran and Pakistan," in Marty and Appleby, *Fundamentalisms*.
5. Majid Tehranian, "Islamic Fundamentalism in Iran and the Discourse of Development," in Marty and Appleby, *Fundamentalisms*.

post-revolutionary Iran. And Lechner[6] offers an interesting insight into the "global turn" in sociology with respect to the analysis of fundamentalism, countering the thesis that fundamentalism is a form of antimodernism. But what interests me more, working from within the tradition-based thinking of Christianity, working as a Christian theologian, are the relays and exchanges, the correspondences and differences between what is going on in còntemporary globalism and the universalist logics of the Christian faith. In a sense what I am asking in this essay is a question about different forms of participation in a cosmic system (or, at least, a system with a cosmic vision). Let me offer two illustrations, each demonstrating a certain parallelism which this essay is concerned to explicate more fully.

Tale of Two Economies I

At the end of Matthew's Gospel the risen Jesus makes the following proclamation: "All authority in heaven and on earth has been given to me. Therefore go and make disciples of all nations, baptising them in the name of the Father and of the Son and of the Holy Spirit" (Matt. 28:18-19). It is one of the foundational texts for Christian missiology. The endings of the two other synoptic Gospels — Mark and Luke — contain similar, but not as elaborate statements (although scholars recognize that the last nine verses of Mark's Gospel are not found in earlier and more reliable manuscripts). What Matthew's statement makes plain is two major theological transpositions affected by the coming of the Christ. First, there is the transposition from the ethnic specificities of Judaism to the universalism of the Christ through the liturgical practice of baptism in the name of the trinitarian God. Second, there is a transposition from a kingdom whose domain is either "within you" or brought "near to you" to a more spatial and territorial understanding of the kingdom. In Matthew's day there were more Jewish people living in the Diaspora than Palestine itself, but nevertheless the picture of the cosmic Christ possessing all authority in heaven and on earth and the strong imperative to go into all nations implies (as the Apostle

6. Frank J. Lechner, "Global Fundamentalism," in William H. Swatos, ed., *A Future for Religion* (London: Sage, 1993), pp. 27-32.

Paul himself inferred) that the community of the faithful would be made up not just of those drawn directly from the Jewish genetic pool and therefore not just within the geography of the Diaspora. The significance of the Council of Jerusalem in which the apostolic church not only recognized Paul but endorsed his ministry among the Gentiles, and the allegorical reading of Abraham's two sons in Paul's letter to the Galatians, cannot be underestimated. The Gentiles were now included in a new covenant, a new dispensation of God's grace. The Jewish Messiah pointed Judaism towards its global horizons, and the kingdom, which Jesus spoke of as "within" or "near," has taken on a colonial dynamic.

The writer of Luke's Gospel dramatizes this theological cataclysm and the spatial determination of the kingdom it effected: "repentance and forgiveness of sins will be preached in his name to all nations, beginning at Jerusalem" (Luke 24:47). Jerusalem, which had gathered together Jewish people from all over the known world for the Passover (when the Christ was crucified), would be the epicenter for the new cosmic reorganization. The writer of Luke's Gospel, in his Acts of the Apostles, narrates how the falling of Christ's Spirit upon the disciples — the anointing of which authorized and empowered them to preach the gospel — came during the Feast of Tabernacles when "Parthians, Medes and Elamites; residents of Mesopotamia, Judea and Cappadocia, Pontus and Asia, Phrygia and Pamphylia, Egypt and the parts of Libya near Cyrene; visitors from Rome (both Jews and converts to Judaism); Cretans and Arabs" (Acts 2:9-11) were all assembled in Jerusalem once more. Peter preached, and "three thousand were added to their number that day" (Acts 2:41). The global mission in the name of a universalist salvation had begun.

As Wallerstein observes with respect to the establishment of the early world-system in the late fifteenth and early sixteenth centuries, the rate of globalization is governed by overcoming territorial particularity by technological means.[7] We will be continually discovering the double axes of technology and expansion. The early church flourished in its own way but became increasingly fragmented under persecution. The

---

7. Immanuel Wallerstein, *The Modern World-System: Capitalist Agriculture and the Origins of the European World-Economy in the C16* (London: Academic Press, 1974), pp. 15 and 16.

degree to which Jerusalem remained its first mother church, followed later by Rome, is still uncertain. But there is little doubt that a major upturn in the expansion of Christianity came with the conversion of Constantine in 312 and the Edict of Milan issued in 313. The Edict, while granting religious freedom throughout the Roman Empire, was the first step in constituting Christianity as the religion of the Empire. It explicitly sought and associated divine favor with the Imperial common weal. Constantine himself wrote that "My design then was, first, to bring diverse judgements formed by all nations respecting the Deity to a condition, as it were, of settled uniformity; and, second, to restore the health tone to the system of the world."[8] His sentiments express here a new political theology being forged at the time by Eusebius of Caesarea in his *Ecclesiastical History:* that Constantine was a second Augustus, and like Augustus (who had created the conditions of worldwide unity and peace for the coming of the Christ), the vehicle for the Providence of the Christian God. Eusebius forged a rhetorical link between the Christian church and the military technologies of the late Roman Empire. He did this by weaving together, in his propagandizing texts, two distinct economies — the theological and the political. Christian cosmology was now inseparable from its teaching on the salvation of the world and imperial ambitions. Constantine himself turned rhetoric into activity, by (a) forging the systemic links that lay the foundations for Christendom and (b) fighting Donatists and Arians, and so establishing the ideological parameters of the *corpus Christianorum*. The Imperial administrative and military networks provided Christianity with the means for expansion; the means of developing a logic at the heart of its monotheistic *credo:* "After the victory of the Milian Bridge [312 CE], Christianity was never again to lack an imperial patron."[9]

With the fragmentation and decline of the Empire itself, Christianity was enabled, even required, to expand and establish (with Latin as the *lingua universalis*) the integrating infrastructures upon which Western European civilization emerged from the Dark Ages into the glories of the various forms of Renaissance from the twelfth century onwards.

8. W. H. C. Frend, *The Rise of Christianity* (London: Darton, Longman and Todd, 1984), p. 487.
9. Frend, *The Rise of Christianity*, pp. 482-83.

Tale of Two Economies II

When Christendom itself dissolved — as fledgling nation-states grew stronger and schism racked the body of the church — Christianity underwent a second major transformation that adapted it for the new forms of expansionism and imperialism that arose in the late fifteenth and early sixteenth centuries with respect to another economy: capitalism. Following the forced entrenchment of the Holy Roman Empire by the advancing Ottoman Turks — where territories of an earlier expansion by the crusades were brought under Arab dominion — Christianity's imperial ambitions were now channeled by both a new colonialism and a universalization of its own identity in terms of "religion." That is, the several voyages — first of exploration and then of colonization (which were undertaken as much on theological as economic and political grounds) — paralleled the rise of the generic category of "religion." "Religion" is what Constantine dreamed of when he sought to "bring diverse judgements formed by all nations respecting the Deity to a condition, as it were, of settled uniformity." Still, in fifteenth-century England, to speak of "religions" was to speak about the various monastic orders; and to speak of secular was to speak of those things outside of such orders. Thus "a secular cleric" was not the oxymoron it would be by the eighteenth century. This followed a line of usage found throughout the Medieval period and summed up by Aquinas: "religion" was a practice or discipline of Christian piety. Christianity itself was not a religion, it was the faith.

But by the late fifteenth century the word was coming to be employed to describe the universal grammar binding various forms of Christian practice by two leading Renaissance thinkers: Nicholas of Cusa and Marsilio Ficino. Gradually, as new lands and new peoples were being encountered, and the journals, letters, and narratives of those encounters were laying the basis for the new science of ethnography, so "religion" became a rhetorical tool for a new universalism. The need, following the warring factions of the Reformation, for a political and theological *détente,* gave "religion" social and political force. Its demythologization and demystification was well underway in the seventeenth century, when the "true religion" was understood by philosophers such as Lord Herbert of Cherbury as that which constituted a universal moral order. With Locke this moral order became the foundation for public truth, individual responsibility, and civil government. Nevertheless, and this remains significant, "religion's" universalism issued in and through Christianity. Religion was demythologized and demystified Christianity. Some would argue, myself among them, that since the development of "religion" as a concept in early nineteenth-century Germany with Schleiermacher and Hegel, it has always remained a Christian concept.

"Religion" became a category that eventually led in the nineteenth century to the study of religions developed by Christian thinkers. The word concentrated and bound together several cultural trends: an anthropological attention to the general condition of being human, a move towards viewing ethics as the common denominator for this human condition, and the development of the concept Nature. Through thinkers like the mid–seventeenth-century Cambridge Platonists, Christianity became conceived in terms of a natural and therefore universal theology. So Peter Sterry could advise in 1675 in his *Discourse of the Freedom of the Will*:

> Look upon every person through this *two-fold Glass, the Blood, and Beauties of Christ. Christ hath died for all*. The *natural being* of every person hath his *Rest* in the *Grave of Christ*, and is watered with his blood. *Christ lives in all*. His *Resurrection* is the *life* of the *whole Creation*. He is the *Wisdom*, the *Power*, the *Righteousness* of God in every work of *Nature* as well as of *Grace*. He is the *Root* out of which every *natural*, as well as *spiritual* Plant springs, which brings forth himself through every natural existence, and brings forth himself out of it, as the *flower*, the *brightest of the Glory of God*.[10]

Hence people everywhere came under the influence of Christ. The Christ-as-Logos Christologies of Alexandrian theology of the third century enter a new stage of development, coupled now with territorial expansion.

The territorial expansion would have been impossible without advances in technology: new weaponry, new measuring instruments like the quadrant and the compass, better forms of shipbuilding, for example. The technically minded John Donne, in a sermon delivered in

10. Peter Harrison, *"Religion" and the Religions in the English Enlightenment* (Cambridge: Cambridge University Press, 1990), p. 127.

1622 to the Honourable Company of the Virginian Plantation, was quick to theologize these developments, speaking of them in terms of God's unfolding Providence: "*God* taught us to make Ships, not to transport our selves, but to transport him."[11] In 1627, the Dutch theologian and lawyer, Hugo Grotius, in the introduction to his influential book *De Religione Christianae,* opens the first section of Book I with a reference to the technocratic fame of Dutch seamen. He writes what will become a systematic account of Christianity in which "variety of opinions is limited within certain bands, in which all men are agreed" so that these seamen in their voyaging may confute errors. "[F]or they can never want matter, but in their long voyages will every where meet either with pagans, as in Chine or Guinea, or Mahometans, as in the Turkish or Persian Empires, and the kingdoms of Fez and Morocco; and also the Jews." The technological possibilities of preaching the gospel to all nations go hand in hand with the development of a theology that makes conversion to Christ a matter of recognizing the truth of the human situation and the created order.[12] A new egalitarianism, a brotherhood of mankind, is announced in which God's justice is rendered evident; the particularities of redemption in Christ are now globally available. Natural knowledge revealed broad *a priori* moral truths, which in Benjamin Whichcote's words are "concurrent with the sense of heathens and strangers, who do agree with us in all instances of morality." Thomas More concurred: "And therefore we cannot say that every Idolatrous Heathen must perish eternally."

There were various strands of Calvinism, Platonism, and Arminianism that gave subtle shades to these emerging theologies of religion — on the whole Roman Catholics and Muslims were still beyond redemption. Furthermore, the development of the generic and globalizing category of religion owed much to the political need for peace in

11. John Donne, *Selected Prose,* ed. Neil Rhodes (Harmondsworth, Middlesex: Penguin Books, 1987), p. 191.

12. The cultural historian, Perry Miller, observes how this theologizing of the technological was evident in the nineteenth century and gave a moral value to transportation: in 1848 "James L. Batchelder could declare that the Almighty himself had constructed the railroad for missionary purposes and, as Samuel Morse prophesied with the first telegraphic message, the purpose of the invention was not to spread the price of pork but to ask the question 'What Hath God Wrought?'" See Perry Miller, *The Life of the Mind in America* (New York: Harcourt, Brace and World, 1965), p. 52.

many Western European countries following years of civil warfare conducted on the basis of conflicting Christian creeds. Natural theology, like the appeal to discover a universal language, an *Ursprach,* by the seventeenth-century Bishop Wilkins, was a response to a set of contingent political circumstances. Nevertheless, what is evident is also a further unfolding of a logic at the heart of the Christian understanding of the redemption of the world.

Wallerstein in his monumental history of world trade and the development of a capitalist world-system views economics as the dynamic for modernization and globalization. He gives hardly any place to theological dynamics which, in fact, governed (even regulated) economic policy throughout the Medieval and Renaissance periods.[13] This is an oversight, for territorial expansion and the development of the world-system was, throughout the fifteenth and sixteenth centuries, a matter for intense theological discussion particularly by the Jesuits who were profoundly involved with missionary ventures. One only needs to read the newly restored journal of Christopher Columbus to observe how central evangelization and conversion was to the enterprise:

> Your Majesties, being Catholic Christians and rulers devoted to the Holy Christian Faith and dedicated to its expansion and combatting the religion of Mahomet and all the idolatries and heresies, decided to send me, Christopher Columbus, to those lands of India to meet their rulers and see the towns and lands and their distribution, and all other things, and to find out in what manner they might be converted to our Holy Faith.[14]

When we return the developments of Western Christianity into the picture we can perhaps understand globalism as issuing from a certain cultural, rather than simply economic program. Wallerstein raises an interesting question as to why Europe rather than China entered the

---

13. Keynes (1936) had taken some account of Medieval economics. He drew his distinction between savings and investment on the basis of his investigations. But his interpretation of usury has been challenged by Bernard Dempsey (1943) and, more recently, Stephen Long (2000).

14. John Cummins, *The Voyage of Christopher Columbus: Columbus' Own Journal of Discovery Newly Restored and Translated* (London: Weidenfeld and Nicholson, 1992), p. 81.

theater of world-trading, exploration, and colonization in the late fifteenth century. Agreeing with and quoting the work of William Willetts, he answers that "this has something to do with the *Weltanschauung* of the Chinese. They lacked, it is argued, a sort of colonizing mission because, in their arrogance, they were already the whole of the world."[15] I would argue that the colonizing mission felt by several European nations — but first and foremost Catholic Spain and Portugal — is endemic to the Spirit of Christianity, which forever saw the other nations beyond itself lacking a salvation it was its duty to offer. Christian missiology thus plays a part alongside embryonic mercantile covetousness and territorial ambitions in the development of the capitalist world-system. After all, these expeditions and explorations were profoundly speculative; they ran risks that required vision and drew on imaginations fired by more than simple acquisitiveness or opportunity costing. As sociologists and historians like Max Weber[16] and R. H. Tawney[17] (1924) pointed out, Western capitalism (and the material exchanges prior to formal monetary systems) is implicated in mindsets, habits, and household disciplines established by Christian practices of the faith. As several economists have also pointed out (Hayek and Hirsch, most prominently) the practice and the theory of economics issues from and proceeds upon a moral legacy of truth and promise, fiduciary and redemptive acts, construals of freedom. It was a legacy first forged in Christendom and later rendered universal when "religion" devolved theological particularity into ethical normativity. A residual Christianity, in terms of its reduction to moral values, still makes possible the persuasive power of economic policy and informs the arguments engendered by any such policy. Economists like Hayek, Novak, and Schumpeter are steeped in liberal ethics. The debates over whether markets have agency, or have outcomes that can be foreseen (and prevented), and the debates concerning scarcity, opportunity costs, and distributional justice are all still dependent on a moral legacy bequeathed by Christianity.[18] A more recent theological voice has drawn

15. Wallerstein, *The Modern World-System,* p. 55.

16. Max Weber, *The Protestant Ethic and the Spirit of Capitalism* (London: Routledge, 1992).

17. R. H. Tawney, *Religion and the Rise of Capitalism* (Harmondsworth, Middlesex: Penguin Books, 1984).

18. The move away from the gold standard in the mid-1970s suggests a major

attention to the cultural currents that bring together Christian theology and economics in terms I will develop below. In a chapter entitled "Christianity and the Capitalism of the Spirit," Mark C. Taylor writes:

> The Spirit of God represented in the eucharistic wafer is the currency of exchange, which establishes the identity of differences within the godhead and mediates the opposition between divinity and humanity throughout the history of salvation. . . . Hegel's speculative philosophy actually anticipates the aestheticization of money, which characterizes postindustrial capitalism. In the late twentieth century, something approximating the Hegelian Absolute appears in global networks of exchange where money is virtually immaterial. When read through Hegel's logical analysis of Spirit, it becomes clear that money is God in more than a trivial sense.[19]

Where Latin American liberation theologians lament the disparity between the monetary and the divine economies, Taylor conflates the two. From the perspective of a Christian worldview economics cannot function as an autonomous force — that would accept the autonomy of the secular, which in turn would constitute a Gnostic heresy. On the other hand, the tradition-based reasoning by Christian theologians has to read economic discourse, insofar as it is possible, in terms of its own tradition. For, following Adam Smith, the discipline has accepted the secular worldview, and developed as a discourse concerned only with the logic of immanent activities that are without transcendent significance. What Christianity seeks, then, with respect to its examination of economics, is threefold: first, the nature of the desire economics represents and the relationship of that desire to the wider cultural and political ethos; second, an understanding of its own history and teachings with respect to the development and effects of that desire; third, a critical judgment concerning that secular desire and its effects. The judgment is necessarily provisional, since all Christian

---

shift in monetary economies from that moral legacy in which "promissary notes" ought to be redeemed, in which there are certain deontological duties that underpin economic exchange mechanisms.

19. Mark C. Taylor, *About Religion: Economics of Faith in Virtual Culture* (Chicago: University of Chicago Press, 1999), pp. 154-58.

judgments await the final unveiling of the truth in the eschaton. The judgment is the telos of the examination, but the beginning of a process of amelioration. For the call would be to a new disciplining of that desire with respect to being faithful to the call of Christ. So, for example, for Christianity, global capitalism can only be a figure, a substitute, a surrogate for a misplaced desire for God. Capitalism cannot be a ground-base, a natural and empirically verifiable dynamic upon which a master-narrative of explanation for cultural change is founded. Substitution and surrogacy are fundamental to the exchange mechanisms described in economics, so it is what capitalism is figuring, what it is a substitute for, that Christian-based thinking investigates. Taylor, for example, like Hayek, figures capitalism as freedom; freedom defined as unfettered desire. The glamour of globalism, the seductive appeal of its internationalism, figure, I suggest, infinite desire — which, at times, is expressed the other way round: a desire for the infinite.

Global Flows: Economies of Signs

To proceed with the examination of globalism, by Christianity, requires returning to one of the fundamental orienting principles of Christian thinking and faithful practice. It is necessary to understand the importance of being caught between a memory of an inaugural past, a certain present realization, and the anticipation for what is not-yet. Christian believers participate in a time-displacement, when viewed theologically. This is a participation in an eschatological mindset rooted in a divine economy, as I shall explain. It is the nature of this participation that we need to explore further, because it is here that we can best understand contemporary conceptions of globalism as revisiting (kindly put), parodying (more harshly put), or peddling secular kitsch versions (most critically put), of Christian conceptions. In other words, developing the last section on the universalism of the category "religion" — globalism can be understood as one more dissemination of a Christian *logos*. Hence, the importance of showing why the generic term "religion" issues from Christianity and still effects a Christianization in the "study of religions" even when those other "religions" are far from being practices of the Christian faith. Put in this way, it could be that Christianity, then, is able to facilitate the most far-reaching critique of globalism (understood both economically and culturally) by exposing its transcendental dreams and concealed aspirations. Globalism is a historical production with a profound Christian pedigree.

The divine economy in the Christian faith is conceived in terms of the nature of the triune God and the operation of the divine in the creation, maintenance, and salvation world. The triune God is not the deist concept of an ultimate point outside and beyond the creaturely realm. Rather, God as source of all is incarnate in the Son, Jesus Christ, by and through whom all things were created, and the Spirit forever negotiates the reciprocity of the love between the Father and the Son. Technically, these are termed the trinitarian processions — each being called forth by, and returning to, the other. The early Greek Fathers described the dynamic of the Trinity as perichoretic — a circling dance. Creation issues from the heart of a profound givenness or emptying of one towards the other in the Trinity, as such "processions" become "missions" or "sendings out." All that is, is then held to be so because of the operation of the divine economy within creation. Things have no value of themselves. In fact, things do not exist in and of themselves. All things only have value with respect to the fact that they are gifted, given from and maintained by the presence of God. It is as if all things, when held up to the light of God, would reveal the watermark of Christ within them. Things cannot be things, that is reified (in both the Latin and later Marxist understanding of that term), unless prized from their participation in the divine economy and, hence, alienated from the ongoing work of the Creator.

The founding exchange mechanisms of economics can only come about, therefore, through such a reification and alienation in which the Good is calculated and calibrated according to "goods." This reification and alienation is much more profound than the capitalist's tearing asunder of the laborer from the products of his or her labor. Marx only uncovered the secular logic of "things." What makes possible his thinking is a certain opacification of the natural which took place much earlier than industrialism. In this opacification of the natural and sacramental, the world is mechanized and understood in terms of positivist facts and calculable empiricisms. Put briefly, the difference between the sacramental and the secular worldviews is a question concerning the nature of the economy in which one is participating: the divine economy or the secular economics. And just as Nietzsche was correct in recognizing that when men killed God they then replaced him, so secular economics reinscribes divine economy within its immanent logics. As such the discourses on contemporary globalism, which speak in heady, ecstatic terms of the collapse of geographical space, the erasure of national and continental boundaries, the electronic flows of capital investment, and the cultural polysemy — of drinking Chilean wines, in (now affordable) Italian clothes, from glasses made in China, while sitting on Shaker-designed chairs produced from Swedish pine and lit by candles refined from North Sea oil — make manifest, materially, the attributes of God: omnipotence, omniscience, and omnipresence. The vast homogenizing, synthesizing, and integrating dynamics of globalism will perfect the realization of Spinoza's monism: God is the one substance of which all else are modifications. Put more briefly, globalism is not a policy or an operation, but more like an environment, an atmosphere. It implicitly possesses and promotes a cosmology. The cosmology has close affinities with the stoic model of the world in which all things are interconnected or analogically related. Globalism is, then, the final step in the cultural logic of secularism in which the world becomes God. It is also, not only from a Christian perspective but from the perspective of *Kulturkritiks* like Adorno, the logic of idolatry.[20]

We find the same logic at work in the development and deepening of cyberspace. Without the telecommunication technologies sustaining virtual reality, globalism would not be possible. Digitalization and simulacra, optic fibers and electronic mailing are the driving force behind the realization of the global project. But, again, beneath the hype of cybernauts immersed in metaphors of light, cruising weightlessly and anonymously along highways of information that dissolve time, location, cultural context, and identity, lie Christian accounts of heaven, life beyond bodily imperfections and limitations, angels and angelic knowledge. Manuel Castells has called real virtuality the final turn of secularism.[21] Globalization and the expansion of the virtually real are not creating parallel universes — the one imaginary and the

20. See Theodore H. Adorno, "On the Fetish Character in Music and the Regression of Listening," in *The Culture Industry* (London: Routledge, 1991), pp. 29-60, where he expounds the logic of commodity production where use-value is minimalized and the "consumer is really worshipping the money he has paid" for the items. "Goods" now become fetishes, erotically charged objects of a displaced desire.
21. Castells, *The Rise*.

other real — they are collapsing the distinction between the imaginary and the real. Hence Castells's "real virtuality." The world is now recreated again, only more perfectly, as simulacra. This is the realization of the ancient dreams for the effect of *poiesis* — in Aristotle and Renaissance Platonists like Sir Philip Sidney: redeeming the world through creating it again, imaginatively. But alongside the virtual perfecting is an explicit costing: digitalization is the final step in commodification. For what was once reified through the opacification of nature is now reproduced virtually in megabytes.

Globalism, then, as the construction of a world-system (of not just economic but cultural interdependence) is one more attempt by human beings to become divine. It is the continuation of a Prometheanism that goes back to the famous *Oration of the Dignity of Man* by Pico della Mirandola at the end of the fifteenth century. And the desire behind the drive is infinite freedom. Freedom, defined as the infinite possibilities for choice; frictionless freedom proscribed by no bounds, either physical, cultural, or historical. This is what sells it and persuades us of its value.

But what is this infinite freedom? It must be that which lies beyond choice; since the expression of choice, since choosing itself, implies limitation. To be able to have all things simultaneously, to possess the fullness of the present as present — only this can fulfill the dreams of infinite choice. Adorno was quick to point out that this was another aspect of fetishism: "The appearance of immediacy is as strong as the compulsion of exchange value is inexorable."[22] Hence one of the key elements of global culture, as Paul Virilio recognized, is speed; perfection is instantaneousness. Perhaps then the desire behind the drive is actually one for oblivion, or what Michel de Certeau calls "white ecstasy." Certeau describes this ultimate *jouissance* in a language culled from various world-faiths. In a conversation constructed between two men meeting on a mountain, Simeon the monk speaks of the "final bedazzlement" in which there is "an absorption of objects and subjects in the act of seeing. No violence, only the unfolding presence. Neither fold nor hole. Nothing hidden and thus nothing visible. A light without limits, without difference; neuter, in a sense, and continuous."[23] This

22. Adorno, *The Culture Industry*, p. 38.
23. Michel de Certeau, "White Ecstasy," trans. Frederick Christian Bauerschmidt

"silent ecstasy," this transcendence that comes from recognizing all particularities are infinitely reproducible and reducible to a digital coding and a pixel imaging; this transcendence that comes from seizing the presence of things in the present and understanding all locations as infinitely transferable; this transcendence that comes from the radical realization of immanence — has other names: Heidegger's and Derrida's "end of metaphysics"; Fukuyama's "end of history"; Jaron Lanier's (the man who coined the term "virtual reality")[24] "experience of infinity"; Deleuze and Guattari's "deterritorialization"; Lyotard's "body without organs"; Baudrillard's "hyperreality"; Arthur Danto's "the end of art"; consumer satisfaction; the apotheosis of free-trade; and the call for the complete transparency of institutional operations by government agencies.

The espousal of radical immanence is, ultimately, the abandonment of oneself to an impersonal and capricious logic that levels everything and locks individuals into a desire for death.[25] It is a contemporary turn in Nietzsche's *amor fati*. Globalism is the ultimate synthesis of the Freudian psyche: the libidinal economy becomes the death drive. Enforced universal democratization is the Freudian *stasis*, the zero degree dressed in the neoliberal language of freedom. Thomas Friedman, who has written one of the most popular books on globalization, observes that he is frequently asked "Is God in cyberspace?" His answer is indicative of one of the axioms of globalization: "There is no place in today's world where you encounter the freedom to choose that God gave man than in cyberspace." Freedom of choice is harnessed to movement here albeit in an illusory manner — illusory because to choose is

---

and Catriona Hanley, in Graham Ward, ed., *The Postmodern God* (Oxford: Blackwell, 1997), p. 157.

24. Jaron Lanier and Frank Biocca, "An Insider's View of the Future of Virtual Reality," in *Journal of Communication* 42, no. 4 (1992): 150-72.

25. With disturbing prescience, prior to the information age Adorno wrote: "Today the curious individual becomes a nihilist. . . . The curiosity which transforms the world into objects is not objective: it is not concerned with what is known, but with the fact of knowing it, with having, with knowledge as a possession. This is precisely how the objects of information are organised today. Their indifferent character predestines their being and they are incapable of transcending the abstract fact of possession through any immanent quality of their own" (Adorno, *The Culture Industry*, p. 85).

not to move, and where one moves to (whether, in fact, we can even talk of "movement" at all) when space has collapsed under a rule of homogenization is a real question. Like creatures released from the pressures of gravity we float, we surf, we ride, we free-fall, we transcend a variety of human finitudes to become divine. To be global is to be divine: the most globalized figures (Hollywood film stars, sports and royal personalities, entrepreneurs like Soros, Gates, and Branson) are the stars in the new global galaxies that inspire cult following, the saints of a new form of veneration.

This is the very point at which Christianity can intervene, recalling globalism to one of its origins and pointing up the differences between parent and progeny. It can partly do this because, in the move from universalism (a hallmark of Christianity as "religion" and a hallmark of modernity in so many different guises) to globalism, Christianity as a practice is shaking off its affiliations with "religiousness" and reclaiming its tradition-based modes of reasoning. The implosion of liberalism under the pressure of pluralism has brought about the demise of theological liberalism, Christian liberalism in this case. And the response to this implosion is not necessarily fundamentalism or biblicalism, but new appeals to reclaiming insights of the past, new analyses of orthodoxies, of subject-forming practices in confessional communities. The new right thinking among evangelical Christians, as they move towards conservative Roman Catholicism, *is* a response to globalization, a purely counter-cultural response (which nevertheless often employs the latest in telecommunication skills). Because, in Christian teaching, the kingdom of God has not yet fully come — because, as I said earlier, Christian thinking is caught between memory, participation, and anticipation — there is always an element that remains counter-cultural. But it is an element, not a policy — an element that gives rise to Christianity as *Kulturkritik*. This will be important for what I wish to argue.

In the wake of the collapse of socialism (whose demise, like liberalism's, came because its operational logic demanded a dialectic between itself and that which was other — capitalism, in this case) a dialectic globalism imploded; in the wake of the collapse of socialism, theological reasoning is, perhaps, the only form of effective *Kulturkritik* with respect to globalism.[26] But effective cultural criticism cannot be done

26. The effectiveness of the *Kulturkritik* practiced by Adorno and Horkheimer

from a faith that polices its narratives and practices in order to create barricading walls against secular incursions. The rejection of theological liberalism in favor of tradition-based reasoning (which requires an academic investigation into the nature of the tradition and the nature of its orthodoxies) need not be simply counter-cultural. There is much within the tradition-based reasoning of Christianity that recognizes it is part of the world, not at war with it. Christianity cannot separate itself from the world. Its thinking epitomizes the tensions that Roland Robertson has termed "glocalization" — the way in which the local and particular are commodified for the global and endlessly reproducible. But in Christian thinking, the local community is given a density of significance in relation to the global body of Christ. From this new standing upon the grammar of the faith Christianity can point to similarities and differences, to degrees of participation. For in Christian thinking, freedom is not defined in terms of an individual's range of choices. Freedom is not customized and viewed in terms of the accumulation of commodities. Freedom is not constituted on the edges of a bad infinite. My freedom to choose affects other people's livelihoods, and maybe their freedom to choose. The Italian clothes I can now afford are made affordable by cheap, possibly sweatshop labor somewhere in the world, hidden so that I might not see it — might not see the consequences of my choosing. Globalism renders all communities and societies virtual realities. It turns individualism into a cosmic principle — hence the spirituality of globalism is inextricable from New Age self-enlightenment technologies and self-designed lifestyles.

Christian thinking counters such an atomism with its own accounts of participation. This does not mean, it cannot mean, that those who practice the Christian faith are not also involved in secular global operations. The new commercial cosmology deems that none of us is exempt — even the poor and destitute become necessary aspects of global economics. But it does mean that Christian living and believing

---

has always been a matter of debate. A dark pessimism and a pervasive nostalgia mark Adorno's writings. While he longs for a transcendence that might refigure the radical immanentism of commodity exchange, he finds no place for such a transcendence. He had looked for it in art, but the mass production of aesthetic objects has now rendered art "impotent really to accomplish the transcendence of existence" (Adorno, *The Culture Industry*, p. 74).

can act as an explicit critique of globalism's aspirations to transcend finitudes. It can do this in several ways, but what is important about these ways is that they are made possible on specific theological grounds, not moral grounds. This is crucial.

There has been a tradition since 1848, when facing some of the human consequences of industrialism, of a Christian social ethics. These ethics have pointed to the human suffering and degradation that result from various economic enterprises and government policies and prophetically called for justice and a fair distribution of the world's finite goods. As such, Christian social ethics formed alliances with a number of liberal humanitarian pressure-groups, dissolving its distinctive theological narratives and accepting a moral common ground. As we saw above, the universalization of Christianity through forming a generic "religion" functions to augment economic globalization. As Stephen Long has put it: "non-confessional theology has the same shape as the formal but contentless character of global capitalism. It recognizes 'value,' but not substantive and particular goods."[27] This is not simply Christianity colluding, this is Christianity co-opted — erasing difference in terms of fellow feeling and cooperation. In the wake of economic globalism and the pluralist culture, that liberal humanist, departicularized Christianity of moral common ground becomes difficult to maintain. It has lost its credibility.

Concurrently, those concerns with scarcity, the calculation of opportunity costs, and redistributive justice are rendered infinitely more complex. For scarcity is about objects and their optimal use. It is associated with a concrete world of finite things. For its operations to be defined it is assumed that both the exchange of these finite things and the world in which they can be exchanged can be represented transparently, objectively. That world no longer is there; that mode of representational innocence is no longer there — if, even with modernity, it was ever there. The goods that globalism trades in are more informational and electronic than material; new forms of poverty, wealth, and scarcity emerge. When scarcity is named we now have to ask where and what is being named, who is doing the naming, how the calculations for optimal use are being made, what is being left out of the equation (since

27. D. Stephen Long, *Divine Economy: Theology and the Market* (London: Routledge, 2000), p. 55.

something always is) and for what reason. "Scarcities" are produced, they are disseminated, they are ideologically freighted. They are not seen and identified from nowhere. They are shifting and shifted throughout global transactions. They are not fixed, nor can they be controlled or even comprehensively surveyed. So how can they be redistributed? The old concept of scarcity belongs to an identity politics that cannot operate in a virtual world. In fact, the virtual world — manned (quite literally) in the majority by cosmopolitan elites — knows no such concept. Its operational logic is excess and abundance: everything is available, at any time.[28] And therefore, as a corollary, what does distributional justice mean in a network society where distribution belongs to flows of space, flows of information, flows of signs, flows of persuasion? What does "social" mean as distinct from "cultural"?[29] What does public policy mean when the public is no longer an identifiable and discrete group of people, and when the power for policy-making, when power per se, is radically decentralized?

The critique of participation in a global culture can no longer be adequately based on liberal ethics, which was quickly assumed into Christian social ethics. The critique on the basis of the tradition-based reasoning is, then, a theological critique that calls into question several issues:

1. The language of transcendence with respect to globalism, which lends globalism a certain New Age spiritual coloring, involves a category mistake. For one cannot be the author of one's own transcendence. There can be certain alterations made to personal consciousness — by alcohol and other chemical substances, by lack of sleep, by the low flickering of fluorescent lighting in supermarkets and shopping malls, by sexual engagement, by speeding or participating in a fast roller-

---

28. Simon Cooper, "Plenitude and Alienation: The Subject of Virtual Reality," in David Holmes, ed., *Virtual Politics: Identity and Community in Cyberspace* (London: Sage, 1997), pp. 93-106.

29. One of the central thinkers on globalism, Immanuel Wallerstein, has recently observed: "Where can we find 'societies' other than in the minds of the analysts, or of the orators? Social science would, in my view, make a great leap forward if it dispensed entirely with the term" (Wallerstein, *The Politics of the World Economy* [Cambridge: Cambridge University Press, 1984], p. 2). Like "community," it trails a moral legacy that can mask its absence. I suggest what Christians need to consider now is not a social ethics but a cultural ethics.

coaster ride, by perspectives that warp spatial dimensions. But these experiences do not transcend the human condition; they alter the consciousness of what still remains, quite adamantly, a human subject. Globalism may infinitely extend the range of experiences open to an individual; it may constitute that individual by various means as a consumer of polyglot experiences — but its processes and operations are all immanent, all planetary, all concerned with a circle of exchange that is never broken and means, economically, there is no free lunch. Transcendence, as grace, is gifted, the recognition of giftedness; it cannot be an object of one's choosing. It cannot be reified at all. This leads us into the next critique of global participation that Christian thinking facilitates.

2. Transcendence is not, for Christianity, the obliteration of the finite. Its central appreciation of incarnation, of the divine made human, offers a positive account of finitude. The finite is completed, redeemed, by the divine — finds its proper direction, employment, and significance. The finite is not a world of things to be overcome. Finitude rather marks the limitations of human longing and ambition; sets them in their place and, in so doing, safeguards the human from the hubristic. The act of hubris is always an act of self-deification. The Christian logos first critiques, then, not the effects or the operations of globalization, but its Promethean drive. It is a drive related to free-market capitalism. But rather than offer some outdated socialist critique of capitalism *as such*, what Christian thinking provides is a certain theological pathology of the drive itself. Novak has consistently reiterated what Pico della Mirandola first proclaimed: "you decide who you are; you create yourself."[30] Globalism runs with that gospel. But it is not a Christian gospel. By critiquing the very drive of globalism Christianity can then examine its effects and operations. This leads directly to its function as culture-critique.

3. Christianity, because it not only shares so much with globalism but is, as I have argued, one of its roots, can point to the absence that haunts and produces global culture. For Christianity understands the virtual nature of the real. Its eschatological account of creation and its history establishes a tension between what was, what is, and what will

---

30. Michael Novak, *A Theology for Radical Politics* (New York: Herder and Herder, 1969), p. 36.

be. Nothing can be accepted merely at face value. Nothing can literally be what it seems to be. There is always a seeming, an appearing as. Put another way, the Christian worldview is fundamentally a semiotic one. Faith is a participation in the reading, production, and unfolding of signs — signs of the kingdom, signs of the incarnation, signs of the gospel, signs that receive their true significance only in the coming again of Christ. The global worldview is also, to follow Baudrillard (and exemplified most clearly in the digitalization of information), constituted in and through an economy of signs. But these signs are divorced from signifieds. They flow endlessly into other signs, referring only to other signs: signs that are simulacra, signs that like fashions, come and go in a hyperventilating ephemerality. Their *telos* is the open desert, the infinite stretches of barely imaginable freedom that drives desire forever onwards and bears eternally the pain of having to choose one thing over and against another. The economy of globalism's signs expresses and perpetuates the empty nihilism of globalism's transcendental dream of liberation.

Conclusion

And hence to judgment: while Christian living in Christ seeks to extend *communitas*, globalism customizes; while the Christian worldview "in Christ" proclaims a participation that renders us members of another and interdependent, globalism interconnects for its own functional purposes atomized VDU's; while Christian orthopraxis seeks that each may become all that God intend they become, globalism effects a policy of divide-and-rule (only no one is ruling now and the tyranny lies with the field of global operations themselves); while the ethics of the Good life "in Christ" preaches one thing, globalism's ethos of death, lack, and anemic infinite extols another.

All this said, let me emphasize again, there is no pure Christian theology and no innocent Christian practice. Christianity and globalism intersect at many and at complex points. But that does not affect the critical role Christianity can and will perform with respect to economic and cultural globalism. And as I also have already said, it has this role because of its own historical involvement in the development of globalism — because so many of globalism's aspirations are parodies of Christian hopes as they were demythologized through the development of "religion" and, finally, secularized. Globalism's figuration of unappeased and unappeasable yearning, will, I suggest, lead to a return to the theological. The theological will, again, guarantee (will be the only means of guaranteeing) communal belonging in the collapse of the social into the cultural. For it will guarantee the identification of differences within the increasing indifferentiation produced by the immanent cultural logics of globalism. That could be worrying. Theologians need to be on guard. The next global wars may not be international, or interracial, they could be interfaith. This is where the work on fundamentalism, with which I began, becomes important as critique itself.

POLITICS, POWER,
AND IMAGINATION:
CRITICAL REFLECTIONS
ON RECONCILIATION

Reflections on the Political Power
of the Theological Imagination

Victoria J. Barnett

Declaring one's personal "location" has become fashionable in academic discourse, but such an opening statement is crucial to this essay. The first morning I sat down to write, I had just finished the morning paper, the front page of which carried a disturbing photograph of sobbing Irish Catholic girls on their way to school, passing through a gauntlet of screaming, rock-throwing Protestants. Not long thereafter, I stopped to buy milk one morning, and the cashier told me that an airplane had just crashed into the World Trade Center. Emerging from the store, I heard a swelling chorus of sirens; when I reached home and turned on the television, I learned that another plane had crashed into the Pentagon, only a few miles from my house. Almost two months later, as I sit down to revise this paragraph, I have just read an article discussing the pros and cons of torture as an acceptable investigative weapon in the fight against terrorism.

So I write in disquieting times, with no idea as to what the future holds. Under such circumstances, my thoughts wander along new, previously unexplored tangents. One certainty is that the sequence of events that began on September 11 holds consequences for people around the world, but the reader of this essay will certainly know more about those consequences than I do at this moment. Another certainty is that, for a very long time, many Americans had the luxury of ignoring political terror and the dilemmas it brings. This is not true of all Americans. African Americans, Native Americans, and the numerous refugees who have come to our shores from all over the world know a great deal about terror. But September 11 brought the issue into the mainstream of public discourse in a new way, and it is already shaping how we think about our democracy.

It's a good time, then, to ponder the territory of the imagination. Several years ago, in more optimistic times, I organized a panel titled "Political Acts of Theological Imagination," and John de Gruchy's name immediately came to mind as an ideal person to speak about the subject.[1] I had been struck by the more or less peaceful revolutions that had occurred in places like Eastern Europe and South Africa, and by the exciting work on human rights that was being done by religious thinkers in a variety of cultures and contexts. Although it found expression in very concrete political movements and events, "theological imagination," it seemed to me, primarily described a *process* that characterized a profoundly hopeful, idealistic, and transformative moment in human history.

The key word here is "transformative," which in recent years has become a catch phrase in discourse about education, law, social change, conflict resolution, and human rights. It is an implicit concept in much of the political theology that emerged in the last quarter of the twentieth century. What it signifies, really, is that moment when human beings see new possibilities, act upon them, and by so doing, transform their own previous ways of thinking and alter the subsequent course of history, in great or small ways. In education, writes Alfonso Montuori, transformative thinking is an important corrective to "methodolatry" and "modeltheism."[2] "Transformative" acts — in the form of truth commissions, acts of reconciliation between former enemies, the establishment of new forms of government, and new understandings of human rights — help lay the foundation for a new future that may prevent us from repeating the horrors of the past. It is a tremendously creative response to human history, and our capacity as religious believers to embrace it relies heavily upon the resources and strength and elasticity of our theological imagination.

1. This panel discussion was held on November 17, 1999, at the Churches' Center for Theology and Public Policy, Washington, D.C.

2. Alfonso Montuori, "Reflections on Transformative Learning," *ReVision* 20, no. 1 (Summer 1997): 34-37.

In many ways, however, "theological imagination" is a problematic concept. I have just described the political products of theological imagination in glowing terms. Yet there are a number of historical events — the Crusades, the Inquisition, and the Holocaust, to name a few — in which religious language, and, often, religious motive, have played a terrible role. Crashing a jetliner into a skyscraper could be described as a horrific "political act of theological imagination," an act both terrible and creative. To the degree that the September 11 hijackers were moved by their religious motives, this deed illustrates faith in its most destructive form — a furious and cold-blooded collision with the world. While religious faith is a force that erases boundaries and creates understanding among peoples, it can also construct bitter boundaries and generate hatred. In a fierce poem, "The thing that eats the heart," Stanley Kunitz evokes the forces of violence and terror ("inflamed with need, jingling its medals at the fang-scratched door") that so shaped the twentieth century. The final line of the poem is startling and haunting: "The thing that eats the heart is mostly heart."[3] Mostly heart. Whether the outcome is good or evil, our works of heart are shaped by passion and, yes, imagination, and one of the tasks of twenty-first-century theologians will be to explore that paradox.

And this is the reason that wise people are cautious when they enter the territory of the political and the religious. Much of the immediate response to the terrorism in my country has come from commentators who stress the importance of private religion and secular tolerance. Religious terrorism, they say, is what comes of seeking political expression for religious faith and its values. Such expression is all too often the mark of fanaticism, a perversion of religion. Thus, writing in *The New York Times,* Salman Rushdie concluded, "The restoration of religion to the sphere of the personal, its depoliticization, is the nettle that all Muslim societies must grasp in order to become modern."[4]

In other words, one conclusion that people draw from political terror is that the best protection against political extremism and the ideological misuse of religion is the embrace of secular, modern society,

3. Stanley Kunitz, "The Thing That Eats the Heart," *The Collected Poems* (New York: W. W. Norton, 2000), p. 115.
4. Salman Rushdie, "Yes, This Is About Islam," *The New York Times,* November 2, 2001, A21.

and that the best cause the religious community could take up right now would be that of secularized civil society. In many respects, I agree with this viewpoint. The U.S. constitution established the separation of church and state not only to protect the religious minorities who had fled to our shores, but to define the ways in which religion is appropriate (or not) in the public sphere. One of the hallmarks of U.S. democracy is its capacity for pluralism, tolerance, and the peaceful coexistence of different faiths and cultures. The side effect of that is that beliefs and practices that might be exclusive or divisive are privatized.

Yet I find the assumption behind the answer (that it is safer to keep religion out of the public sphere because of the myriad problems that arise, from fanaticism to state co-option of religious authority) problematic. Historically, of course, it's often been true. The political expression of religious faith can take very destructive forms, such as the kind of totalitarian theocracy we see in places like northern Sudan. Even in places like Northern Ireland where religion is not the direct cause of the troubles there, it still becomes an identifiable and divisive mark of those troubles.

The dilemma is that many of our greatest political achievements — the end of slavery, the bill of rights, the human rights movement, the end of apartheid in South Africa — are also, directly or indirectly, products of "theological imagination." Moreover, many of them were initiated and led by troublemakers who had decided to challenge the established order. Religion is often domesticated (or privatized) through its integration into the values of political and cultural order. There is nothing inherently wrong with this state of affairs, if the means and ends of a society are just and moral. But there are times when it cannot be integrated or domesticated — times, for example, when the answer is not the reform of a system (like apartheid or segregation) but the end of it.

And there are other times, like the present, when religion has something to say in the public sphere that no one else is saying, when, in fact, theological imagination may be what we need to get past ideological dead ends. I like to read history, and one of history's peculiar consolations is the news, both reassuring and disturbing, that we have been through this before. Each manifestation of evil, war, and pestilence is peculiar to its age, but the dilemmas with which it confronts people of faith are often quite similar. And one of those dilemmas is that our sense of the apocalyptic or, at the very least, of a profound shift in the course of human affairs, leads us to grab on to clear-cut solutions. Something within us changed profoundly as we watched the airplanes fly into the buildings. Traumatized, wounded, frightened people struck by terrorism want more than anything else to "do something" — which perhaps comes from a deeply psychological need to "undo" what has happened.

But human history has experienced such seismic shifts before, and we experience lesser shifts all the time. One of the most widely quoted poems in the twentieth century was William Butler Yeats's "The Second Coming," in which one line after another describes such cataclysmic shifts. Sudden historical transitions unleash a sense of helplessness, in language and belief. How to describe the indescribable? What can the language of justice or charity achieve? Of what use are any of our social or political mechanisms? Not surprisingly, in such moments people turn to religion for guidance, but religious leaders themselves feel the same helplessness. How can they go on as before? Many of the turning points in the history of the church and its theology emerge in such eras. The writings of thinkers like Dietrich Bonhoeffer or Martin Luther King can be read as "theologies of crisis." Caught up in moments of tempestuous political change, confronted by the violence of political evil, they concluded that their church could no longer go on as before. Writing from a Nazi prison, Bonhoeffer wrote of the necessity for new kinds of faith "in a world come of age."

As the U.S. theologian Frederick Herzog once put it, "theology moves forward when great questions arise." Herzog recalled the words of Abraham Lincoln, who at the height of the Civil War "tried to appeal to the creativity of the American people: 'The dogmas of the quiet past are inadequate to the stormy present. The occasion is piled high with difficulty, and we must rise with the occasion. As our case is new, so we must think anew, and act anew. We must disenthrall ourselves.'" And, Herzog concludes, this "disenthrallment" is what can lead us to "a new birth of conscience."[5]

I suspect that this new birth of conscience begins in our dialogue with the world, when something triggers our imagination. Martin Lu-

5. Frederick Herzog, "New Birth of Conscience," *Theology Today* 53 (January 1997): 477-84.

ther King wrote his "letter from a Birmingham jail," and his words resounded in the hearts of numerous people who were then moved to act. We see an image of poverty and, with the power of the imagination that enables us to envision "a new heaven and a new earth," decide that it is unacceptable, that we need to change the structures that created it. Hope and imagination, Paul Ricoeur once wrote, are the cathartic forces that can transform evil. Imagination enables us to see what is being covered up, to hear the voices of the victims, and unmask the euphemisms for injustice, murder, and oppression. All of these actions are simply ways of standing in solidarity with "the other," which is simply a way of loving our neighbors as ourselves. And it is in the moment that we discover within ourselves the creative power to meet the challenges of history and change it — that we become protagonists.

In Yeats's "widening gyre" we are cast into chaos, but human beings have shown, again and again, that out of chaos we can create not only order but justice, not only things of usefulness but of beauty, not only acts of desperation but of grace. In faith we seek not just a beauty that will offset the pain and ugliness of this world, but the kind of beauty and grace that emerges from the meaningful struggle for authentic life. This kind of beauty is as necessary to us as the oxygen we breathe. We need meaning. We need to feel that we are a part of creation, and that our lives are worth something. The brutality and coarseness that scar the lives of so many in the world today reveal what happens to human beings when they are deprived of it.

And that is why we continue to seek beauty — not just in the obvious places, such as nature or works of art, but in our encounter with the world. By understanding this dialogical nature of imagination we realize that beauty — even theological beauty — does not exist in opposition to the world, but in interaction with it. Writing about this, Robert McAfee Brown pondered the difference between the existentialism of Albert Camus and the Christian perspective: "Camus and the Christian have different questions. For Camus, the question is: How can beauty and the oppressed be understood together? For the Christian, the question is: How could they possibly be understood separately?" Our task, Brown continues, is clear:

> Where there is beauty apparent, we are to enjoy it; where there is beauty hidden, we are to unveil it; where there is beauty defaced, we

are to restore it; where there is not beauty at all, we are to create it. All of which places us, too, in the arena where oppression occurs, where the oppressed congregate, and where we too are called to be.[6]

In other words, theology is a "contextual" art. Yet I am not so interested here in the context as in the act (or leap) of imagination (or faith) it provokes. "Theological imagination" is not so much a new way of doing theology as a different level of understanding what we do. Academically, it doesn't replace solid scholarship and hermeneutics; in terms of the lived religious life, it's not a substitute for discipline, good works, or prayer. In reality, it builds upon those things. Like the dancer's grace that is the product of years of training, imagination has to have its feet on the ground. That is, it has to be grounded in the world in order to see its possibilities.

How do religious people address the ugliness that is a part of all political forms of evil, including apartheid, slavery, genocide, and terrorism? The latter half of the twentieth century saw a number of paradigm shifts within my own Christian tradition in response to evil. The theological legacy of the Holocaust for Christians has inspired an ongoing re-examination of traditional teachings and doctrines about Judaism. The churches' experiences in places such as Nazi Germany, Communist Eastern Europe, military dictatorships in South America and parts of southeast Asia, and the apartheid regime in South Africa, led religious people in those countries to rethink the relationship between the church and state authority, the options for resistance, and the possibilities for a lived faith that could give rise to new political visions. In my own theological education I had the good fortune to study under professors like Gustavo Gutierrez, Robert McAfee Brown, Dorothee Soelle, and other tremendously creative thinkers who devoted their careers to shifting the paradigms, as it were.

Yet every religious tradition, often in its mystical traditions, has mechanisms for shifting the paradigms: ways of faith that lead to new ways of seeing. And each religion, I believe, is inherently subversive; the essence of religious belief is this subversive energy. For Christians it begins with the "baby who is the small center of sanity in a large and

---

6. Robert McAfee Brown, *Creative Dislocation — The Movement of Grace* (Nashville: Abingdon Press, 1980), pp. 141-42.

crazy world,"[7] and ends with a concept of a god who does not rule but gives us free will, who is not to be found in a palace but in the ghettos, with the poor and outcast. I think that is what the phrase from the Beatitudes, "the meek shall inherit the earth," is all about. Meek here doesn't mean weak, or intimidated, or cowardly. It doesn't even necessarily mean soft-spoken or gentle. It means a way of acting where strength is not openly flaunted but dwells within, without form but with a firm core — of belief, or faith, or goodness.

Thus, while the very concept of "theological imagination" might seem esoteric, the matter of which it is constructed and exercised is very mundane. Sometimes I think that religious belief itself may be the ultimate example of theological imagination. I recall reading a biblical story to my son when he was very young, and when I had finished, he gave me a sly look and said: "But we don't really *know* whether any of this is true, do we, Mama?" And the fact is, we don't know. I read my children countless fairy tales and myths, but I told them the biblical stories as if those were true, thus making an important distinction for myself and for them. Much of my own life and work has been grounded on the premise that there is indeed a God and that the universe makes sense — the premise that, in the words of the poet Robert Penn Warren, "there is something hidden in the dark."[8] If the world's religions are merely the works of the human mind, then the human mind is capable of imagining great and complex deities and, based upon these, of creating cathedrals, works of art and philosophy, liturgy and theology, and inspiring tremendous acts of charity, justice, liberation, and transformation. Even if this were all an illusion, it would still be something in the dark.

Yet it still wouldn't get at the essence of the theological imagination, or the mystery of faith, which is that it is both gentle and hard, resilient and relentless: what the poet Dylan Thomas once described as "the soft, unclenched, armless, silk, and rough love that breaks all rocks."[9] These paradoxical qualities help explain why faith can coexist

7. Brown, *Creative Dislocation*, p. 27.

8. Robert Penn Warren, "Three Darknesses," *New and Selected Poems* (New York: Random House, 1985).

9. Dylan Thomas, "There Was a Saviour," *The Penguin Book of Religious Verse*, ed. R. S. Thomas (Baltimore: Penguin Books, 1963).

with doubt. Ultimately, I think, the only kind of faith is the one that can coexist with doubt. Surely one of the most powerful and moving statements in the Gospels is that of the father of the epileptic child in Mark 9:24: "I believe, Lord. Help my unbelief."

That is the kind of faith I am trying to describe — one with a place for doubt. In the final analysis, doubt is what gives us enough room for "acts of theological imagination." Those acts may be simple, but they are always subversive. We read stories to our children, confident that their minds will glean some enduring truth from between the lines. We learn to live — since it is as much a part of our created nature as blood and bone — with "the thing that eats the heart." And, in an age of suicide bombers and stone-throwers, we seek to embrace "the soft, unclenched, armless, silk, and rough love that breaks all rocks."

Reconciliation as Metaphor

Charles Villa-Vicencio

Asked about reconciliation, Archbishop Desmond Tutu replied: "It is a miracle." The question is whether, reaching beyond the Archbishop's theology, the miracle can be deconstructed. It is a bit like trying to talk about God in a secular world. Erik Doxtader captures the dilemma in a thoughtful way: "When distanced from the divine, released from the notion that it is strictly a gift and action of God, the faith of reconciliation appears poetic. Reconciliation promises a beginning, the creation of that which we can neither hold nor control. It is something that goads our imagination and extends our knowledge. We quantify reconciliation at the risk of rendering it banal."[1] And yet silence is not tenable. We are compelled to speak. We are constrained to find lucid content to a poetic concept, driven by the realization that ultimately the well-being of our lives and that of the broader community depends on relationships with others.

A tight definition often goes a long way to bedeviling the reconciliation process. To define hope too tightly, to destroy the metaphor, to overlook the inherent ambiguity of the healing process is to undermine the very goal of reconciliation — which is to bring people together. To name the ideal is to own it. To own is to limit. To define too closely is to reduce poetry to the rules of grammar. It is to turn creative

---

1. Erik Doxtader, "Is It 'Reconciliation' If We Say It Is? Discerning the Rhetorical Problem in the South African Transition." An unpublished paper.

imagination into pie in the sky and hope into illusion. It is to ignore what the existentialist (and atheist) philosopher Max Horkheimer called a "theological moment," without which "no matter how skilful, [politics] in the last analysis is mere business."[2] So, perhaps (but only *perhaps*) it is better to live with definitional ambiguities — embracing rather the power of metaphor in imaginative pursuit of what is more than what exists at any given time.

Reconciliation must by definition reach beyond the restrictive ghetto of any creed, culture, or ideology. It must necessarily be both conceptually and substantially available to everyone. Long held to be a religious concept, in order to attain universality it must acquire secular meaning too.

A simple, even a complex, definition of reconciliation that fails to provoke imagination and unlock yet-to-be-discovered possibilities of life, fails to enable suffering individuals and wounded people to move forward. Ideological wars over definitions of reconciliation, of what is and is not required for it to happen, are enough to persuade all but the most rigid zealots that precise definitions and formulas concerning reconciliation often do more harm than good. The goal of reconciliation is the transcendence of an impasse that has capacity to destroy.

Reconciliation defies reduction to a neat set of rules. It is more than theory. There are no simple "how to" steps involved. It includes serendipity, imagination, risk, and the exploration of what it means "to start again." It involves grace. It is a celebration of the human spirit. It is about making what seems impossible possible. It is about the complex business of real people engaging one another in the quest for life. It is an art rather than a science.

Confronting the Theological Demons[3]

The dominant theological paradigm of reconciliation that entrenches a sequence of *confession, repentance, restitution,* and *forgiveness,* to be fol-

---

2. M. Horkheimer, "Die Sehnsucht nach dem ganz Andern" (Hamburg: Furche, 1975), p. 60.

3. Writing invariably includes an autobiographical subtext. This section of this essay is an attempt to acknowledge mine. While working in the Truth and Reconcilia-

lowed by *reconciliation*, has left a heavy imprint on both theological and secular debate. It is this that causes some to dismiss the very notion of reconciliation as unhelpful in political debate on group and national conflicts. It is perceived as a kind of utopian dream that contradicts what mere mortals (saints apart) are capable of.

The obvious appeal of the above theological sequence to those who have suffered gross violations of human rights is grounded in an understandable and natural propensity of victims and survivors to seek satisfaction. The quest in what follows is for a viable political ethic that seeks not *revenge* that may well provide short-term relief, but *satisfaction* of the kind that results from enduring peace which is dedicated to the restoration of human dignity and the beginning of a more equitable society. Put differently, the goal is authentic and lasting reconciliation, which is inevitably a slow process that goes beyond an all too often passing embrace.

This is a goal driven by an energy that stands at the intersection between theology and experience. It is an ethic that takes seriously the biblical invitation to reconcile as well as the experience of those who have suffered most, who either simply cannot reconcile or, alternatively, demand a price that their perpetrators are not prepared to pay. There is, suggests Donald Shriver, "nothing more 'natural' in human relations than revenge, and nothing less political."[4] Miroslav Volf speaks of being "caught between two betrayals — the betrayal of the suffering, exploited and excluded, and the betrayal of the very core of my faith."[5] How, politically, can we construct an ethic that affirms the understandable and legitimate demands of the violated who want ac-

---

tion Commission, I was asked by a journalist whether my theological career had prepared me for my work as Research Director of the Commission. I told her that while I scarcely used a theological word or symbol in my work, it was probably the most theological exercise I had ever been engaged in. The Institute for Justice and Reconciliation, where I presently work, is a secular organization. It at the same time confronts me with theological questions on a regular basis. Having been an ordained minister and taught theology for going on thirty years, this is inevitable. "You can take the boy out of the institutional church. You cannot take theology out of the boy."

4. Donald Shriver, *An Ethic for Enemies: Forgiveness in Politics* (New York/Oxford: Oxford University Press, 1995), p. 13.

5. Miroslav Volf, *Exclusion and Embrace: A Theological Exploration of Identity, Otherness, and Reconciliation* (Nashville: Abingdon, 1996), p. 9.

knowledgment of their suffering, repentance, and justice — while affirming the theological injunction to forgive?[6]

It is argued in what follows that this becomes possible where new ways of engaging former enemies and adversaries *begin* to occur. This is invariably a slow and contested process, giving rise to a sense of interdependence between adversaries and former enemies. It requires tolerance, within which empathy and understanding begin to emerge, leading perhaps to the beginning of a relationship. Confession, repentance, restitution, and forgiveness (the "big four") are almost invariably left until later — as the completion of the reconciling process. Indeed, some would argue they are only authentically possible in the wake of a reconciling process that has at least been initiated. There must be a context of grace or acceptance (a psychologically and politically safe place) for individuals or communities to make themselves vulnerable in confession (acknowledgment) and repentance (transformation) — the more explicit theology of which will be returned to at the end of this section of the essay.

The inherent danger of postponing the "big issues" can, of course, result in the searing legacy of bad memories. And yet, the politics of reconciliation is about the gradualism of what is conceivably possible at any given time. It is argued in the pages that follow that initiating the peace process — the first step on the reconciliation continuum within a given context — is as important as the ultimate success of the process. Indeed, most nations and individual relationships survive quite well on less than the ideal. The pursuit of the ultimate goal is at the same time necessary to ensure that the initial step in the process does not become the final one. A lack of movement beyond the first hesitant step in rapprochement (what are often referred to as "confidence-building steps") can only serve to fuel the suspicion of the critics of political gradualism, who reject the process as little more than the rearranging of furniture on a vessel that drifts ever closer to disaster.

Not to deal with the past in an overt and conscious manner, not to demand repentance from the perpetrator and forgiveness from the victim or survivor, is an appealing option to nations confronted with a

---

6. See Hannah Arendt, *The Human Condition: A Study of the Central Conditions Facing Modern Man* (Garden City, N.Y.: Doubleday Anchor Books, 1959), p. 214. See also Desmond Tutu, *No Future Without Forgiveness* (New York: Doubleday, 1999).

deeply divided past. Spain is a prime example of largely successful political amnesia. Post-Nazi Germany dealt with its past with caution and hesitation. The President of the then Federal Republic of Germany, Richard von Weizsäcker, in 1995 made an important speech concerning Germany's Nazi past, in which he said that while there was no "zero hour" for the German people in moving from the past to the future, there was a "fresh start."[7] France, Italy, and other European countries, as well as post-Stalinist Russia, have dealt with their pasts with equal caution. More recently, former eastern bloc countries have more or less followed suit. Politically a "fresh start" is more important than what von Weizsäcker called the "zero hour" in which all past sins are supposedly washed away. The question is, to what extent is the one related to the other? Nations in transition from past autocratic and oppressive rule to democracy and human rights cannot but be sensitive to the question of how much introspection there should be concerning the past. They need similarly to ponder how much acknowledgment and restitution is required. A politics that reconciles is necessarily a politics of the middle ground.[8]

Most people predicted a disaster for South Africa in the late 1980s. Many within the faith communities and in secular society, understandably and with justification, called on the apartheid leaders to submit to unconditional surrender. This, it was insisted, was the only legitimate and realistic way to move forward. The breakthrough, however, came not as a result of any Damascus Road experience or capitulation of the old regime. It came as a result of a series of encounters within which protagonists on opposing sides began to make contact with one another. Tentative, fragile steps were taken that led to "talks about talks." In the process, cautious relationships were forged. This opened the way to a search for peace and the beginning of a reconciling process.

John Paul Lederach reminds us that "it is a paradox of sorts that human concern for and interest in reconciliation is as old as the hills and at the same time in a pre-infancy stage." It is further, he suggests, "conceptualised from within particular religious frameworks."[9] To

---

7. Shriver, p. 84.

8. See Erik Doxtader, "Middle Voices in Transition: The Form of Public Speech in Post-TRC South Africa," *The Public* 8, no. 3 (2001): 23-34.

9. John Paul Lederach in Raymond G. Helmick and Rodney Petersen, eds., *Reli-*

marry the theological and the political, the need for which has already been emphasized, the pastoral or facilitating promotion of reconciliation requires a less immediately demanding approach than what is commonly perceived as prophetic theology, or the kind of ultimatums that characterize secular crisis politics. In the South African context Nelson Mandela reassured the faithful in the liberation movements who had long demanded the ignominious and total surrender of the apartheid regime that he was pursuing the same goal by an alternative (and arguably more effective) means, made possible in South Africa by the normalizing of the political process.

The quest, in the pages that follow, is for an approach to peacemaking that distinguishes between goal and process, while recognizing that the one is inherently linked to the other. In so doing, it seeks the ground of peacemaking in emerging trust that reaches beyond mere techniques of conflict management and the persuading of former enemies to sign a peace accord (as important as this is). The aim is a paradigm of peacemaking that recognizes the need for a growing relationship of trust that both makes the peace accord possible and is aimed at enduring political stability beyond the accord.

Miroslav Volf reminds us that there are no "autonomous and self-constituting entities" in human relations, we are inextricably bound to others with whom we have historical and contemporary contact.[10] It is through human *encounter* that the healing process begins. This does not suggest that repentance, justice, and other important dimensions of human relations are to be suspended indefinitely or played down in any other way. The struggle against injustice is part of the more fundamental pursuit of *reconciliation*. There is no question about this. The pursuit of *justice* is a goal that needs to sustain the reconciliation process. It is not, however, necessarily something that must precede the process as a price to be paid for what is to follow.

The need is for what has been called "a relationship-centric approach to reconciliation."[11] Conversion is not a sudden act of moral insight. It is a process of learning. It is the beginning of a new way of liv-

---

gion, Public Policy and Conflict Transformation (Radnor, Pa.: Templeton Foundation Press, 2001), pp. 183, 184.

10. Miroslav Volf, in Helmick and Petersen, p. 40.

11. Lederach, in Helmick and Petersen, p. 185.

ing. It involves different attitudes towards and relationships with those from whom one often continues to be estranged. It is a relationship that places dialogue and reciprocity at the center of the struggle to be fully human, suggesting that people are incomplete to the extent that they are alienated from one another. Often neglected at the height of war, rebellion, and conflict, it was a principle that underlay the South African transition from apartheid to democratic rule. It involves an anthropological reality grounded in a philosophy of *ubuntu*, which states that a person is only a person through other people.[12] This quest for humanity is never in isolation from others. It is inherently in communion with others, where the mutual shaping one of the other is possible. As such, it is necessarily opposed to a sense of fatalistic surrender to estrangement. It involves the creation of the kind of future that pursues the creation of a society that transcends exclusion and alienation, in reach of inclusivity and reconciliation.

There are numerous obstacles that undermine this process. These include bad memories, deep and abiding levels of hurt, the need for acknowledgment of past suffering, reparation, justice, and a host of related concerns. No one has the right to prevail on victims and perpetrators to forgive or to be reconciled, let alone to suspend their quest for justice. The question is whether victims and survivors can be enabled to move on, *to get on with the rest of their lives* in the sense of not allowing anger or self-pity to be the all-consuming dimension of their existence — as a basis for pursuing justice in a strong and viable manner. It does *not* mean forgetting the ghastly deeds of the past. This is usually not possible and probably not helpful. It does *not* mean necessarily becoming friends with the person responsible for one's suffering, nor does it mean *forgiving* that person. Very few accomplish this. Perhaps most people can only deal with their past suffering intermittently. At times they are able to rise above past suffering, at other times they fall beneath its sway.

The theological demands for confession, repentance, resistance, and forgiveness are important. They are enduring and need to be addressed. Any suggestion that they are a necessary precondition for the possibility of getting reconciliation underway is, however, likely to be counterproductive in deeply divided societies. An alternative approach,

12. Tutu, p. 31.

which identifies reconciliation as *process* rather than *goal*, is more helpful. This *pastoral* approach is not an alternative to, but an inherent part
of, a viable *prophetic* ethic of reconciliation and forgiveness. It may well
be the more viable way of attaining the elusive goal of justice.

Theology is at its creative best where and when it embraces the
realm of the artistic — in liturgy, symbol, and ritual, where imagination
and new possibilities dwell, rather than the *realm of dogma* and legal
codes. The former offers the possibility of forging new options through
the celebration of human creativity and compassion; the latter lends itself to the kind of rigidity that defends past practices and entrenched
rules concerning what is possible in the future. Religion that is reduced
to legalism and moralism, stripped of its flexibility, humanism, aesthetics, intellectual quests, and spiritual devotion, is essentially a thing
of power, not of the soul. It is a limited and time-bound agenda that
turns away from what Horkheimer called the "theological moment"
that takes us beyond "mere business."

The truth of the matter is that many church leaders in South Africa find themselves trapped in a different approach to reconciliation
and forgiveness. A reading of a series of interviews conducted by Bernard Spong with church and other religious leaders suggests that repentance needs necessarily to precede reconciliation — as a necessary
price to be paid.[13] There is a concern throughout the interviews about
"cheap grace," which is attributed to a failure of individuals and the
church as a whole to "publicly confess their involvement in the evil of
apartheid." It is argued that a failure "to provide adequate restitution
and compensation" to victims and "to compensate for the legacy of the
past" undermines any possibility of reconciliation. These, suggests one
of the interviewees, are "the requirements for reconciliation." "In the
end," says another, "reconciliation . . . is really only going to happen
when people experience economic transformation and economic justice." The concerns of the leadership and their understanding of the
goals that need to be pursued are both noble and necessary. They offer,
however, little to no suggestion as to how we should get the nation to
this point of realization. Bluntly stated, they offer a theology of law in
the name of a prophetic theology. One is left asking whether there is

13. Interviews conducted on behalf of the American Association for the Ad-
vancement of Science, 2001.

not, in addition to the "prophetic demands" for which church leaders are sometimes renowned, also the need for a creative and imaginative pastoral theology of grace that seeks to enable the sinner to repent. An old lady in the Buitenkant Street Methodist Church once asked me to remember that "you catch more flies with honey than with vinegar"! My "prophetic" zeal made it difficult for me to understand her.

There is a new challenge facing the church. It is to wrestle with the question of *how* to enable the nation to realize the goals it has explicitly set itself in its Constitution. Those were, of course, the heady days of the first democratic elections that saw Nelson Mandela become the nation's first democratically elected president. The emotional dedication that accompanied these events is, for many, a distant memory.

In addressing the importance of the Truth and Reconciliation Commission as it was beginning to be conceptualized, Dirkie Smit reminded us of the roots of the gospel:

> According to the Christian gospel it only becomes possible for this truth — about who we really are, about our pasts, about the suffering we have inflicted upon others and the guilt we have brought upon ourselves — not to become unbearable, not in fact to become something that we must push aside, repress, avoid and deny, when we acknowledge the more comprehensive truth of the love, mercy, forgiveness and acceptance of God.[14]

Smit argued that true self-knowledge, consciousness of sin, and genuine repentance are only possible as a *consequence* of God's forgiveness — *not* as a condition for forgiveness. Quoting Ted Jennings's *The Liturgy of Liberation,* he suggests "the only sin we know is sin that has already been forgiven. We do not see the problem until we have seen the solution."[15] The question is: What does this imply for pastoral practice? It has something to do with persuading those who refuse to accede to the demands made by the church leaders that there is a friendly, reconciling, and potentially forgiving context that can make this hap-

14. Dirkie Smit, "The Truth and Reconciliation Commission — Tentative Religious and Theological Perpsectives," *Journal of Theology for Southern Africa* 90 (March 1995): 6.
15. Smit, "The Truth and Reconciliation Commission," p. 7.

pen. This may just provide the grace to enable South Africa's most recalcitrant racists, self-satisfied white liberals who seem to suggest they
bear no guilt or responsibility for the past,[16] and culpable black collab-
orators that it is time to come to the party!

The pertinent question is *how* to demonstrate to the most fearful
and recalcitrant members of the society the generosity of those who,
having suffered most in the past, are committed to building an inclusive society. Here lies an opportunity for the church. Suffice it to say,
the extent to which whites and others refuse to respond to the grace inherent in the new South Africa is likely to be the extent to which reconciliation is likely to wither away.

Nation-building is ultimately about more than theology and spirituality. In the world of politics, it is about "the art of the possible."
The question of *how* to attain a given end is as important as the end itself. The need is for a theology that understands this process and contributes to it. It is a process that requires theologians to take seriously
the challenge presented by Dietrich Bonhoeffer more than a half a century ago from his prison cell, which was to proclaim the gospel in secular language. Effectively, this involves using language that is understood by secular society. It probably also means refraining from the
kind of acontextual dogmatism that seeks to prescribe how, when, and
where repentance, forgiveness, and repentance should occur.

Implicit to the preceding argument is a theology of grace. It is not
a theology of cheap grace. Its end is restitution and justice. What distinguishes it from a more rigid theology of law is process. It is about
how to reach the agreed end. It is pastoral. It is pragmatic. It is also goal
oriented. The latter means that any neat distinction between the pastoral and the prophetic cannot in practice be sustained.

The pertinence of Dietrich Bonhoeffer's classic text, *The Cost of
Discipleship*, will never diminish. There *is* a cost. The cost is perhaps beyond the human capacity to pay. It is a gift of God that enables true repentance. Volf suggests that resistance to repentance is "not just because we do not like being wrong, but that almost inevitably the others

---

16. The response of some to the *Home for All Campaign* initiated on Reconciliation Day in 2000, inviting whites to acknowledge their responsibility to rebuild the
nation, illustrates the refusal of many whites to even acknowledge the benefits of the
past, let alone to "repent" of their ways.

are not completely right either."[17] Indeed it could probably be shown that most confessions contain a measure of ambivalence. They come with a mixture of repentance, self-defense, a measure of self-justification, reluctance, and a desire to see the other person(s) show an equal amount of introspection and humility.[18] True repentance is even more difficult if the former perpetrator sees him or herself as a victim resulting from the context of, for example, the changed political situation. A series of interviews with former South African security force personnel — perpetrators of gross human rights violations — bears ample witness to this phenomenon.[19] A pertinent contextual theological question to be addressed in contemporary South Africa concerns the kind of theological and ethical praxis that is required to enable sincere, lasting, and significant repentance.

Discerning the Metaphor

Resisting banality, determined to transcend the logic of "what seems possible," and eager to find some pointers to practice that unites rather than alienates, the indefinite facets of reconciliation are considered rather than defined in what follows. This is an attempt to understand (rather than explain) reconciliation as a concept that lures, eludes, and intrigues. It constitutes an exercise in unpacking the metaphor rather than naming it.

Consideration of reconciliation techniques is imperative, talk about reconciliation is important, and the identification of lessons learned from reconciling initiatives is essential. The spirit nevertheless blows where it wills and reconciliation happens in different places in different ways. Vigilance is needed in order to discern the possibilities of reconciliation where and when they occur. And tragic is the initia-

17. In *Exclusion and Embrace*, p. 119.

18. Carl Jung's writing on post–World War II confessions is worth considering in this regard. See "Epilogue to 'Essay on Contemporary Events,'" in *Collected Works of C. J. Jung*, ed. H. Read et al. (New York: Pantheon Books, 1964), vol. 20, pp. 227-43. Quoted in Volf, *Exclusion and Embrace*.

19. The results of this work, being undertaken by Paul Haupt and Nazeema Ahmed, through the Institute for Justice and Reconciliation, are due to be published in 2002.

tive, whether theologically grounded or not, that seeks to curtail these possibilities in the name of one or another prescribed code or doctrine.

- Reconciliation does *not necessarily involve forgiveness.* The holocaust survivor, Simon Wiesenthal, published his memoir, *The Sunflower,* twenty-five years after being liberated from impending death.[20] He tells of an occasion when he was sent to work in a makeshift hospital for wounded German soldiers. A nurse escorted him to a mortally wounded soldier named Karl, who was struggling to die. Karl told Wiesenthal that he needed the forgiveness of a Jew in order to die in peace. He spoke of his years in the Hitler Youth and sorrowfully confessed to having been sucked into the treachery of Nazi slaughter. The dying German soldier asked the embattled Jew for forgiveness. Wiesenthal questioned how he, a beleaguered Jew, should respond to a repentant, dying Nazi soldier. Should he have killed him? Could he forgive or deny forgiveness on behalf of other Jews? Without a word he walked out of the room, leaving the soldier to die alone. Haunted by the experience, when the war ended he went in search of Karl's mother. She confirmed for him Karl's story and the apparent sincerity of his confession. For the rest of his life Wiesenthal questioned his actions in having walked out on a repentant, dying, Nazi soldier. Wiesenthal, at the same time, pondered the lack of obvious regret by so many Nazis who were brought to trial and by a German population that wished to forget rather than to make amends. What should he have done? He was *not* ready to forgive. He *was* tempted to break or interrupt the continuum between hatred and revenge. He went in search of Karl's mother. It was the beginning of a relationship — an attempt to transcend estrangement, which could, in different circumstances, have been taken further.
- Reconciliation *interrupts* an established pattern of events. Wiesenthal's search for Karl's mother suggests as much. Reconciliation is a first step beyond enmity. It makes "time for speech," sometimes in the midst of violence, without any guarantee as to whether such talk can have any long-term benefit.[21] Seen on a continuum ex-

---

20. Simon Wiesenthal, *The Sunflower* (New York: Schocken Books, 1976).
21. Doxtader, "Middle Voices in Transition," pp. 23-34.

tending from temporary suspension of the logic of established patterns of cause and effect to a rupture of such patterns that contains the possibility of new life, the interruption offers no guarantee of enduring success. It happens in different ways, at different levels of intensity. An important exercise in capturing the scarcity of reconciliation initiatives, and the lure of such moments in time, is to collect and reflect on stories of reconciliation, exploring their relevance to other situations in life. Theologies of reconciliation are more about stories than about theory.

- Reconciliation is *process*. It is a process that begins perhaps with no more than a measure of intrigue, curiosity, or perhaps morbid fascination as to what it is that makes the alienated person who he or she is. "It started by me wanting to see what the people who killed my daughter looked like," observed Ginn Fourie, mother of Lyndi, who was killed in an armed attack on a Cape Town pub. "I wanted to know what made them the kind of people they were."[22] In her case, the encounter with the killers led to her forgiving them and the beginning of a different kind of relationship with them. In the case of Simon Wiesenthal, it did not go that far. Reconciliation is often as painful as it is costly. It is not for the fainthearted or easily defeated. And clearly some have no obvious desire to go in search of it at all.

- Reconciliation involves *understanding*. Understanding does not necessarily lead to reconciliation. When, on the other hand, the story of a perpetrator is thoughtfully told, heard, and deeply understood, it can soften the perception the victim, survivor, or observer has of the perpetrator concerned. It opens space for the possibility of a new kind of interaction between adversaries. Many perpetrators are themselves victims of one kind or another — of propaganda, religious indoctrination, fear, disillusionment, and a culture of submission. "Some of us were more eager than others to please our political bosses, but not a hell of a lot of policemen followed the textbook and blew the whistle on what was happening," a senior policeman in the former South African Police observed.[23] Jozef Garlinski, a Polish underground fighter who survived Au-

---

22. In conversation with the author. Cape Town, 1999.
23. In a private conversation.

schwitz, tells of the horrendous evil he both witnessed and himself suffered. He ends his account by saying, "please remember those young SS officers could have been your sons or mine."[24] In understanding the perpetrator, we begin to understand the forces that make for evil. We discover the power of these forces and we begin to realize that the enemy (the German, the Serb, or the Afrikaner) does not have a monopoly on moral insanity. We discover that maybe there is a "little perpetrator" in each of us. It is this that makes unconditional negative judgment of another a little more complex and opens the possibility of a basis for interaction in the present that could lead to a new kind of future.

• Reconciliation requires *acknowledgment.* As understanding does not necessarily lead to reconciliation, so truth is not necessarily a conduit to reconciliation. There are, however, few who have suffered deeply who are able to begin to rise above this suffering without having at least a rudimentary knowledge of the cause and circumstances surrounding these events. They want to know who killed their spouse, child, or parent. They want to know why. Silence, for the victim or survivor, concerning the past often results in a wall of *inertia* — an inability to move on. There is a sense of paralysis that entraps the victim in his or her sense of defeat. Ashley Forbes, a torture victim of the notorious torturer, Jeffrey Benzien, was critical of the decision by the South African Truth and Reconciliation Commission to grant Benzien amnesty, arguing that he failed to make full disclosure. Nevertheless, he observed: "I forgive him and feel sorry for him. And now that the TRC has showed what happened, I can get on with the rest of my life."[25]

Acknowledgment does *not* mean forgetting the ghastly deed. It does *not* mean necessarily becoming friends with the person responsible for one's suffering. It does mean a break with overt enmity, and the beginning of a different kind of relationship, signaled in Forbes's words "I feel sorry for him [Benzien]." Not all survivors of torture accomplish this. Consider the words of Kalu: "What really makes me angry about the TRC and Tutu is that

---

24. Jozef Garlinski, *Fighting Auschwitz* (London: Ortis Books, 1994), p. 139.

25. Quoted in *Sunday Independent,* 6 December 1998. In an article by Wilhelm Verwoerd.

they are putting pressure on me to forgive. . . . I don't know if I will ever be able to do so. I carry this ball of anger within me and I don't know where to begin dealing with it. The oppression was bad, but what is much worse, what makes me even angrier, is that they are trying to dictate my forgiveness." Her words capture the pathos involved in the long and fragile journey of healing. No one has the right to prevail on Kalu to forgive. Would acknowledgment of the truth about the past help her to deal with the "ball of anger"? It is an open question.

- Reconciliation *takes time*. I visited Rwanda, where I was asked to speak about reconciliation. "We are still burying the dead and looking for justice," I was told.[26] Reconciliation may come later. It would have been obscene to ask Jews to be reconciled with Germans in 1945. The miraculous thing is that there were some Jews who were able to explore the meaning of reconciliation in the immediate wake of the holocaust. There are some Rwandans who argue that reconciliation, in the modest sense of an *interruption* to Hutu-Tutsi violence, is the only alternative to genocide. In South Africa, after twenty-seven years Nelson Mandela came out of jail seeking reconciliation — and there are others in South Africa who are ready to forgive. Icons of hope are important. But for most people, only a first enquiring venture beyond hatred is possible. The reconciling process takes time.

What Then Is Reconciliation?

Engraved into the South African social consciousness, the concept remains emotionally or mentally beyond the understanding of many, but at the same time it refuses to go away. The affirmation of the concept by former President Nelson Mandela and the championing of reconciliation by Archbishop Desmond Tutu in his role as chairperson of the TRC has allowed few if any South Africans to ignore it. Some embraced it. Others rejected it. Few have been able to ignore it.

What then is reconciliation? We have suggested certain pointers: interruption, something less than forgiveness, process, understanding,

26. In Kigali, June 1999.

acknowledgment, patience. To the extent that *a word is what it produces,* it has something to do with the engaging of people in an attempt to overcome enmity. This could be grounded in self-interest, in curiosity, or in intrigue. Ultimately it involves grace.

Whatever the immediate motivation, at a deeper level reconciliation gives credence to the African expression of *ubuntu.* It suggests that people are incomplete to the extent that they are alienated from one another. It is an African spirituality that is akin to a spirituality grounded in the Western theological tradition that comes to expression in the writing, for example, of St. Augustine. Seeking to develop a way forward amidst the escalation of violence and enmity that led to the fall of Rome in 410, he gave expression to an enduring dimension of Western spirituality in his confessional meditation: "Thou hast made us for thyself and our hearts and minds shall know no rest until they find their rest in Thee."[27] Grounded in the New Testament imperative, as it is, we are reminded that the biblical "Thee" is inextricably related to a "thou." Love of God and love of neighbor cannot be separated. Suffice it to say, within the kind of spirituality that links the love of God and the love of humanity, which lies at the heart of African and Western spirituality (and elsewhere), there resides within humans and nations a desire for living in peace with one another, which seeks to transcend even the most hostile conflicts. Often neglected at the height of war, rebellion, and conflict, this hope drives conflict resolution, peacemaking, and the need for coexistence. It is an anthropological incentive, grounded in a spiritual reality that those who would live in peace with their neighbors would do well to ponder.

When individuals and nations are consumed with anger, faced with the possibility of annihilation and yet neither willing nor able to capitulate, reconciliation is often the only alternative to the impasse. Trapped within a deadlock of destruction or submission, the quest for a way out of despair (what Karl Barth simply called "the night")[28] is to

27. Augustine, *Confessions* I.i.1 (Oxford: Oxford University Press, 1991), p. 3. Clearly it is necessary to note the obvious limitations of Augustine's interpretation of his own spirituality as identified, for example, in Rosemary Ruether's "Augustine and Christian Political Thought," *Interpretation* 29 (1975): 258. Few live up to the standard of their own insights!

28. Karl Barth, *Epistle to the Romans* (London: Oxford University Press, 1960), p. 43.

find an alternative to what seems like the iron grip of fate. It is this kind of impasse that resulted in the South African settlement that led to the political transition of 1994. In the words of Shakespeare's Macbeth: "as two spent swimmers, that do cling together," black and white South Africans realized that a settlement of one kind or another was imperative. It was the only option capable of bringing to an end an ever escalating war that threatened to destroy the very identity, infrastructure, and promise of a nation yet to be born. The archbishop's "miracle" is that both sides somehow came to believe that new life could still emerge, phoenix-like, out of the strife that characterized the apartheid years.

Reconciliation begins where people who are at enmity one with the other learn to deal with conflicts in a humane manner, at the heart of which is civility and creativity. It suggests that being human involves a process of engagement between strangers and adversaries, however difficult, as a basis for the possibility of a relationship and a space within which to deal creatively with issues (material and subjective) that make us less than human. It involves refusing to heighten the potential for self and mutual destruction.

In South Africa reconciliation involves the perpetrators of gross violations of human rights, as well as beneficiaries and bystanders, but also victims and survivors, dealing with the dehumanization that has come to characterize *their persons.* Njabulo Ndebele, powerfully and yet simply, suggests that reconciliation has essentially to do with "who we can become."[29] It involves committing ourselves to overcoming the dehumanization that has shaped our lives as well as our dehumanizing attitudes towards others. Wole Soyinka ponders the nature of the "slave condition."[30] It is a denial of humanity — "a psychological mutilation of the human entity," which in diverse (subliminal) ways can linger for generations in the psyche of oppressed and subjugated people. He insists it is necessary to "seize and alter that destiny." In the South African context, Steve Biko articulated this better than most:

> All in all the black man [sic] has become a shell, a shadow of a man, completely defeated, drowning in his own misery. . . . The first step

29. In his address at the Institute for Justice and Reconciliation's award ceremony of the Reconciliation Award given to Tim Modise, 8 March 2000.
30. Wole Soyinka, *The Burden of Memory: The Muse of Forgiveness* (Oxford: Oxford University Press, 1999), p. 70.

therefore is to make the black man come to himself; to pump back life into his empty shell; to infuse him with pride and dignity, to remind him of his complicity in the crime of allowing himself to be misused and therefore letting evil reign in the country of his birth.[31]

Reconciliation involves the humanization of the victims and survivors of slavery, colonialism, racism, and apartheid. It involves people who have been treated as less than human and who sometimes internalize that dehumanization, seizing their humanity and their destiny. Antjie Krog in *Country of My Skull* speaks of the importance of one who has suffered being able to shift from a pre-linguistic state within which one is overwhelmed by the extent of the suffering, to the point where one can take control of the suffering, at least, to the point of being able to speak about it. A "particular memory at last captured in words can no longer haunt you, push you around, bewilder you, because you have taken control of it — you can move it wherever you want to."[32] Maybe we should say we can begin to wrestle with the possibility of "moving" it. This, she suggests, is what the TRC was all about. This was, in a sense, what Biko's words, quoted above, are all about. It's what Habermas[33] is talking about when he speaks of taking a measure of rational control through speech, redeeming the "inner foreign territory" of the perverse unconsciousness by bringing it to words — by naming the beast.

It also involves perpetrators, beneficiaries, and bystanders dealing with the dehumanization that has come to characterize *their persons*. This often involves claims to rightful privilege, arrogance, greed, indifference, ignorance, and fear. In the South African context, the transcendence of such dehumanization might need to involve a "white consciousness" that seeks to strip away the layers of deceit that have come to characterize "white superiority." This "superiority" has, in different ways, survived the momentous events that heralded the demise of apartheid in 1994 — in much the same way that the "slave condition" survived emancipation in the previous century.

31. Steve Biko, *I Write What I Like* (Oxford: Heinemann, 1987), p. 29.

32. Antjie Krog, *Country of My Skull* (Johannesburg: Random House, 1998), p. 42.

33. See Jürgen Habermas, *Knowledge and Human Interests,* trans. J. J. Shapiro (Boston: Beacon Press, 1973). Also "Systematically Distorted Communication," *Inquiry* 13 (1970).

An Abiding Divergence

Directly related to a theory of reconciliation grounded in anthropological desire is, of course, the challenge of justice, without which the goal of the reconciliation process cannot be fully attained. It is an inherent part of reconciliation. At worst it renders reconciliation no more than a façade that is not reconciliation at all. As a case can be made for a human inclination towards self-fulfillment in relation to others, so there is a penchant within most people that seeks material and legal satisfaction for loss suffered. The weight of wrong suffered is at times such that it lends credence and understanding to an ingrained human desire for revenge.

The nature of the relationship between noncodified social rules and legal norms in society is complex and need not be entered into here.[34] It is enough to note that it is in relation to this kind of reality that Martha Minow defends organized (state) retribution as an exercise in taming, balancing, and recasting the personal animus involved in vengeance.[35] By institutionalizing feelings of anger, resentment, and even hatred, the state exercises procedural controls over individual and group anarchy. In Susan Jacoby's words, it is an alternative to the "wild justice" of the vigilante.[36] The refrain of critics of the TRC is, "I want justice." But, if justice is no more than "an eye for an eye and tooth for a tooth," there is an entrenched divide between justice and reconciliation that can only have the most disastrous implications for deeply divided societies like South Africa and a host of other countries in political transition. In the sense of breaking with, or interrupting, the logic of revenge, reconciliation is the creation of time and space in which to find new ways of dealing with past grievances.

It is this space that, in South Africa, has given rise to competing

34. See Richard Wilson, "Reconciliation and Revenge in Post-Apartheid South Africa: Rethinking Legal Pluralism and Human Rights," pp. 11-14. Paper delivered at the workshop held by the Centre for the Study of Violence and Reconciliation, History Department, "The TRC: Commissioning the Past," University of Witwatersrand, Johannesburg, June, 1999.

35. Martha Minow, *Between Vengeance and Forgiveness* (Boston: Beacon Press, 1998), p. 12.

36. Susan Jacoby, *Wild Justice: The Evolution of Revenge* (New York: Harper and Row, 1983), p. 10.

notions of justice that at least partially satisfy the human impulse for satisfaction. The development of notions of restorative justice as an alternative to retribution has generated extensive debate in this regard.[37] The unresolved debate concerns the extent to which retribution necessarily entails vengeance. The need, not least in a deeply divided society, is to define "reconciliation" and "justice" in non-exclusive ways. Indeed they often feed off one another. The threat of punishment in South Africa has, for example, in several ways contributed to the success of the TRC and the possibility of former perpetrators and their victims finding a basis for coexistence.

The TRC model of justice is not perfect. Howard Zehr suggests that from a restorative justice perspective the South African TRC "is flawed, opportunities have been missed, but the importance of this understanding [of justice] — not only in South Africa, but for the world — must not be underestimated. It is a bold step on an uncharted path."[38] The TRC was assigned the important task of instituting *corrective moral justice* by putting the record straight, in the sense of naming both perpetrators and victims, as well as pronouncing a "just cause" in the conflict under review. It had no power to execute *punitive justice,* nor did it have the power to execute *distributive justice,* in the sense of correcting material imbalances.

We are back with the "time and space" that must be used to redress the material and other imbalances that brought the nation to the brink of collapse in the late 1980s and early 1990s. The TRC has made certain recommendations in this regard, which include recommendations of material payments to those whom it found to be victims of gross violations of human rights. The state and the nation as a whole have been regrettably slow to respond to these recommendations, which means, somewhat ironically, that the TRC process may not ultimately succeed. This is up to the state and the nation as a whole. It is a

37. John Braithwaite, *Restorative Justice: Assessing an Immodest Theory and a Pessimistic Theory,* Australian Institute of Criminology, Australian National University, 1998; Jennifer J. Llewellyn and Robert Howse, "Restorative Justice: A Conceptual Framework"; Tony Marshall, "Restorative Justice — An Overview," *Criminal Justice Quarterly* 5 (1993): 2-3; Charles Villa-Vicencio, "Why Perpetrators Should Not Always Be Prosecuted," *Emory Law Journal* 49, no. 1 (Winter 2000).

38. Howard Zehr, "Restorative Justice: When Justice and Healing Go Together," *Track Two* 6, nos. 3 and 4 (December 1997): 20.

process that includes material redress — both individual and at the level of social services for all victims of apartheid. It must necessarily also include the healing of memories. It must further enshrine in the national consciousness the memory of past abuse, through the establishment of museums, monuments, memorials, and other national symbols. If the national memory is to be powerful enough to check future atrocities, future generations must encounter the memory of past atrocities. This memory must, as in the case of the holocaust, be ingrained in the consciousness of every South African. The burden of this essay is to enquire how this may be accomplished. It is about the process of reconciling a nation.

To the extent that the nation establishes material redress, national memory, and the will to resist those forces that made for apartheid, it will have achieved a level of justice that will not satisfy the thirst for revenge of all, but may have begun to redress the needs of most. It is here that the possibility of a creative encounter between justice and reconciliation resides. It is about promoting a process that focuses less on who we are and more, in the words of Njabulo Ndebele, on "who we can become."[39]

---

39. In an address at the Institute for Justice and Reconciliation's "2001 Reconciliation Award" to Tim Modise, 8 March 2001. Picking up on this thought, Antjie Krog suggests the "healing stream" initiated through the Truth and Reconciliation Commission has been undermined by the failure of the government to follow up on the recommendations of the TRC. In so doing, she writes, "it allowed the healthy stream of accountability that was starting to flow through the country to dry up. It curtailed compassion and left us stunted. We are no longer a country becoming," *Sunday Independent,* December 2, 2001.

Using Exegesis: On "Reconciliation" and "Forgiveness" in the Aftermath of the TRC

Cilliers Breytenbach

Introduction

A general dissatisfaction exists with the results of contemporary academic exegesis. What is meant by academic exegesis? For the moment it will be adequate to say that by "academic exegesis" I refer to the interpretation of the Bible, as it is practiced by mainstream biblical scholars. Leaving the nuances between the different approaches aside, exegesis aims to understand the biblical text in its historical context. It aims to either reconstruct the author's or the implied author's intention, but when it is influenced by the reception theory, it strives to reconstruct how the audience or the implied audience understood the text. We will then, when doing exegesis on a letter from Paul, try to understand what Paul, as entailed in the text, could have meant. We can also try to reconstruct the situation in which the members of the Corinthian house churches heard Paul's letter being read aloud and how they imagined the meaning or message of what Paul had written. I refrain from going into detail, knowing that there is much more to say. The main concern regarding exegesis is to understand and to interpret the documents in the New Testament as the written remains of an act of communication that took part between an author and his/her addressees during the first two centuries CE.

One could of course — and some of us are doing it — regard the documents of the New Testament as being directly addressed to us.

This results, for example, in the reading of Paul or the Gospel of John as if we as readers are the implied addressees or reader/s. There is nothing wrong with such a point of view. Bible study groups will continue reading the Bible in this way. This kind of reading, however, does not result in an interpretation of the text, but rather directly results in using the text. By distinguishing between the interpretation and the use of a text, I follow Umberto Eco's interpretation theory. Eco's now famous lecture on the "Limits of Interpretation"[1] (delivered at Konstanz on the Bodensee, where Jauss and Iser initiated "Rezeptionsästhetik") has argued convincingly that the "Opera aperta," the open works, have their boundaries. The task of exegesis is to create an interpretation, in other words, to use the linguistic evidence to supply a literal interpretation of the semantic meaning and the pragmatic intention of the text, where "text" refers to the remains of what is left from the original act of communication. Exegesis focuses on the text and aims to reconstruct the intentio operis. Such a (re)construction of the intention of a text is a hypothesis of the exegete. But he/she also regards it to be an interpretation of the text. It is not my intention to explain the way in which the exegete as modern informed reader makes sense of the text. It suffices to state two important facts: (1) A text is a complex and structured linguistic sign that can be described in (text-)linguistic terms; (2) a New Testament text is a remnant from antiquity that still exists for our eyes to be read. The process of semiosis through which the modern exegete constructs the once meant meaning and intended intention can be explained in terms of a semiotic or text-semiotic theory.[2] The main task of New Testament exegesis is to use the literary leftovers from Christian antiquity and to attempt to construct the sensus litteralis of a particular text that can be tested, and hopefully approved of by other exegetes scrutinizing the same ancient texts, reconstructed from papyri that date back to the second and third centuries CE.

---

1. Umberto Eco, *I limiti dell'interpretazione* (Milano: Gruppo Editoriale, 1990).
2. Cilliers Breytenbach, "Exegese des Neuen Testaments. Auslegung sprachlich strukturierter Texte," in A.-K. Finke and J. Zehner, eds., *Zutrauen zur Theologie. Akademische Theologie und die Erneuerung der Kirche* (FS Christof Gestrich) (Berlin: Wichern Verlag, 2000), pp. 273-86.

Fundamental Uses of New Testament Exegesis

Exegesis forms the foundation for New Testament Studies. It ventures to interpret the text and then to formulate that interpretation in order to share it with others. Exegetes normally publish these interpretations in the form of commentaries or monographs. But what is the use of the interpretations and results of exegesis?

First, it provides the basis for Bible translation. Without the text-critical, historical, and philological study of the manuscripts of those documents that comprise the New Testament, there will be no text to translate. No dictionaries will exist to provide us with the meaning of words, and no atlases, encyclopedias, and other databases to explain to the modern reader the customs and beliefs of the first Christians.[3]

Second, in those traditions where Sunday sermons ought to be a reflection on some passage in the Bible, exposition of the biblical text in commentaries is vital to help the preacher understand the literal meaning and intention of the pericope, e.g., in the Lutheran tradition, from the "Perikopenreihe." This usage stands next to the translation as one of the primary uses of exegesis.

But apart from translation and exposition, what other uses result from exegesis? It depends on where, when, and by whom the results of exegesis, namely interpretations, are used. I suggest that we distinguish at least four secondary uses, as elaborated in the following section using examples relating to South Africa.

Secondary Uses of New Testament Exegesis

1. The In-house Use of New Testament Exegesis

The way in which New Testament scholars themselves make use of the results of their exegesis determines the usefulness of their work in theo-

---

3. Some dispute this fundamental role of historical-critical biblical studies. I have a challenge to put to them. They should give those ministering the gospel, or those engaged in daily Bible study facsimile copies of the Hebrew Isaiah scroll from the Qumran caves or copies of the Greek papyri with parts of New Testament documents on them. Then they should ask them what they have understood.

logical faculties, the universitas litterarum, the Christian churches, and the public. Exegetes do not only do exegesis. Primarily they are historians, constructing the history of early Christianity, for example, the history of the development of their literature, the social history of early Christian groups and communities, the development of the perceptions they had about God, the Jewish law, Christ, salvation, their own future, and their relations to the nonbelievers. The history of the first Christians is part of the history of the ancient Mediterranean world, in fact very closely associated with ancient Judaism during the early years of the Roman Empire. Thus the study of early Christianity forms part of the study of the literature, the religion, and the social structure of the Greek-speaking parts of the Roman Empire. It is a matter of choice which aspect of the history of early Christianity one focuses on. Some construct the literary forms in the New Testament and their development against the backdrop of the literature of Hellenistic Judaism and other contemporary genres. Traditionally this subdiscipline was called "Introduction to the New Testament," but for various reasons I prefer to speak of the "history of early Christian literature."

Because Christianity is essentially a religion, a great deal of effort goes into the construction of the systems of belief in early Christianity. In a history of early Christian faith, the interpretation of the texts of the New Testament is used to construct the origin and initial development of religious perceptions in Christianity. Usually this subdiscipline is called the "Theology of the New Testament," but if one looks at the publications in this field, one should rather rename it as the "History of Early Christian Religion."[4]

But of course, the first Christians were mainly Jews, living in real time and space in the Greek cities of the Mediterranean world. The literature they left us formed part of ancient societies. Their beliefs, expressed in their literature, can therefore not be isolated from their own social history. This means the history of early Christian literature and religion must be embedded in a construction of the social history of early Christianity as a Jewish religious movement in the Graeco-Roman

4. Cf. H. Broers, *What Is New Testament Theology?* (Philadelphia: Fortress Press, 1979); R. H. Fuller, "New Testament Theology," in E. J. Epp and G. W. MacRae, eds., *The New Testament and Its Modern Interpreters* (Philadelphia: Fortress Press, 1989), pp. 565-84; H. Räisänen, *Beyond New Testament Theology* (London: SCM Press, 1990).

world.[5] It is to the detriment of all three subdisciplines when they are practiced and taught in isolation from one another. There ought to be, in New Testament studies, only two disciplines, i.e., the exegesis of the texts and the use of those interpretations to construct the histories (literary, religious, and social) of early Christianity. The question can be asked: What is the purpose of history writing? According to Paul Ricoeur, the narrative of the historian stands "for" the past. It takes the place of the past that has truly passed.[6] Drawing on Ricoeur, one might say that history writing on early Christianity represents the origin of Christianity for contemporary Christian societies, enabling Christians to find their own identity with reference to their roots. Because Christianity is a historical religion, heavily dependent on the use of its original literary forms, it is bound to take cognizance of its own origins. New Testament exegesis provides a historical narrative representing those origins.

2. The Use of New Testament Exegesis for Theology

Exegetes thus use their exegesis for history writing. Much more can be said about such an undertaking, but I'll leave it there and ask: Are exegetes not rather theologians than historians? They are, after all, appointed to teach in theological schools or faculties. In what way can they contribute to theology in general?

The trademark of New Testament studies has, unfortunately, become specialization. Especially in the Anglo-Saxon world, we have schol-

5. Cf. Paul Ricoeur, *Time and Narrative,* vol. 3 (Chicago: University of Chicago Press, 1988), section 2.
6. This can be illustrated with reference to what was traditionally called the "Theology of the New Testament." The major trend has been to follow the proposal made by William Wrede as early as 1897 that a "Theology of the New Testament" should rather be presented as the development of the history of early Christian religion. It should commence with Jesus of Nazareth and should include the non-canonical documents of the second century. Very few books of such a broad scope have been published recently. Cf. H. Räisänen, "'Theologie des Neuen Testaments' und ihre Alternative heute," in U. Mell and U. B. Müller, eds., *Das Urchristentum in seiner literarischen Geschichte* (Beihefte zur Zeitschrift für die neutestamentliche Wissenschaft 100 — FS J. Becker) (Berlin: de Gruyter, 1999), pp. 517-42.

ars studying and teaching Pauline literature, for example, explaining his religion or system of belief, constructing the history of this great apostle to the Gentiles and of the churches he founded. Other scholars concentrate on the Johannine literature, others on one of the gospels. There are very few New Testament scholars who still oversee the whole field of New Testament Studies. Notwithstanding all the benefits of specialization, this has one very negative consequence: publications that cover the whole field of early Christian studies have become a rarity. In general, exegetes have managed to use their interpretation of individual documents to provide theologians with descriptions of the belief systems or thought patterns of individual authors. The problem, however, is that theology in general and those preaching the gospel are not well served by this "use of exegesis." It is very difficult to mold modern theologies this week on Paul, next week on John, and the week after on the teachings of Jesus of Nazareth. In order for modern Christianity to define its own identity with reference to its origins in the apostolic age, exegetes need to use their interpretation of the texts in a way that yields a comparative description of the differences between the theological traditions within the New Testament. This comparison should also turn its focus on the common presuppositions shared by all authors. A Theology of the New Testament, according to a noteworthy proposal by Ferdinand Hahn, presupposes a history of early Christian religion, but moves beyond that. It constructs "one" Theology of the New Testament on the basis of the underlying principles of the thought patterns of early Christianity.[7]

Following Hahn, we should distinguish between a historical approach, in which the history of early Christian religion is constructed in all its phases and developments, and a Theology of the New Testament. The latter ventures to describe the central themes of those documents contained in the New Testament in such a way that not only their differences, but also their common presuppositions become apparent. This is a hermeneutical task that goes well beyond that of mere

7. Cf. Ferdinand Hahn, "Urchristliche Lehre und neutestamentliche Theologie. Exegetische und fundamentaltheologische Überlegungen zum Problem christlicher Lehre," in W. Kern, ed., *Die Theologie und das Lehramt* (Quaestiones disputatae 91) (Freiburg: Herder Verlag, 1982), pp. 63-115; Ferdinand Hahn, "Vielfalt und Einheit des Neuen Testaments. Zum Problem einer neutestamentlichen Theologie," *Biblische Zeitschrift Neue Folge* 38 (1994): 161-73.

historical reconstruction and will make use of exegesis in such a way that it will benefit all theological disciplines.[8]

3. The Use New Testament Exegesis May Have Within Christian Communities

Exegetes are not only servants to those engaged in systematic or practical theology. Neither do they write just the first chapter of a history of Christianity. They can also as theologians and believers (if they choose to be included in the latter group) become involved in contemporary theological debates. This would require them to present sections of early Christian history of religion in such a way that it honors its debt to the people of the past, and has a bearing on the central questions in contemporary Christianity.

There are many examples of how this can be done. Some exegetical studies promoted the process of finding a new consensus on the doctrine of justification between the German Lutheran churches and the Roman Catholic Church.[9] Constructions of the initial phases of the Christian mission by the congregation in Antioch and the Pauline mission in Galatia have shown that racism has no place in Christianity. The fact that during the Galatian crisis Paul adheres to the decision by the apostolic convent in Jerusalem in 48 CE is of fundamental importance to Christianity in general. Paul's position was clear. Faith and the resulting baptism, by which the converts from paganism are integrated into the body of Christ, is the only prerequisite to being adopted as a child of God and to belonging to the children of Abraham. Circumcision is an unnecessary precondition; the apostolic convent did not demand that the Gen-

---

8. If one wants to move in this direction, one should oppose the increasing specialization in New Testament teaching and research. Senior lecturers and professors in New Testament Studies should be required to publish in more than one area and it should be demanded from them to teach the whole subject. Doctoral programs should cover all the writings of the New Testament. Only then will they be able to produce New Testament Theologies that would promote a fruitful discussion within a school or faculty of theology.

9. Cf. Th. Söding, ed., *Worum geht es in der Rechtfertigungslehre? Das biblische Fundament der "Gemeinsamen Erklärung von katholischer Kirche und Lutherischem Weltbund"* (Quaestiones disputatae 180) (Freiburg: Herder Verlag, 1999).

tile Titus be circumcised. One does not need to become a Jew to be a child of God.[10] That means that the culture in which Christianity originated, the Jewish culture, its customs and its laws, is not an essential part of Christianity. Even though Jesus was a Jew and no Christian, even though the first generation of Christian leaders — Mary, Mary of Magdala, Peter, Barnabas, Paul, Apollos — were all Jews, the churches of God in Antioch, Galatia, Macedonia, Corinth existed beyond the synagogue. If Christianity was not even bound to the culture in which it germinated, how could it be bound to Western culture? Christianity moves on, leaving cultures behind, deeply influencing the cultures it encounters. Because personal faith in the gospel is that which makes somebody a Christian, efforts to make culture, gender, social class, or race a prerequisite to belonging to a specific church, or to partaking in the Lord's Supper, are fundamentally un-Christian. Apartheid was not a heresy only because it contradicted the love-commandment or presupposed that black and white can not be reconciled, it was fundamentally in conflict with Christian identity as formulated by Paul. Apartheid claimed to classify people in terms of their birth — Paul would say "according to the flesh." All Christian churches should have opposed a system that forced their members apart along racial lines, since they have all been baptized (integrated) into the one body of Christ and drenched by the same Spirit. The Spirit of God who resurrected Christ determines Christian identity, which is not divided along sexual, social, or ethnic lines.[11]

The fruits of exegesis can be presented by historians of early Christianity when they engage in current theological debates within Christian communities. Where possible, they can relate their reconstruction of the origins of Christianity to contemporary theological debates within Christianity. In doing so, they use exegesis to contribute to the formulation of contemporary Christian belief. When this is not done by New Testament Studies, the voices from the period in which

10. Cf. Cilliers Breytenbach, "The Freedom of God's Children — Reflections of Paul's Epistle to the Galatians," in K. Nürnberger, ed., *A Democratic Vision for South Africa* (Pietermaritzburg: Encounter Publications, 1991), pp. 109-14.

11. Cf. 1 Cor. 12:13; Gal. 3:28. For more detail see Cilliers Breytenbach, "Die Identiteit van 'n Christenmens. In aansluiting by Paulus," in Cilliers Breytenbach, ed., *Church in Context: Early Christianity in Social Context/Kerk in Konteks. Die vroeë Christendom in sosiale verband* (Pretoria: NG Kerkboekhandel, 1988; German translation in Threskeutike kai ethike enkyklopaideia 33, 1989), pp. 51-64.

Christianity first took shape either fall silent or are drowned out by the clamor of the current debate. In both instances it harms Christianity, whose self-definition is based on Scripture documenting the period of its initial formation.

The Benefit Public Discourse May Have from New Testament Exegesis

In societies where religion plays a vital role, concepts of religious origin may sometimes dominate public discourse. It seems to me that in the wake of the "Truth and Reconciliation Commission" (TRC) the notions of "reconciliation" and "forgiveness," generally recognized to be of Christian origin, have done just this. It might be because ex-theologians like Dr. Alex Boraine and the retired Archbishop of Cape Town, Desmond Tutu, led the proceedings, that forgiveness, confession, and reconciliation (all at "home in the religious sphere")[12] became so important. It is surely too early to judge the outcome of the TRC. Historians will have to wait until the past is less present in living memory before they dare to give the TRC its place in South African history. But even before the TRC finished its report, it became abundantly clear how unclear the notion of "reconciliation" is.

This should not surprise us. Even within Christianity "reconciliation" is no clearly defined concept. And in the New Testament? Here reconciliation is confined to Paul (1 Cor. 7:11; 2 Cor. 5:18-20; Rom. 5:10-11; 11:15) and the deutero-Pauline letters of Colossians (1:20-22) and Ephesians (2:16). Since I have discussed the origin of this concept and its use by Paul and his followers extensively elsewhere,[13] I can be very brief. Originally reconciliation is no theological concept. It is almost never used metaphorically to depict the relationship between the gods and humans. It plays virtually no role in the Old Testament, but is of Greek origin, becoming prevalent after Alexander the Great's empire collapsed into countless wars. There was a great need for diplomacy to overcome

---

12. Desmond Tutu, *No Future Without Forgiveness* (London: Rider, 1999), p. 71.

13. Cf. Cilliers Breytenbach, "Reconciliation: Shifts in Christian Soteriology," in W. S. Vorster, ed., *Reconciliation and Construction* (Pretoria: University of South Africa, 1986), pp. 1-25.

the consequences of war, and former warring factions had to move from enmity to friendship; they had to be reconciled. In Greek, reconciliation has to do with the change from enmity to friendship; it refers to the change from strife and hostility to peace, between individuals, or between citizens of warring cities and nations. To be reconciled is to have peace and friendship between former enemies. In the Graeco-Roman world reconciliation required that those who were taken captive during a war be released from slavery and that amnesty be granted for the wrongs inflicted during the conflict. Reconciliation aims at ending hostilities and replacing them with a prosperous life in peace or concord.

This is why Paul could introduce the notion of reconciliation into theology. He uses this language of Hellenistic diplomacy to depict his role as apostle in 2 Corinthians 5:18-20. He thereby transfers political terminology to the relationship between God and humankind. He is a messenger who offers the message of reconciliation to humankind, telling them that through the death of Christ, God has reconciled his hostile enemies — human sinners — to himself. When judging men and women, God will not take their sins into account.

Reconciliation is thus not really a concept of Christian or even religious origin.[14] And even more important: It is used in the Pauline literature with reference to the relationship between God and humankind where God changes the sinner, who lived in enmity towards God, into a friend who lives in peace with God. Precisely because of the use of this notion within Christian soteriology, it becomes virtually impossible to take Paul's notion of reconciliation as point of departure to discuss reconciliation between the victims and the perpetrators of state violence during the apartheid era. It is so deeply attached to Paul's explanation of the saving effect of Jesus' death that it makes little sense to detach the notion of God reconciling humans from New Testament soteriology and to reintroduce it into interpersonal or interracial relations in the public sector, where many of the persons involved are not confessing Christians. From the Hellenistic philosophers and historians it is clear that without reconciliation, without the change from hostility and strife to friendly relations, there is neither peace nor prosperity. This is exactly what the constitutional base of the TRC expresses.[15] To realize

14. Cf. Desmond Tutu, *Future*, pp. 45-46.
15. Cf. Desmond Tutu, *Future*, p. 35.

this, one does not need Paul, because the notion of political reconciliation was not his idea. There is little that the Pauline adaptation of this
notion can contribute to easing political tension. One should rather
take Paul's example and do what Paul did: adapt the original political
notion. In doing so, it is important to note that the idea of reconciliation is traditionally at home in the process of peacemaking. Conditions
of peace agreement or reconciliation are a political matter and must be
negotiated between the parties involved.

So whence the strong religious orientation in the TRC? It seems
to me that the notion of forgiveness had a great influence on the chairperson of the TRC and was conflated with the idea of reconciliation by
the archbishop in the light of the African tradition of *ubuntu*.[16] I would
suggest, then, that we discuss the notion of "forgiveness." By promoting the use of this genuine theological concept in the aftermath of the
TRC, exegesis might make a useful contribution to the current debate.

The notion of forgiveness in a Christian sense is always the remission or acquittal of debt or trespasses. Early Christianity inherited this
notion from John the Baptist and Jesus of Nazareth.[17] John the Baptist,
for example, proclaimed that those who repent, i.e., change their hearts
and minds and turn back to God, would be forgiven by God (LukeQ 3:3
and Mark 1:4). Jesus of Nazareth taught his followers to pray to God as
a Father, "to forgive us our debts" (Q 11:4/6:12). Importantly, though,
the Jewish-Christian tradition qualifies the forgiveness. In the first instance John conditions the state in which one may expect forgiveness:
Only those who confess their trespasses, who with a humiliated spirit
and a contrite heart pray to God, will be forgiven. Jesus gives the example of the Pharisee and the tax collector in the temple. The latter
prayed: "God be merciful to me, a sinner!" (Luke 18:13). It is needless to
ask for forgiveness without a sincere sense of guilt and remorse.

In the second instance Jesus stated the condition under which
the debt is remitted. According to the synoptic tradition, he connected
the petition for the remission of debt or the forgiveness of trespasses
to the willingness of the supplicant to forgive others (cf. Mark 11:25):

16. Cf. Desmond Tutu, *Future*, pp. 34-36.
17. Cilliers Breytenbach, "Vergeben/Erlassen," in L. Coenen and K. Haacker,
eds., *Theologisches Begriffslexikon zum Neuen Testament* (Neukirchen: Neukirchener
Verlag, 2001), pp. 1737-42.

"and forgive us our sins, for we ourselves also pardon every one indebted to us" (cf. Luke Q 11:4), or "and forgive us our debts, as we also forgive our debtors" (Matt. Q 6:12).

In the third instance, it is important to note that the forgiveness of sins or the remission of debt is not an effect of the death of Jesus. Judaism of the period of the second temple cherished Israel's belief that the Lord is "a God merciful and gracious, slow to anger and abounding in steadfast love and faithfulness, keeping steadfast love for the thousandth generation, forgiving iniquities and the transgression of sin" (Exod. 34:6-7). Jesus stands firmly in this tradition, in which the offender should pray to the merciful God for forgiveness.

For those who have decided to deal with the horrors in the past of our beloved country from within their Christian tradition, I believe these three principles are very important. First and foremost, there should be mercy and forgiveness because God is merciful, or as Archbishop Tutu has said: "In this theology we can never give up on anyone, because our God was one who had a particularly soft spot for sinners."[18]

Second, although the TRC for good reasons did not make remorse and contrition prerequisites for granting amnesty, the national process of reconciliation will not succeed unless a considerable number of the former National Party supporters show genuine remorse. Those who kept the National Party in power at the polls have to carry the political responsibility for the atrocities done by a state that was representing them. In view of the truths that emerged during the TRC sessions, a contrite acknowledgment of this political guilt is a prerequisite for reconciliation with those who suffered under the system.

Third, the exegete must tell those who have been wronged that if they want to live in the tradition of Jesus Christ, they can expect the same measure of forgiveness from God that they are willing to give those who have trespassed against them.

In short, these are the focal points of the early Christian tradition of forgiveness, and I suggest that those who partake in the ongoing debate of "reconciliation" in South Africa, and who want to contribute to the debate by drawing on their religious tradition, might find them useful. Linking up with this tradition, they might find exegesis useful in the political realm.

18. Desmond Tutu, *Future*, p. 74.

Reconstructing the Doctrine
of Reconciliation within Politics

Ralf K. Wüstenberg

Theoretical Presuppositions

Theological discussion on the continent of Europe about the relation between theology and politics has been conducted mainly in terms of ethical theories such as Luther's doctrine of the "two realms" or "two-fold reign of God."[1] This doctrine came under particular criticism when supporters of the Nazis misused it during the Third Reich. In reaction Karl Barth and others confronted the Lutheran doctrine with a different one, namely that of the *Königsherrschaft Christi* (the kingship or royal sovereignty of Christ). This doctrine, on the basis of a more Reformed reading of the New Testament, asserted the kingship of Christ over both the church *and the world*.

While this essay cannot go into the complex and diverse discussion of these influential ethical theories,[2] it seems necessary to highlight a central difference between them. Whereas Luther's political

---

1. Cf. Martin Luther, *Secular Authority. To What Extent It Ought to Be Obeyed, 1523,* *WA,* vol. 11, pp. 249ff. (*WA* = *Weimarer Ausgabe,* the standard edition of Luther's works, Weimar 1883-.)

2. I have discussed the issue in greater detail in my (unpublished) Habilitation-thesis, *Die politische Dimension der Versöhnung — Eine Systematisch-theologische Studie zum Umgang mit Schuld nach den Systemwechseln in Südafrika und Deutschland (The Political Dimension of Reconciliation: A Systematic Theological Study on Dealing with Guilt in South Africa and Germany).*

RALF K. WÜSTENBERG

ethic grants to the state a degree of autonomy in making decisions in the area of politics,[3] Barth's approach stresses that it is both possible *and necessary* to draw analogies between personal Christian ethics and political ethics.[4] Both theories, however, see danger in a too simple and direct equation of ethics in the private sphere and ethics in the political sphere.

Such a direct equation could be made in two ways: either by claiming for political insight the right to be determinative in the theological field or on the other hand by claiming for theological or religious insight the right to determine decisions in the area of politics.

Examples of both of these ways of making such an equation and their dangers are patent. During the Third Reich many Christians in Germany allowed their theology to be steered by a political agenda. The so-called *Deutsche Christen* are the most obvious example of this. On the other hand in our own time radical Islam poses the question whether its theocratic approach is not an example of steering politics according to a religious agenda.[5]

Although both theories avoid certain pitfalls, both also suffer from apparent shortcomings. In particular, both appear to suffer from shortcomings that inhibit a constructive theological discussion of current political events:

1. Both ethical theories make use of terms and metaphors — like the concept of a *Reich* (empire or kingdom) in which God reigns, or the concept of the *Königsherrschaft* of Christ — that clearly derive

3. The key points in Luther's position are the following: (a) God is the Lord of both kingdoms, but rules each by different means (the law and the gospel) for different ends (peace and piety). (b) All Christians live in both kingdoms simultaneously — in the kingdom of God in that they are righteous, and in the kingdom of the world in that they are sinful. (c) The two kingdoms are to be sharply distinguished from one another, in such a way that the realms of law and gospel are to be neither separated (as in secularism) nor equated (as in ecclesiocracy).

4. Cf. especially Karl Barth, "The Christian Community and the Civil Community," in W. Herberg, ed., *Community, State and Church: Three Essays by Karl Barth* (Garden City, N.Y.: Doubleday, 1960), pp. 149-89, a translation of *Christengemeinde und Bürgergemeinde* (München: Chr. Kaiser Verlag, 1946).

5. Consider, e.g., the authoritarian religious rule of the former Taliban regime in Afghanistan.

258

from a pre-democratic tradition and so are alien to modern democratic thought.

2. Both theories are *ethical* theories, reflecting the question "to what extent a secular authority ought to be obeyed."[6] They do not reflect the (in a way more specifically *theological*) question of how Christian ideas may themselves already impact on or affect political decision-making. Thus they fail to reflect or to provide clues to the key questions that need to be posed in the interdisciplinary discourse that is necessary to achieve greater theological insight (*Erkenntnisgewinn*) in this area. We noted that both theories avoid directly equating political and theological ethics. But the question is how far they help in the search for *indirect* links or common shared religious and political language and thus enable a genuine dialogue between theology and politics.

Such indirect links can be established in two ways:

1. On the one hand there is the possibility, which needs to be investigated, of "baptizing" political language, so that political terms can be used in the theological arena to express the insights of the new reality that Christ brings about (2 Cor. 5).
2. On the other hand there is the reciprocal need to investigate two possibilities:
   • whether theological ideas have already been transposed into political language, so that they can be recognized in the political arena, and
   • whether theological language can be reconstructed, so that it can be used in the political arena.

In order to explore such indirect links we have to examine very sensitively what goes on in the political field. It is just here that the problem lies. For no method has been developed to determine how political events can be examined in theological terms. Thus neither political theory deals with the fundamental question of the possibility of reconstructing theological ideas in the context of politics.[7]

6. See above the subtitle of Martin Luther's pamphlet.
7. The reason for this is easy to find: for both theories this was not a question

Let us consider the above weaknesses of the two ethical theories in the light of Dietrich Bonhoeffer's ethical paper on "The Ultimate and Penultimate Things."[8]

1. The distinction between "ultimate and penultimate things" is clearly a more adequate terminology for the interdisciplinary discourse of theology with political science than the distinction between "two kingdoms" or "two realms." For Bonhoeffer the "ultimate things" are the last things, temporarily and in reality. In temporal terms justification by faith is clearly both the turning-point and the end-point of a process in which every Christian constantly finds him/herself (in that he/she is *simul iustus et peccator*). The assumption is that a real time span precedes any act of justification. In terms of reality, justification by faith is an ultimate or last thing because nothing can be regarded with greater seriousness than this event.[9]

The advantage of Bonhoeffer's distinction lies in its dynamic. "Ultimate things" and "penultimate things" for him do not describe certain spheres, empires, or kingdoms. Instead they are categories that describe events both theologically and in terms of political reality. This makes possible a clear distinction between the ultimate and the penultimate. (Here Bonhoeffer allows for what is valid in Luther's approach.) On the other hand Bonhoeffer avoids separating ultimate things from penultimate things. (Here he allows for what is valid in Karl Barth's approach.) The "world can continue being the world," but (as a penultimate thing) is at the same time related to what is "ultimate" (analogously to the

---

in their time. The problem of reconstruction was not a problem for Luther; nor was it a real question for Barth during the Church Struggle in the Third Reich. At that time the urgent issue was the proclamation of a *status confessionis*.

8. Cf. "Die letzten und die vorletzten Dinge," Dietrich Bonhoeffer Werke 6 (Munich: Christian Kaiser, 1986-), pp. 137-62. This is the standard critical edition of Bonhoeffer's works. An English translation of the DBW is in progress (Minneapolis: Fortress Press, 1996-).

9. This reminds one of Anselm of Canterbury: God is "a being than which none greater can be thought" *(aliquid quo nihil maius cogitari possit)*. See *Proslogion*, I, 93, 20f., ET E. R. Fairweather, ed., *A Scholastic Miscellany: Anselm to Ockam*, LCC, vol. 10 (Philadelphia: Westminster, 1956), p. 73.

way in which the law and the gospel are distinct and yet related). Penultimate things have to be delivered from the temptation to understand themselves as "ultimate" or "last" things, because it is only from the "ultimate," from the justifying and reconciling Word of God, that light falls on the penultimate, on the dimensions of this world — particularly on the political.

2. As far as the second weakness that we noted in the two ethical approaches is concerned, Bonhoeffer comes to our aid by clearly assuming a "connection" between what is "ultimate" and what is "penultimate," even though he leaves it to posterity actually to explore and work out this connection, i.e., to discover with the help of theology what is ultimate in what is penultimate, including in political reality.

Theological Exploration

Following the path outlined by Bonhoeffer, we will now seek to find the "connections" between "ultimate things and penultimate things" by searching for indirect links between political and theological language. In order to do so we need to focus on a specific issue in theology. An obvious issue is the doctrine of reconciliation. Let us then explore the possibility of reconstructing the doctrine of reconciliation within the political realm.

We shall deal with the problem in two steps: first spell out the need to define what is meant by reconciliation in the theological context and then explore the political dimensions of the same term.

Any attempt to lay down the principles of the Christian doctrine of reconciliation naturally tends to focus more on the various relations to which the doctrine applies rather than on actual definition of the concept. A Christian understanding of reconciliation proceeds from a number of assumptions and has a specific range of meanings:

- The Christian doctrine of reconciliation assumes that our communion with God has been destroyed by human sin.
- Reconciliation then means the restoring of our relationship with God through Jesus Christ.
- Reconciliation in Christ makes communion with God possible

261

again in that Christ atones for the guilt that comprises the barrier between God and humankind. God thus makes a new beginning with the world "in Christ."

- Reconciliation is between God and the sinner, not with sin. On sin the judgment is final.
- God's reconciliation means that Christ has made human beings able to live in community with God and with each other again.
- In reconciling the world with himself God has left "fingerprints"[10] or traces of this in his creation and leaves it to us to discover these.

Reconciliation has, in summary, to do with "change." "Change" is the original meaning of the Greek word (καταλλαγή) that Paul introduced in the well-known passage in 2 Corinthians: "God . . . reconciled us to himself through Christ and has given us the ministry of reconciliation: that is, in Christ God was reconciling the world to himself, not counting their trespasses against them and entrusting the message of reconciliation to us" (5:18-19).

It is interesting to note that καταλλαγή was originally used in the Greek world for rather banal dealings like "changing money." Later it played a key role in complex diplomatic processes, e.g., when hostile cities made peace with each other again.[11] Paul himself takes over the word "reconciliation" (καταλλαγή) from such political language in order to convey a theological meaning, namely to express what happens between God and humankind in Jesus Christ and what the new relationship that results means. Thus whereas it formerly referred to a diplomatic process between human beings, it now takes on a radical meaning in the changed ontological setting of the new being in Christ (2 Cor. 5:17). The political meaning of reconciliation has, so to speak,

10. Note the suggestive title of the recent book by Robert Farrar Capon: *The Fingerprints of God* (Grand Rapids/Cambridge: Eerdmans, 2000).

11. See Cilliers Breytenbach: *Versöhnung. Eine Studie zur paulinischen Soteriologie* (Neukirchen: Neukirchener Verlag, 1989). Breytenbach argues with some force that when Paul transferred the concept of reconciliation to the theological field in order to express the relationship between God and human beings, it had lost its social and political dimension. On the other hand Breytenbach seems to fail to see the rich possibilities that his exegetical results open up for reconstructing the theological dimension of reconciliation in politics.

been "baptized" by Paul. What is now meant by the term is the fundamental change from being a sinner to becoming a righteous person before God, from being God's enemy to becoming reintegrated into loving community with God. (It is important to note that the active subject in this act of reconciliation is God!)

Let us return to Bonhoeffer and assume that there is a connection between "the ultimate and the penultimate things," between eschatological reconciliation and political reconciliation. The key question is: How do we uncover the "connection" between theological and political reconciliation so as to reconstruct the eschatological meaning of reconciliation, reconciliation in the "new creation" of which Paul spoke, in the political processes of reconciliation?

The attempt to answer this question in methodological terms brings us to a critical point. How can we explore what political reconciliation means? What method is adequate for this undertaking? As we noted above, no such method has been proposed for theological research. We therefore have to undertake empirical field studies in order to explore the political dimensions of reconciliation.

The political sciences provide methodological assistance in this venture;[12] they also point toward empirical fields that are of particular relevance and interest for us. Political reconciliation has played an important role in instances of political transition to democracy after authoritarian rule. Research on political transformation *(Transformationsforschung)* has examined well-known examples of political transition in countries such as Chile after the end of Pinochet's dictatorship, South Africa after the end of apartheid, Germany after the fall of the Berlin wall, and East-bloc countries after the collapse of Communism. In all these countries the question has posed itself: How should we deal with guilt for the crimes committed under the preceding authoritarian rule? And to what extent and under which conditions can the way of reconciliation overcome the divisions of the past?

---

12. I have made use of political methods for exploring the process of political transition in a different article. See "Reconciliation with a 'New' Lustre: The South African Example as a Historical and Political Challenge for Dealing with the German Democratic Republic's Past," *Journal for Theology of Southern Africa* 113 (July 2002). The interdisciplinary dialogue between the study of jurisprudence and political science in particular provides a catalogue of key categories that make it possible to reflect on political reality from a theological point of view.

RALF K. WÜSTENBERG

Let us assume for a moment that there is a political field in which both concepts, namely guilt and reconciliation, play a key role. Let us also allow that political reconciliation can be related to guilt, i.e., that reconciliation in politics provides one way of dealing with moral guilt. Both considerations imply that it is possible to equate a moral understanding of guilt with the theological understanding of sin. But can it be taken for granted that both mean the same thing? In what we have stated above we have assumed that political reconciliation and theological reconciliation are different things. Likewise the merely ethical sense and the theological sense of guilt need to be distinguished. The notion of sin implies more than an offense against moral values or ethical guilt: it involves a person's whole relation with God. Moreover, a person does not become a sinner when he or she behaves in an unethical way. Their sinful behavior is both the result and the manifestation of being sinners and as such members of sinful humankind.

On the other hand, if we assume that there is a connection between political and theological reconciliation and likewise between guilt before human beings and sin before God, how shall we pursue Bonhoeffer's question about the connection between the ultimate and the penultimate things?

Broadly speaking, there seem to be two conditions:

1. The "condition for the possibility" (to use Kant's language) of guilt in people's relation to one another is sin (i.e., their being sinners) before God.
2. The condition for the possibility of reconciliation between human beings as a political reality in the penultimate is a reconciled relationship between them and God in Jesus Christ in the realm of ultimate things.

Both of these conditions assume a relation between ethical guilt and sin on the one hand and between political reconciliation and reconciliation as an eschatological reality on the other. In a broad sense they provide a framework for dealing on a theological basis with guilt and reconciliation in the political sphere.

Let us now explore, in a more detailed way, the possibility of reconstructing the Christian doctrine of reconciliation within the political sphere, using South Africa as an example. As is well known, the guilt incurred during the apartheid era was dealt with in the framework of a truth commission. Victims could tell their stories of oppression before the Truth and Reconciliation Commission (TRC), and perpetrators of human rights violations were required to tell the truth in order to get amnesty. I am going to argue that a Christian agenda underlay the political and juridical process in the TRC and that one can show from its proceedings how political and theological language are transferable.

Let us examine the amnesty procedure more closely. According to the TRC law,[13] applicants for amnesty had to make "full disclosure of all relevant facts" that led to a human rights violation. The law did not (and could not) require "repentance" in the theological sense (*passiva contritio*) as a condition for reconciliation in analogy with the dialectic of law and gospel. If a perpetrator made a full disclosure without showing any regret, he qualified for amnesty, so long as certain other requirements in the TRC law were met.

There were a number of such cases of full disclosure, and most of them ended with amnesty. Many of them, of course, were viewed critically in South Africa, especially by the victims. They asked, How can we forgive the perpetrator if he does not regret what he did? I have dealt elsewhere with this issue and the important questions it raises from a theological perspective.[14]

In what follows I will concentrate on one example that yields answers to the question of the possibility of transferring political language into the theological sphere. Let us focus on the political and juridical understanding of truth-telling on the one hand and a theological understanding of truth in relation to remorse on the other by following a dialogue at a TRC hearing.

Jeff Benzien, a highly decorated police officer in the apartheid era, applied for amnesty in July 1997. During the TRC hearing, held in Cape Town, three of his former victims were present. According to the amnesty law, the victims were allowed to put questions to the applicant. One of the torture victims, for instance, asked Benzien to demon-

13. The Promotion of National Unity and Reconciliation Act No. 34 (1995).

14. See my article, "Philosophische und theologische Grundprobleme beim Verstehen des südafrikanischen Versöhnungsprozesses," in *Religion and Theology: A Journal of Contemporary Religious Discourse* 7, no. 2 (2000): 169-91.

strate a special torture technique that he had used on victims during interrogation.

Like many other hearings, the Benzien hearing also developed its own genuine dynamic once it began. Juridical matters, moral values, and theological implications seemed to take turns in being central. Clearly, Benzien's main purpose for testifying before the TRC was to get amnesty. The TRC's main function in turn was to prove whether Benzien met the (juridical) criteria for amnesty. But once the discussion began with the victim, the process of truth-finding involved more than just trying to find out the facts:[15]

> *Mr. Jacobs* (victim): I was your first survivor of this torture method of yours, you would concede that, you say?
> *Mr. Benzien:* Yes.
> *Mr. Jacobs:* Yet you appeared very effective at what you were doing (. . .)
> *Mr. Benzien:* I can't answer that — how effective it was.
> *Mr. Jacobs:* Are you a natural talent at this, I mean, do you think? (. . .)
> *Mr. Benzien:* I wouldn't know if I have got a natural talent for it; it is not a very nice talent to have.
> *Mr. Jacobs:* Okay. (. . .) If it is not a very nice talent to have, you went on, if [as?] you say, from nine o'clock till two o'clock, which is quite a few hours; you went on for long with something you are not very comfortable with. How do you explain that?
> *Mr. Benzien:* Mr. Jacobs, the method employed by me is something that I have to live with, and no matter how I try to interpret what I did, I still find it deplorable. I find it exceptionally difficult, sitting here in front of the news to everybody. I concede that no matter how bad I feel about it, what was done to you and your colleagues must have been worse. Believe me, I am not gloating or trying to prove that I am somebody who I am not.
> *Mr. Yengeni* (victim): What kind of man uses a method like this

15. The punctuation of the original record is slightly amended in its reproduction below.

(. . .) to other human beings (. . .), listening to those moans (. . .) and taking each of those people near to their deaths — what kind of man are you (. . .), what happens to you as a human being?

Mr. Benzien: Mr. Yengeni, not only you have asked me that question. I, Jeff Benzien, have asked myself that question to such an extent that I voluntarily approached psychiatrists. (. . .) If you ask me what type of person is it that can do that, I ask myself the same question.

Passages in the dialogue such as those in which Benzien states, ". . . it is not a nice talent to have" and "I find it exceptionally difficult, sitting here in front of the news to everybody" are already noteworthy from a theological point of view. Whereas the former statement indicates a turn-about in that it gives the deed a new moral interpretation, the latter statement on the face of it expresses shame. "Shame" expresses something more: the "inner person" *(innerer Mensch),* to use a term from Reformation theology, is involved. Shame expresses renunciation not only of the deed but also of the kind of person one is. It not only expresses renunciation of the deed in its moral aspect *coram hominibus;* with shame the person becomes aware of standing *coram deo.* It affects the person himself. A change in the inner person becomes evident. "The conscience becomes fearful."[16]

In the last statement in the dialogue above *Benzien* places himself as a person in question: "I ask myself the same question," he declares. It becomes clear that repentance *(passiva contritio* in Lutheran terminology) is concerned not only with individual moral offenses: it flows from a remorse *(Zerknirschung)* that the law (in the moral-theological sense) brings about by revealing that everything in a human being is under the curse of sin. *Benzien* "wakes up" from the apartheid dream, the nightmare of apartheid that theologians have categorized as a sin

---

16. Article 12 of the Augsburg Confession (CA) of the Lutheran Church. "Repentance" consists according to CA XII, 4-5 of two parts: *"altera est contritio seu terrores incussi conscientiae agnito peccato, altera est fides, quae concipitur ex evangelio seu absolutione et credit propter Christum remitti peccata et consolatur conscientiam et ex terroribus liberat."* It is interesting that "liberation" marks the endpoint of the argument! Quoted from *Die Bekenntnisschriften der evangelisch-lutherischen Kirche* (Göttingen: Vandenhoeck & Ruprecht, 1986), p. 65.

against God.[17] To that extent it is a waking up from sin, i.e., from hostility against God. Repentance or conversion is a "waking up" *(Erweckung)* that Karl Barth expounds in a way pertinent also to this context: "The sleep from which a person is awakened, according to Scripture, is a going along a wrong path, a going in which one is oneself turned the wrong way and stuck in being turned the wrong way."[18]

Benzien's awakening occurred not from fear, constraint, or intimidation but voluntarily, even though the announcement of conditions for the granting of amnesty (on the juridical level) initiated the process that led to it. "Truth" received another dimension, an accusing function, through personal confrontation with the victim (the moral level). The victim placed the person behind the deed "in question." The perpetrator was shaken awake. This shaking awake parallels the spiritual function of a sermon calling to repentance (the theological level).

These theological observations describe an end-point. For we are dealing here with a development or process, one that advances from the juridical to a moral to a theological understanding. On the juridical level Benzien sought to meet the criteria for amnesty by revealing what he did to his victims. Truth on this level is factual truth. On a moral level the revelation of all relevant facts — in our case the detailed description of Benzien's torture techniques — led to a moral judgment of what happened that contrasted with the attitude he had had during the apartheid era. This moral self-judgment was intensified by personal confrontation with the victims and their account of how they experienced what had happened. Truth took on a further function, namely that of a moral accusation *(Anklage)*. The victims questioned the *person* behind the *torturer.* What person can do these things? The perpetrator was "aroused from sleep" through the distinction between person and deed.

In this process of being aroused from sleep one can rediscover the theological function of a "sermon calling to repentance" *(Bußpredigt).* Here we are no longer concerned with a moral paradigm, in the light of which the deed implies only an offense against moral values (= ethical guilt). Instead the law (in its theological sense, as *usus secundus legis)*

---

17. See as a predecessor of the *Kairos Document,* e.g., John de Gruchy and Charles Villa-Vicencio, eds., *Apartheid Is a Heresy* (Cape Town: David Philip, 1983).

18. *Kirchliche Dogmatik (Church Dogmatics)* IV/2 (my translation).

leads the person to the turning point where he despairingly but profoundly questions himself. The "old" person is placed under question. On a theological level we are here concerned with the appeal for repentance that precedes conversion in the biblical meaning of the word. In the naming of the injustice *(Benennung des Unrechts)* by both victims, Mr. Yengeni and Mr. Jacobs, we hear the "call to repentance" *(Bußruf)* of the gospel and the prophets.

The example of the Benzien hearing shows that reconciliation (together with repentance, which is a component of reconciliation) involves being confronted by the truth, that is, by the identification of injustice *(Benennung des Unrechts)*. To that extent we can argue that truth (which functions in the same way as a sermon calling to repentance) "provides the way" (Bonhoeffer) for reconciliation. In *this* sense the political formula "no reconciliation without truth" can be transferred into theology.[19]

In conclusion, it is important to note that the movement we have observed from the juridical to the moral to the theological understanding of truth about reconciliation does not aim at introducing a new Aristotelian metaphysics. On the contrary, as we have shown, there is no straight path leading from political reconciliation to its theological meaning. There is instead an ontological breach at the point where we enter the theological understanding of the process. As we have stated, there is no direct link between political and theological language. But coming from the theological angle enables us to discover "connections" between the "ultimate" and the "penultimate things," either by way of transferring political into theological language or by way of reconstructing a theological motif within political reality.

In our case we were able to reconstruct the theological depth of

19. The formula "reconciliation through truth" represents, from a theological point of view, a formula with three unknowns. What it means depends on

    a. the view of reconciliation,
    b. the understanding of the preposition, and
    c. the meaning of truth.

Because of this danger of ambiguity the formula "reconciliation through truth" is not on principle reciprocally transferable. For example, a theological reconstruction of the political formula is possible only where the preposition "through" is understood in the sense of Bonhoeffer's "preparing of the way" *(Wegbereitung)* and not as a methodology.

repentance as a "sign of transcendence" (P. L. Berger) in the midst of political reality, at a hearing of the TRC. The quality of the "sign of transcendence" lies precisely in what repentance makes possible, according to the Bible, namely, freedom — in the sense that in reconciliation between God and humankind a change of perspective takes place. Thus "reconciliation through truth" does not mean theologically being stuck in moral accusations; what it does is highlight the overcoming of moral guilt. That truth is truth only when it sets free is clear from the Gospel of John (8:32). "The truth will make you free," said Jesus. "Free for what?" asks Miroslav Volf, and provides the answer: "free to make journeys from the self to the other and back and to see our common history from their perspective as well as ours, rather than closing ourselves off . . . ; free to live a truthful life and hence be a self-effecting witness to truth rather than fabricating our own 'truths' and imposing them on others; free to embrace others in truth rather than engage in open or clandestine acts of deceitful violence against them."[20]

20. Miroslav Volf, *Exclusion and Embrace: A Theological Exploration of Identity, Otherness, and Reconciliation* (Nashville: Abingdon, 1996), pp. 272f.

Seeing Things Differently: On Prayer and Politics

Dirkie Smit

"Seeing the World sub specie Christi" (Bonhoeffer)

"Christian piety at its best has made a significant contribution to the social transformation of the world," states John de Gruchy.[1] And it may be impossible to understand his wide-ranging contributions to social theory without appreciating their spiritual roots in Christian piety, prayer, and worship. De Gruchy has written several pieces dealing directly with this relationship.[2] The theme, however, runs through all his work, including recent publications on democracy and aesthetics.[3]

Like several well-known Christian ethicists today, de Gruchy seems convinced that Christian ethics depends fundamentally on seeing — on perception — which is not surprising, since Bonhoeffer al-

---

1. John W. de Gruchy, *Cry Justice!* (London: Collins Liturgical Publications, 1986), p. 23.

2. Including his introductory essay, "Christian Spirituality and Social Transformation," in *Cry Justice!*, pp. 23-46, and his essay on "Prayer, Politics, and False Piety," in Allan A. Boesak and Charles Villa-Vicencio, eds., *When Prayer Makes News* (Philadelphia: Westminster Press, 1986), pp. 97-112, also published as *A Call to End Unjust Rule* (Edinburgh: St. Andrew Press, 1986).

3. In particular, notions of seeing, vision, and beauty are intimately related with struggles for justice, both in *Christianity and Democracy* (Cambridge: Cambridge University Press, 1995) and *Christianity, Art and Transformation: Theological Aesthetics in the Struggle for Justice* (Cambridge: Cambridge University Press, 2001).

ready claimed that "seeing the world sub specie Christi is the paramount theological activity for Christians."[4] In his seminal analyses of the process of ethical decision-making, Heidelberg ethicist and Bonhoeffer scholar H. E. Tödt also argued that "seeing" constitutes the first and crucially important aspect of this process.[5] In fact, it is in all probability the influence of the Reformed tradition, and particularly "the massive and incisive contribution of Karl Barth to ecclesiology," albeit read through the lenses of Bonhoeffer's "basic 'Barthian' orientation to theology" that led de Gruchy to these convictions.[6]

One of the painful effects of apartheid was the fact that South Africans did not "see" in the same way. De Gruchy was a theologian in a society in which people lived in different worlds and perceived life, history, one another, in radically diverse ways. They also saw ethical issues in these diverse ways. Even what were regarded as ethical problems, dilemmas, and challenges differed drastically. They obviously also disagreed with regard to appropriate responses to moral challenges and solutions to ethical dilemmas, but, even before they disagreed about responses and courses of action, they already disagreed fundamentally about what they saw or failed to see, what they experienced and accepted as moral challenges and what they ignored or overlooked. Even social theories reflected the visions of those that were looking. De Gruchy would continually struggle with these social realities and their impact on theology.

It is therefore not surprising that a language of an ethics of being — of community, character, narratives, saints, disciples, and friendship — has also become popular in South African ethical circles. Several recent doctoral theses share a common moral language, namely the language of an ethics of being, arguing that it is in communities of charac-

---

4. Dietrich Bonhoeffer, *Creation and Fall* (London: SCM Press, 1959), pp. 7-8.
5. See, e.g., Heinz Eduard Tödt, "Towards a Theory of Making Ethical Judgments," in David K. Clark and Robert V. Rakestraw, eds., *Readings in Christian Ethics*, vol. 1 (Grand Rapids: Baker, 1994), pp. 291-97.
6. John W. de Gruchy, *The Dynamic Structure of the Church* (unpublished dissertation, University of South Africa, Pretoria, 1972), p. i. Any brief look at his curriculum vitae demonstrates the pervasive influence of both Barth and Bonhoeffer on his thought, and his continuing interest in the Reformed tradition. It was very appropriate when he was awarded the Barth prize in 2000 in Berlin. See also his autobiographical essay "How I Changed My Mind," forthcoming in *Journal for Theology of Southern Africa*.

ter that responsible people are to be formed. The challenges facing South African society at the beginning of this century will also require an ethics of being, of role models and inspiring characters, of commitment and responsibility, of mutual acceptance and living with the other. The new South Africa needs new South Africans, people who can see. But where do we learn to see?

"Seeing Things Differently" (de Gruchy)

Seeing Things Differently is the title of de Gruchy's recent volume of sermons. "The title, it seems to me, sums up a central theme in the Christian gospel, namely that we are called to 'become like children' in order to see things from a totally different perspective, that is, the perspective of God's gracious reign over the whole of reality."[7] This suggests at least one possible reason why Christian worship is so crucially important for Christian ethics. Christian worship is one of these "social locations," perhaps one of the most important places and occasions where Christian believers learn to see.

It is, of course, not without reason that de Gruchy uses this title for a book of sermons, rather than a book on worship or liturgy. In the Reformed tradition, since Calvin, it has been customary to give preference to the ear over the eye as the primary human instrument for knowing, including knowing God. This was particularly important in the Reformed understanding of worship. A bias for the visible significantly shaped medieval theology and spirituality. The ultimate religious experience was to be a beatific vision. In this, Calvin brought a major change. We are blind, he repeated. We cannot see. Therefore God speaks to us, and we hear before we can see. And in the worship service, the living God is speaking to us. We hear, and only then do we see. As Nicholas Wolterstorff explains,

> The medieval Christian longed for the full vision of God. The Reformed Christian longed for the full coming of the kingdom of God. The medieval Christian sought to approach God. . . . The Re-

---

7. John W. de Gruchy, *Seeing Things Differently* (Cape Town: Mercer Books, 2000), p. vii.

formed Christian sought to respond to the acting God. The Roman tradition tried to see God; the Reformed, to hear God. Their contrasting liturgies are manifestations of these contrasting visions of what it is that we and God have to do with each other.[8]

For de Gruchy, in hearing we also learn to see. Through sermons, we learn to see differently. This was how Calvin understood the function and the authority of the Scriptures. They become the spectacles, the lens through which we can see. "The Scriptures are not something to look at but rather look through, lenses that refocus what we see into an intelligent pattern."[9] And it is primarily in the worship service where we listen to and hear God's Word, which then helps us to see properly.

In this, de Gruchy may also have been influenced by Karl Barth. In twentieth-century Protestantism, Barth — somewhat paradoxically, since he is often quoted as showing little interest in the practical details of the liturgy — is regularly called upon as a major witness in this regard. Already in *Fides quaerens intellectum*,[10] his early and seminal study on Anselm, Barth gave an indication of the importance of faith and prayer for theological reflection. And in the lectures on ethics from the same period he made the same point. In the *Church Dogmatics,* already in the first volume,[11] Barth began to develop this fundamental conviction systematically. Bromiley remarks that one of the unappreciated aspects of the *Church Dogmatics* is this ultimate orientation of theology to worship.[12]

In Barth's influential publications on the relationship between church and state, to which de Gruchy often refers, he showed that prayer negates itself if it does not become action. In his 1937-1938 Gifford Lectures on the knowledge of God and the worship of God in the Reformed tradition, Barth distinguished different forms of the ser-

8. Nicholas Wolsterstorff, "The Reformed Liturgy," in Donald McKim, *Major Themes in the Reformed Tradition* (Grand Rapids: Eerdmans, 1992), p. 291.

9. Clifford Green, *Imagining God* (San Francisco: Harper & Row, 1989), p. 107, discussing Calvin.

10. Karl Barth, *Fides quaerens intellectum* (Zurich: EVZ-Verlag, 1958/1931).

11. Karl Barth, *Church Dogmatics* I/1 (Edinburgh: T. & T. Clark, 1936).

12. Geoffrey W. Bromiley, *Introduction to the Theology of Karl Barth* (Grand Rapids: Eerdmans, 1979), p. 249.

vice of God, including the worship of the Christian life, the worship service, and the so-called political worship. He now presented the liturgical assembly as "the concrete center" of the church's life, and claimed: "The church service is the most important, momentous and majestic thing which can possibly take place on earth."[13]

Duncan Forrester comments: "When Karl Barth published his Gifford lectures . . . some English-speaking readers were surprised to discover, in a book which they assumed was about the relation between theology and ethics, substantial discussions of the cultic service of God (Gottesdienst) alongside the treatment of the political service of God."[14] In *The Humanity of God* Barth explicitly endorsed the *lex orandi, lex credendi*–principle: "It is imperative to recognize the essence of theology as lying in the liturgical action of adoration, thanksgiving and petition. The old saying, *lex orandi lex credendi,* far from being a pious statement, is one of the most profound descriptions of theological method."[15]

Since the Introduction to *Evangelical Theology* Barth was to make it very explicit that the first and basic act of theological work is prayer.[16] Faith and ethics flow from prayer. Finally, one should remember the way he summarized the proper response to the gospel as prayer, as calling on God, and then interpreted the first petitions of the Lord's Prayer in such a moving and powerful way, also with regard to ethics in *The Christian Life.*[17] Indeed, to clasp hands in prayer, according to Barth, is the beginning of an uprising against the disorder of this world. John de Gruchy clearly has his spiritual roots in this tradition.[18]

---

13. Karl Barth, *The Knowledge of God and the Service of God* (London: Hodder and Stoughton, 1938).

14. Duncan Forrester, "Ecclesiology and Ethics: A Reformed Perspective," *The Ecumenical Review* 47, no. 2: 148.

15. Karl Barth, *The Humanity of God* (Richmond: John Knox Press, 1960), p. 90.

16. Karl Barth, *Evangelical Theology: An Introduction* (New York: Holt, Rinehart & Winston, 1963), p. 160.

17. Karl Barth, *The Christian Life, Church Dogmatics* IV/4 (Grand Rapids: Eerdmans, 1981).

18. For his own views on appropriating Barth in South Africa, see "Racism, Reconciliation, and Resistance," in Charles Villa-Vicencio, ed., *On Reading Karl Barth in South Africa* (Grand Rapids: Eerdmans, 1988), pp. 137-55, concluding with a discussion of intercession and prayer.

"Thinking Our Way into God's World" (Hall)

But why? Why is worship so important for teaching us to see, to look in the right direction? What is supposed to take place in Christian worship? One very suggestive way of answering the question why worship is so important for ethics is to consider what some call "die Ungleichzeitigkeit der Religion" in Christian worship. This refers to the fact that Christian worship has to do with time, with a combination of remembrance, hope, and experience. In worship, Christians remember. Because of that, they hope. And because of that, they are changed, transformed, in the present. Wolfgang Huber explains this with great clarity, almost defining the specific task of Christian ethics in this way.[19] The "non-contemporaneity" of the Christian faith with everyday realities, the distance, the tension, between the Christian faith and the present, makes ethics possible — and necessary. This tension, caused by the distance-in-time, is creative ("schöpferisch"). In this definition of ethics, three dimensions of (the believing community's experience of) time are therefore intimately related with one another. The reason for this is given in the nature of Christian faith itself. It has to do with tradition (memory), hope (future), and therefore with creative tension (present). In all of this, worship plays a crucial role. Douglas John Hall, in the subtitle of his work on prayer, summarizes this idea by saying that Christian worship is about "thinking our way into God's world."[20]

In recent years, South African ethical scholars have also drawn attention to this crucial link between the experience of time in Christian worship and ethics. Robin Petersen, in his doctoral thesis from the University of Chicago, "Time, Resistance and Reconstruction: Rethinking Kairos Theology" (1995), argues that this is the way to understand the liturgy and the religious experience of the African Independent Churches in South Africa and their response to life. However,

19. "Theologische Ethik hat ihre besondere Aufgabe darin, die schöpferische Ungleichzeitigkeit des Glaubens im Blick auf die ethische Probleme der Gegenwart zur Geltung zu bringen," "Erinnerung, Erfahrung, Erwartung. Die Ungleichzeitigkeit der Religion und die Aufgabe theologischer Ethik," in Christian Link, Hrsg., *Die Erfahrung der Zeit* (Stuttgart: Klett-Cotta, 1984), p. 322.

20. Douglas J. Hall, *When You Pray: Thinking Your Way into God's World* (Valley Forge, Pa.: Judson Press, 1987).

more must be said. It is not enough merely to claim that Christian worship is important for ethics, since it liberates the worshipers from the givenness of everyday reality and brings them into a creative tension between past, future, and present, so that they learn to look in the right direction. A crucial question remains, of course, namely: What does the worshiping community see that is so different, or that provides for a different perspective?

"Holiness Joins Liturgy and Justice" (Wolterstorff)

There are many different ways of understanding the relationship between Christian liturgy and public life, between Christian worship and the world. In recent years, various scholars have contributed to this discussion, often in radically different and even conflicting ways. The powerful comments during his last days in prison by Bonhoeffer, linking prayer and doing what was right, have, of course, led to a long tradition of reflection. South Africans often remember Paul Lehmann's attempt to work out the implications of politics as the business of liturgy. And then there is Theodore Jennings's inspiring book on liturgy and liberation, dedicated to South Africans.[21]

One instructive way to explain this relationship has been offered, in several valuable contributions, by Nicholas Wolterstorff, who links liturgy, holiness, and justice in a number of ways. In his discussion of the social ethics of — what he calls world-formative — Reformed Christianity, *Until Justice and Peace Embrace,* Wolterstorff already dealt at length with the importance of worship and liturgy as the distinctive element of Christian existence, arguing that "a rhythmic alternation of work and worship, labor and liturgy is one of the significant distinguishing features of the Christian's way of being-in-the-world." Liturgy, said Wolterstorff, authenticates Christian action in the world.[22]

In several more recent essays, he has explained and developed this

21. Paul Lehmann, "Praying and Doing Justly," *Reformed Liturgy and Music* 19, no. 2: 79; and Theodore W. Jennings, *The Liturgy of Liberation* (Nashville: Abingdon, 1988).

22. Nicholas Wolterstorff, *Until Justice and Peace Embrace* (Grand Rapids: Eerdmans, 1983), pp. 146-61.

point in some detail. In "Liturgy, Justice, and Holiness"[23] he starts with the observation that holiness is a preoccupation of the Christian liturgy. Many people, he says, may feel "that when it comes to holiness we have left behind such earthly, horizontal concerns as justice and entered a higher realm, the realm of the transcendent, of the divine." Wolsterstorff's argument is that there is no such dichotomy between holiness and justice. "God's justice is a manifestation of his holiness; our justice is a reflection of God's holiness. When we deal with justice, we are dealing with the sacred. Injustice is desecration. The preoccupation of the liturgy with holiness does not separate liturgy from justice. On the contrary, holiness binds liturgy and justice together."

Wolterstorff argues that the acknowledgment of God's holiness is inseparable from an imperative for our holiness. Almost no one will dispute that the liturgy is for making us holy, he claims. But, he continues, what does holiness mean? In fact, nothing in the language of liturgy and devotion is more alien to our contemporary secular mentality than speech about holiness. "Once upon a time the concept of holiness was fundamental to the way in which human beings thought about reality and experience. This time — for us at least — is past," he says.

In a major part of his article, Wolterstorff discusses the meaning of holiness by making use of Jonathan Edwards *(Religious Affections)*, Rudolf Otto *(The Idea of the Holy)*, Karl Barth *(The Discussion of Holiness)*, and particularly Mary Douglas *(Purity and Danger)*. He then turns to the Old Testament:

> [I]t is not at all difficult to see why justice is treated as a manifestation of holiness. The unjust society is a society in which wholeness and integrity are lacking. For it is a society where people exist on the margins, on the periphery, hanging on rather than being authentically incorporated into the life and welfare of the community. Such a society fails to mirror the wholeness of God. And when we as Christians recall that this God whose holiness we are to reflect in our lives and our societies is himself a trinitarian community, then it is obvious that the unjust society is an unholy society. It does not mirror God's communitarian wholeness. (p. 18)

23. Nicholas Wolterstorff, "Liturgy, Justice, and Holiness," *The Reformed Journal* (December 1989): 12-20.

In the final part of his article, he moves to the New Testament, and to different forms of brokenness in the world, that we are "in one way or another" to embrace as followers of Jesus Christ. In Jesus we find

> a radically new understanding of how we are to reflect God's holiness. In Jesus we find, if you will, a new hermeneutic of the Torah's concern with holiness. . . . The holiness of a community resides centrally in how it treats human beings, both those who are members of the community and those outside, even those outside who are "enemies." And specifically, the holiness of a community consists . . . in the members of the community embracing the broken ones, and working and praying for their healing. . . . We learn from Jesus that a community which shuns the broken ones can never be a whole community — that is, can never be a holy community. The holy community is the merciful community, the just community. (p. 20)

Wolterstorff concludes that God asks us for more than liturgical acknowledgment of God's holiness, namely to struggle for justice. "Holiness joins liturgy and justice. In the liturgy we hymn God's holiness. In lives of justice and mercy we reflect God's holiness. In the liturgy we voice our acknowledgement of God's holiness. In the struggle for justice we embody that acknowledgement."

In a second article, "Justice As a Condition of Authentic Liturgy,"[24] Wolterstorff focuses more explicitly on this relationship between liturgy and justice. So often, he says, people find it difficult to see that liturgy, justice, and evangelism are all of crucial importance for being the church. People concerned with one of the three often find it difficult to understand the importance of the other two. This, contends Wolterstorff, leads to aberrations.

Wolterstorff briefly explains what he means by liturgy and justice. Almost everyone in the Christian community, he continues, operates with some view on what would deprive liturgical actions of their authenticity. He gives several popular examples. Turning to the biblical writings, he argues that there "the authenticity of the liturgy is conditioned by the

24. Nicholas Wolterstorff, "Justice as a Condition of Authentic Liturgy," *Theology Today* 48, no. 1 (April 1991): 6-21; see also his "Worship and Justice," in McKim, *Major Themes*, pp. 311-18.

quality of the ethical life of those who participate." He discusses several well-known passages from the Old Testament, showing that "liturgy in the absence of justice does not please God; it nauseates God." This does not mean, according to him, that justice is to displace liturgy. The relationship for which he argues is rather a "not/unless" one — not authentic liturgy unless justice. The connection is given, according to him, in the idea of the covenant, where the pattern is deliverance, obedience, blessing. "The prophetic critique of the cult is grounded in the conviction," says Wolterstorff, "that the point of the liturgy is to give symbolic expression to the commitment of our lives to God."

Again, he demonstrates that exactly the same ideas are present in the New Testament as well.

> Worship acceptable to God, authentic worship, is the worship of a pure heart. And the only pure heart is the heart of a person who has genuinely struggled to embody God's justice and righteousness in the world and genuinely repented of ever again doing so only half-heartedly. The worship of such a person consists then of giving voice and symbolic expression to the concerns and commitments of the heart. This . . . is the biblical vision.[25]

Once again, it is clearly no coincidence that Wolterstorff is also from the Reformed tradition and community. Reformed theology has continuously shown a particular preference for issues of justice and transformation and issues of holiness, covenant, and vocation. Reformed communities in history often related their Sunday worship with public responsibility and involvement in public, social, economic, and political life. They have often been under the impression that Paul sends the believers in Romans 12:1 into the world in order to practice their "true worship," their real service of God, after having listened to the good news of chapters 1-11, concluding with the major doxology at the end of chapter 11. It is because of this that Barth could argue, commenting on this passage in Romans, that one must read both the Bible and the newspaper in order to understand the gospel.[26]

Discussing "The Reformed Liturgy," Wolterstorff points to the

25. Wolterstorff, "Justice as a Condition of Authentic Liturgy," p. 21.
26. Karl Barth, *The Epistle to the Romans* (London: Oxford University Press, 1968/1933), p. 425.

remarkable fact that, partly as a result of this view of worship, Reformed people often show a lack of interest in liturgy as such: "The liturgy as the Reformers understood and practised it consists of God acting and us responding through the work of the Spirit. . . . [F]rom the beginning it has been characteristic of the Reformed churches to insist that our response of working in the world is not inferior to our response of worshiping in church. Work and worship are but different modes of obedient gratitude."[27]

Two further illustrations of this Reformed tendency to link worship with justice and ethics can suffice. In the new Church Order of the Uniting Reformed Church in Southern Africa, the link becomes clear from the way in which the responsibilities of the local congregation are described,[28] and in the ecumenical movement worship has also played

---

27. Nicholas Wolterstorff, "The Reformed Liturgy," in McKim, *Major Themes*, pp. 290-91.

28. These responsibilities are described in Article 4: "The congregation forms a community of believers in a particular place to serve God, each other and the world. Service of God has a bearing on the whole life of the congregation and therefore includes service to each other and to the world." The Article then describes these three related forms of service: "The heart of this service of God is to be found in the coming together of the congregation round the Word of God and the sacraments. There God is worshipped and praised. His Word is listened to, the sacraments are received and all needs are brought to God in order to strengthen the believers in their faith and to prepare them for their service to each other and the world." This worship service, therefore, leads to the second form of service: "The believers accept mutual responsibility for each other in their spiritual and physical needs. The congregation lives as a family of God in which all are inextricably bound to each other and share each other's joy and sorrow. Each considers the other as higher than him- or herself and no one only cares about her or his own needs, but also about the need of others. In this way they share each other's burdens and carry out the law of Christ." And worship leads to the third form of service: "The congregation's service to humankind and the world consists of proclaiming God's reconciling and liberating acts in and for the world; of living out the love of Christ in the world; of calling humankind to reconciliation with God and mutual reconciliation and peace; of following God, who is in a special way the God of the destitute, the poor and the wronged; by supporting people in any form of suffering and need; and by witnessing and striving against any form of injustice; by calling upon the government and the authorities to serve all the inhabitants of the country by allowing justice to prevail and by fighting against injustice; by witnessing against all rulers and those who are privileged who may selfishly seek their own interests and thus control and harm others" (Church Order, URCSA, Belhar: LUS).

a crucial role in ethical discussions.[29] Directly or indirectly, de Gruchy has been involved in or responded to both these initiatives. In his *Liberating Reformed Theology* he argues extensively for the ecumenical importance of the Reformed Confession of Belhar, on which the URCSA Church Order is based, and he actually took part in the ecumenical process of the Johannesburg Consultation on "Costly Obedience," where the relationship between worship and morality played a crucial role.[30] In light of this, it should also be immediately clear why de Gruchy chose the title *Cry Justice!* for his book on prayer and politics in South Africa.

"Liturgy Has Been Used to Prevent the Gospel from Taking Hold" (de Gruchy)

However, Christian worship has been and still is an ambivalent phenomenon. In reality it is often more a reflection of society than a critical and creative interruption of society. Worship often legitimates society instead of subverting and interrupting it. Christians often endorse and celebrate the values and virtues of their diverse societies, forming people according to the expectations of their groups and communities, and not according to the gospel.

29. The link between liturgy and life has been stressed in recent ecumenical documents. Reformed churches, theologians, and theology have made important contributions. Best and Heller claim that there still is a "need to develop more fully the relationship of worship to work for justice, witness and service, to the Christian commitment that God's will be done 'on earth as it is in heaven'" (Thomas F. Best and Dagmar Heller, *So We Believe, So We Pray* [Geneva: WCC Publications, 1995], p. xii). A case in point is the appropriation of the (Reformed) notion of covenanting, the appeal to Christians and churches to covenant with one another in collective endeavors to work towards common moral visions and goals, and the role of worship in this process. Biblical ideas on the covenant, propagated by Reformed churches, have played a major role in ecumenical thought over the past two decades. See also the thesis of de Gruchy's doctoral student, David N. Field, *Reformed, Modernity and the Environmental Crisis* (unpublished, University of Cape Town, 1996) for a suggestive application of these ideas.

30. See his *Liberating Reformed Theology* (Grand Rapids: Eerdmans, 1991), particularly pp. 189-235, and Thomas F. Best and Martin Robra, eds., *Ecclesiology and Ethics* (Geneva: WCC, 1997), pp. 50-91.

This is an awareness present in de Gruchy's thought from the earliest days. The Christian church betrays society when it is no longer the church and when it no longer worships as the church. The Christian church betrays society when it merely becomes a mirror image, a reflection, of everyday life, of reality outside the place of worship, no longer informing social life from the "strangely different" perspective of the gospel. In fact, this self-critical reflection on the church's actual form and life in the light of what the church should be formed the heart of de Gruchy's contextual theological reflection from the beginning, from his doctoral thesis on the lack of unity in the church, through the struggles of the church to be the church accounted in *The Church Struggle in South Africa*, to the heresy of *Apartheid Is a Heresy*, and to the deliberately ambiguous "liberating" of *Liberating Reformed Theology*.[31]

This betrayal can take many forms, and in South Africa it took its own peculiar forms. De Gruchy discusses some of these in his essay on "Prayer, Politics, and False Piety."[32] He argues that false piety takes on many forms, "but it inevitably replaces the God who is beyond human control with a god who can be manipulated to serve and sanction self-interest. False piety reduces God to a deus ex machina at our disposal, a god whom we can use for our own ends and one upon whom we can call to sanctify what is in our best self-interest. The god of false piety takes on the characteristics of the particular race, group, or class to which we may belong, and when we enter into battle this god is undoubtedly on our side."

He specifically discusses "two interrelated though apparently opposite manifestations of false piety," namely "its privatization and its patriotic appropriation by the nation or the state." He explains that "[t]he life and worship of churches, and the preaching of its pastors, is often determined in practice much more by popular demands than by biblical and theological integrity." Further, if the church becomes a haven of refuge from responsibility in the world, if sermons are geared to "massage the spiritual ego and sanction self-interest, if the liturgy whether traditional or contemporary becomes a mechanism of escape

---

31. See also *The Church Struggle in South Africa* (Grand Rapids: Eerdmans, 1979) and John W. de Gruchy and Charles Villa-Vicencio, eds., *Apartheid Is a Heresy* (Cape Town: David Philip, 1983).
32. In Boesak and Villa-Vincencio, *When Prayer Makes News*.

rather than the worship of God as Lord, and if priest, preacher, and people somehow combine or conspire to make it so, then false piety not only flourishes, it becomes the norm."[33]

In conclusion, the Reformed tradition, particularly through the lenses of Barth, and Barth through the lenses of Bonhoeffer, continued to have a formative impact on de Gruchy's thought. Typically Reformed questions concerning the calling of the church to be involved in public life have played a crucial role in this process. Since his doctoral thesis he has been interested in the relationship between "event" and "institution," first with regard to ecclesiology itself, but then also with regard to society as such.[34]

Through the years, de Gruchy has dealt with this calling under many different rubrics and from many different theological perspectives — including confessing Christ, the mission of the church, serving the good news, representing the kingdom, and many others — but time and again the implications were clear. Somehow the event of the church — worship, preaching, and piety — had to impact on the structures of the church and eventually also on the structures of society.

The essays on social theory in this Festschrift draw attention to a characteristic of de Gruchy's own work. His analyses "from the other side," of the different systems of life under conditions of modernity, have become much more sophisticated in terms of available social theories over several decades, but they were always informed by the event at the heart of the church, by a way of "seeing things differently," like children. Without taking his Reformed-Barth-Bonhoeffer roots into account, it will probably never be possible to fully appreciate John de Gruchy's life-work and contribution.

33. In Boesak and Villa-Vicencio, *When Prayer Makes News*, pp. 97-112.
34. See the concluding chapter of *The Dynamic Structure of the Church*, pp. 194-283.

Contributors

Barnett, Victoria J. — Washington, D.C., U.S.A.

Begbie, Jeremy — University of Cambridge, England

Bethke Elshtain, Jean — University of Chicago, U.S.A.

Breytenbach, Cilliers — Humboldt-Universität zu Berlin, Germany

Cochrane, James R. — University of Cape Town, South Africa

De Gruchy, Steve — University of Natal (Pietermaritzburg), South
Africa

Durand, Jaap — Stellenbosch, South Africa (Retired from University
of the Western Cape)

Green, Clifford — Hartford Theological Seminary, U.S.A.

Huber, Wolfgang — Bishop, Evangelische Kirche Berlin-Brandenburg,
Germany

Kwenda, Chirevo V. — University of Cape Town, South Africa

Pangritz, Andreas — University of Aachen, Germany

Rasmussen, Larry — Union Theological Seminary, New York, U.S.A.

Smit, Dirkie — University of Stellenbosch, South Africa

Ulrich, Thomas — Berlin, Germany

Villa-Vicencio, Charles — Institute for Justice and Reconciliation, Cape Town, South Africa

Ward, Graham — University of Manchester, England

Welker, Michael — University of Heidelberg, Germany

Wüstenberg, Ralf K. — Dietrich Bonhoeffer Visiting Professor in Systematic Theology at Union Theological Seminary, New York, U.S.A.